The Way of the Wild Soul Woman

"In *The Way of the Wild Soul Woman*, Mary Reynolds Thompson reveals the manifold ways in which women find themselves reflected in the land, and find the land reflected in themselves. This wise and potent guidebook is a howl from the wild soul, a clarion call for transformation, a prayer to the soul of this beautiful, animate earth."

—Sharon Blackie, author of *If Women Rose Rooted* and *Hagitude*

"*The Way of the Wild Soul Woman* is a potent portal for liberating our full flourishing through five archetypes of Mother Earth. Enter its luminous and rich terrain if you're truly ready to reclaim your wholeness, and to blossom into who you were born to become. This book is an offering and a guide that's profoundly useful, as the invitation into archetypal relationship with the Earth bypasses our mind's layered and self-limiting conditioning and helps us connect viscerally to the source of what's most sacred. Healing our own nature through deeply aligning with nature offers a pathway that resonates with soulful inquiry and the author's unique and vulnerable journey. It's a thrilling invitation for every woman, girl, or human who wants to strengthen their archetypal 'feminine,' and step more deeply into healing relatedness with our Mother, the Earth."

—Nina Simons, cofounder of Bioneers and author of *Nature, Culture and the Sacred*

"A unique and imaginative approach to healing the wounds inflicted on all of us by a misogynistic culture. Invoking natural landscapes along the way, these chapters invite us to restore the close connection to nature that is our birthright."

—Susan Griffin, author of *Woman and Nature, A Chorus of Stones*, and *Out of Silence, Sound. Out of Nothing, Something*

"In our deepest interior reflections, we know we are being summoned to balance a world in great peril, and for this we need the full aliveness of women—fierce, wild, tender, and wise. With gorgeous poetics and brilliant personal insights and stories, *The Way of the Wild Soul Woman* takes us on a sacred pilgrimage to the center of living landscapes that strengthen and teach us so that we can heal and stand up for all that we hold dear. Mary Reynolds Thompson is the perfect guide to take us on this timely and necessary journey."

—**Osprey Orielle Lake**, founder of Women's Earth and Climate Action Network (WECAN)

"Mary Reynolds Thompson has given women a map of the journey home to our wild, Indigenous selves. Skillfully weaving wisdom, stories, and practices, she points us toward the exits from our cultural captivity and whispers—no, shouts—'Go!' As *The Way of the Wild Soul Woman* makes clear, there's a new world waiting to be born, and it will only emerge through our own rewilded voices, hearts, and hands. Let's do this!"

—**Lorraine Anderson**, editor of *Sisters of the Earth* and *Earth and Eros*

"The path of the Wild Soul Woman echoes the way of the psyche and how women learn. I wept, I felt emotions I didn't know were there, I raged, I had amazing dreams, I journaled, and the book opened up new parts of me."

—**Valerie Andrews**, author of *A Passion for This Earth*

"The world has long had the Hero's Journey as a model, but we women were excluded. All that is ended now with Mary Reynolds Thompson's rich and life-changing *The Way of the Wild Soul Woman*. Here, finally, is a guide for our journey. From our barren Desert Woman beginnings to our bountiful and complete Grassland Woman, we travel through myth and mystery, ritual and rites, poetry and dreams, with practical guides and soulful blessings for our ultimate transformation to Wild Soul Woman. I cannot wait to share this book with other like-spirited women. Together we will travel, together we will heal the world, and together we will find Home."

—**Judy Reeves**, author of *Wild Women, Wild Voices*

"A powerful initiation to the Wild Soul Woman through an embodied exploration of her five archetypes. Mary Reynolds Thompson sounds a clarion call to reconnecting with ourselves and the Earth. Back to belonging. Back to life."

—**Lucy H. Pearce**, author of *Burning Woman, Creatrix,* and *She of the Sea*

The Way of the
Wild Soul
Woman

**5 Earth Archetypes to Unleash
Your Full Feminine Power**

Mary Reynolds Thompson

FINDHORN PRESS

Findhorn Press
One Park Street
Rochester, Vermont 05767
www.findhornpress.com

Text stock is SFI certified

Findhorn Press is a division of Inner Traditions International

Disclaimer
The information in this book is given in good faith and intended for information
only. Neither author nor publisher can be held liable by any person for any loss or
damage whatsoever which may arise directly or indirectly from the use of this book
or any of the information therein.

Cataloging-in-Publication data for this title is available from the Library of Congress

ISBN 979-8-88850-033-0 (print)
ISBN 979-8-88850-034-7 (ebook)

Printed and bound in the United States by Lake Book Manufacturing, LLC
The text stock is SFI certified. The Sustainable Forestry Initiative® program
promotes sustainable forest management.

10 9 8 7 6 5 4 3 2 1

Illustrations by Kathleen Brigidina
Text design and layout by Christy Day, Constellation Book Services
This book was typeset in Adobe Caslon Pro and Benton Sans

To send correspondence to the author of this book, mail a first-class letter to the
author c/o Inner Traditions • Bear & Company, One Park Street, Rochester, VT
05767, USA and we will forward the communication, or contact the author directly
at **www.maryreynoldsthompson.com**.

For all the courageous women who are throwing off their shames and chains for love of Self and Earth, I dedicate this book to you.

Together, we can change the world.

Contents

4

Mountain Woman

5

Grassland Woman

6

Walking the Way of the Wild Soul Woman

Foreword

I remember the first time Mary sat me down to talk about the difference between metaphors and archetypes. If we'd been in the same room as opposed to on the phone, she would've seen me looking completely nonplussed. To be sure, I had my own version of what an archetype was, but clearly, she was living in a different relationship to the concept. For starters, archetypes were vastly more than just "concepts." She seemed to have an intimate relationship with them that bordered on awe. I was intrigued.

Mary talked about metaphors and archetypes in terms of voltage: the raw power of a construct or experience to deliver a felt change or tangible transformation. As far as she was concerned, archetypes trumped metaphors by a factor of ten. The more I listened and received Mary's transmissions, the more I knew there was a gaping hole in both my understanding and my lived experience. Instinctively, I could feel what she was talking about, but I had no frame of reference for it. I had no map, no compass or key—but I wanted all three.

What ensued from that point was nothing short of delicious. Having already bonded as two British women managing the social and climatic realities of living in California, we dived into a true shared passion: exploring the role of nature in self-liberation. We are nature after all, so surely leaning back into the arms of our natural selves would be fundamental to the emergence of a truer, healthier human?

Then we turned to women. Women and nature share a common history of suppression and domination to the detriment of all life, not least our own. So then, how might embracing deep nature-based archetypes inform or support the rewilding of womenkind?

As a woman who often relates more to mountains, trees, and rivers than to other humans, Mary seemed to be offering a path of greater intimacy to everything I already loved. As the founder of TreeSisters, a UK-based charity sitting at the intersection of feminine leadership and forest restoration, I was fascinated by the prospect of exploring Mary's landscape-based archetypes as guides on a woman's journey home to her own wildness. I also had no concept of how that could be done, or even what it meant, but I was up for the ride.

What started to emerge through the development of an online course, and the magical dance of collective discovery that ensued for so many of us, evolved into the truly life-changing, and deeply significant body of work that is offered to you here. I know nothing else like it. Here, for me, is the map, the compass, and the key.

This is an achingly beautiful, poignantly intimate, and seismically transformational return to our original nature as part of nature. Here, you walk back into the arms of the landscapes out of which we emerged, as if walking into the embrace of ancient ancestors; women who carry the wisdom and sentience of the land itself and can show you to yourself. You are invited to drop all pretense that the conditioned human construct has anything to do with who we really are as women at all.

This archetypal journey provides opportunities for a series of profound initiatory meetings, if you choose them. Through the reflections of these ancient beings of land and water you can meet yourself, honestly, nakedly, and with profound humility, so that an undoing and a becoming can happen through and to you.

To get through what's coming, we need to have access to deeper strength, resilience, creativity, knowing, wisdom, compassion, and love than ever before. We need to let go of who we are not and dare to dance the dance of the Wild Soul Woman within.

I wish that experience for you.

~ Clare Dubois

Introduction

Song of a Wild Soul Woman

Women are rising.
Wild, windswept, born of ocean,
aflame with light, rooted as trees,
we are rising.
We are rewilding ourselves. Emerging from Earth, clad in moss and bark.
We are unrecognizable, except to each other.

We move in the shadows of forests and the deep,
cool undercurrents of streams.
We reach out our arms to the mountains,
dare to stand, cracked and dust-whorled like deserts.
We green ourselves with grasses, root ourselves in moist soil.
We are wondrous. We are rising. We are wild.

We see each other, feel for each other, hold each other up.
Like waves in an ocean we are a celebration of nature's powers and impulses.
We ebb and flow according to our own rhythm.
We will not be dictated to.

A woman no longer separate from the flesh of Earth, becomes her,
speaks for her, lifts her throat
and sings of fire below and stars in her hair.

We are granite and grandeur,
full-fleshed and woven through with wildflowers.
We bloom according to our own ways and whims and wants.
False things fall down in our presence. We are pregnant with life.
A Wild Soul Woman is a woman of belly and breath and boundlessness.

She makes her own way through ancient lands
with soft footsteps, lays down fresh tracks.
Barriers break apart before her.
Instinctively she moves on fin and wing and prayer.

She is the echo of a deeper voice that speaks from the fiery cave.
She is molten, flowing, shapeshifter.
She listens to the wisdom of stone.
She is living proof of a language that banishes all sense of loneliness.
The Earth warms her, welcomes her, enfolds her.
She grows tall amid the fields, greets the wind and the grasses,
the soft grace of rainbows.

She is fire woman and rain woman and earth and air, with plenty to spare.
This is not just my song or your song. This is the song of the Earth.
And the song of every Wild Soul Woman.
We are wondrous. We are rising. We are wild.

We are wondrous. We are rising. We are Wild. The Song of a Wild Soul Woman is a clarion call. A call to remember that you carry within you the mystery of forests and the granite of mountains. Your true nature *is* Nature: wild, windswept, vast as the plains. You are not small or insignificant. You are not the one that your parents fashioned you to be, or society dictated you should be, and you are not the label that your work confers on you. You are a Wild Soul Woman: rooted, powerful, authentic, and instinctual. And yet, how easily we forget!

For too long we women have contorted ourselves in order to succeed, or just survive, in a world that puts profit before beauty, competition before collaboration, exploitation before reciprocity. In this world, we have been repressed, domesticated, exploited, and abused. In this world, nature suffers, too. Rivers are drying up, mountaintops are being leveled, and forests are being felled. And the fertile spirit of life has been so wounded that we find ourselves, along with all existence on this planet, struggling to flourish.

But the call of your Wild Soul will not be silenced. With a howl from the heart, women are crying out for a different way of living. One that honors the Earth, and all beings—feathered, furred, leafed, petaled, and scaled. We are crying out for poetry, for meaning, and for pleasure. On a full-moon night when our blood stirs, we sense that the culture is too shallow and tame to contain us.

Our present story will continue to a bleak and lonely end if humans do not restore their connection to the Earth. This is vital. We all need to do our inner work and bring our full being into the world. But until we arrive at a place of sacred balance between the masculine, feminine, and Nature, we women must travel our own path. It is essential that we first find our own way back to ourselves. And for that, we need a new story.

The hero's journey, the dominant narrative of cultural and personal transformation in the West, has little to offer us. We are not damsels in need of rescue or passive bystanders patiently awaiting the hero's return. We want, above all, to be the protagonists of our own tales, the creators of our own adventures. Instead of slaying dragons, what if we embodied their ferocity and fire in service of all life? We are not separate from the forces of nature, nor do we wish to be.

And if our stories need to change, so, too, must our cultural metaphors. A woman seeking to regain her wildness will not find it in the upward masculine path of striving. True success does not lie for us in breaking the glass ceiling or simply "leaning in" to the status quo in order to rise up. No. The soul path of the feminine is downward, inward, to the ground of the Earth and into the very terrain our culture is attempting to exploit or silence.

In order to become Wild Soul Women, we need to understand the immensity and potency of the wild woman archetype that is rising into consciousness at this time. And we require an initiation of our own—one that is feminine, instinctual, Earth-conscious. That experience is the heart of this book.

—

In 2015, I was asked to lead an online course for TreeSisters, a global non-profit with a mission both to empower women and reforest the tropics. The course was to be based on a journey of transformation through five archetypal landscapes: Deserts, Forests, Oceans and Rivers, Mountains, and Grasslands. I'd explored them in my earlier book, *Reclaiming the Wild Soul,* and now the opportunity to work solely with women filled me with a surge of excitement and curiosity. Women's relationship to Earth has always been different from that of men. Our moon cycles, pregnancies, childbirth—all these things align us with the rhythms and textures of the natural world. But landscapes, too, reflect different aspects of our true nature—and together we would find out how.

In our first class, I shared my earliest childhood memory. It was a summer afternoon, the sun slanting through the window warming my back, birds singing, and the light, shimmering and golden. I longed to merge with the vibrancy around me, and so I attempted to wriggle out of my crib, only to get my head stuck between the bars. Hearing my cries, my mother rushed to my side and tried to push my head back into the crib. When she was unsuccessful, I became inconsolable. Even after the bars were removed and I was finally freed, the trauma remained. Throughout my life, I have suffered from neck problems, which I gradually recognized as a fear of sticking my neck out. But more than that, this experience left me with a terror that in attempting to secure my freedom, I would die.

Breaking free isn't easy. We don't always see the barriers that stand in our way, much less know how to remove them. Reaching for something beautiful, something just beyond our grasp, can seem dangerous, if not impossible. Until, that is, we realize the structures and strictures that keep us imprisoned are man-made.

Together, we can tear them down.

After I told my story, it became clear that the women gathered shared a common belief, regardless of age, ethnicity, or country of origin. All felt cut off from the full depth and breadth of their creativity and aliveness within a patriarchal worldview that undervalues women's contributions and desires, and continually fails to support our innate wisdom. They, too, lacked a model for their own energetic way of being in the world. As I helped them to connect with the five landscapes as liberating archetypes, they began to feel freer and more able speak out for their beliefs. In laying claim to their wild nature, they realized the strength that emanates from a woman's body, and from her very soul, is grounded in the Earth. In fact, each landscape, each magical formation of the Earth, reflects a different stage of growth. When we explore them all in depth, something extraordinary happens. We have a template for unleashing our full power.

Despite the advances of feminism in the past half century, women in our culture are still trapped in limiting roles. We are expected to be the good mother, the loyal (but often unpaid or underpaid) worker, and the ceaseless nurturer. The Earth is similarly viewed as an inexhaustible resource, the "Good Mother" at whose breast we can continually suckle. Women and Nature are expected to provide for others' needs, even to the point of complete depletion. As Ruth Bader Ginsburg told the Supreme Court, "The pedestal upon which women have been placed has all too often, upon closer inspection, been revealed as a cage."[1] It will require great courage to liberate ourselves from our noble role as the all-giving, all-nurturing ones.

Another cost of patriarchy is that we tend to look negatively on the unpredictable, wrathful, eruptive side of the feminine, insisting that these energies be controlled or tamped down, just as we have tried to subdue the Earth. The 16th century philosopher Francis Bacon encouraged men to torture nature—to put her on the rack and extract her secrets,[2] in an era when women were being hunted down and tortured for their secrets during the European witch trials. Bacon's imagery set the scene for the scientific revolution of the Enlightenment, yet in this view both nature and women were only fit for domination, interrogation, penetration. With a history of such violations, no wonder women fear living fully or speaking out.

I believe there is healing in rediscovering our relationship to nature while rejecting the stereotypes placed on us by Western culture. I believe that Earth's loving and caring aspects are interwoven with her ferocity. That women are a rich tapestry of all that is deeply alive, intelligent, instinctual, and feral. That we are too complex and multi-talented to be neatly boxed and labeled. And that if we are to break down the bars of the cage, we must examine our bonds with everything: the Earth, our own bodies, and each other.

Teaching my first Wild Soul Woman course, I was struck by the creativity—art, poetry, dreams, spontaneous rituals and prayers—that emerged from the group. The five Earth archetypes provided an avenue for women to give expression to something they had been dimly aware of but now was bursting forth into everyday awareness: The wisdom of the Earth was within them, and when they aligned with her different aspects, they were stronger, truer, more authentic. As they released themselves from a worldview that kept them within the narrow confines of what it means to be a woman, incredible energy was birthed.

As the weeks went on, we began to talk about Desert Woman, Forest Woman, Ocean and River Woman, Mountain Woman, and Grassland Woman. Not abstracted from the Earth but arising out of her, these archetypes activated a profound and tantalizing awareness of the mythic dimensions of our lives. The challenges we were experiencing didn't instantly dissolve, but our relationship to ourselves was changing. We were able to meet uncomfortable feelings and difficulties with a different set of responses: creative, courageous, and liberating. It was clear: These archetypes held the key to our collective healing.

These, then, are the Wild Soul Woman Archetypes that I will expand upon in this book. They will resonate within, calling you into the depths of your true nature.

As that first circle of women claimed their own voices and empowerment, I began to see the Wild Soul Woman Archetypes as a framework for female initiation. There is a natural progression from the Barren Worlds of Desert Woman, to the Dark Womb of Forest Woman, to the Breaking Waters of Ocean and River Woman, to Giving Birth as Mountain Woman, to Nurturing the Newborn as Grassland Woman.

The journey we are embarking upon is one of creation, where you will let go of what is not working in your life and give birth to your full, feminine power. And while the path is strewn with challenges, you will not travel it alone. At each step you will be guided by these archetypes, and by the stories of other women who have reclaimed their feminine souls, finding a strength that resides far beyond the reaches of patriarchy.

And after that, my sisters, well, *anything* is possible.

Your Journey

Either you will
go through this door
or you will not go through.

—ADRIENNE RICH

The five archetypes that animate your soul are literally as old as the hills. Before there was a human presence on Earth, over the course of hundreds of millions of years, these landscapes were establishing their own cycles, rhythms, and relationships. The ebb and flow of tides, the spin of seasons, the infinite beauty of birth and decay, the fierce uplift of mountains. These ancestral bodies and their natural processes gave birth to us. And their psychological, energetic, and emotional patterns are woven into the depths of your being.

Archetypes influence behavior. Even more importantly for our purposes, they stir the imagination and engage the emotions. We can only learn so much from facts, figures, and abstract concepts. To make fundamental change in our lives, we need this deeper knowing. The archetypes of the wild soul will reveal your inner landscapes and bring new understanding with the force of an erupting volcano or a downpour in a drought-ridden land. They are set to shake—and wake—you up.

Over time, I have worked with thousands of women around the world, including many who are LGBTQ or gender-fluid. And all have benefited from learning about these archetypes. Anyone interested in the wild feminine will find a place for themselves in this work. Earth's archetypes serve the good of all.

Buscar la Forma is a term used by midwifes. It means that every woman must find her own way of giving birth. The midwife's task is not to control the process, but to assist with whatever decision the mother-to-be makes. So let me say it loud and clear: Your journey is yours alone, unique and extraordinary to you. As you recast yourself as a Wild Soul Woman, you must trust your own instinctual rhythms and set your own pace.

When embarking on a journey, especially one that might be arduous at times, it is reassuring to have a sense of what lies ahead. In that spirit, let me introduce you more fully to the archetypes and the stages of growth they represent.

Desert Woman: Barren Worlds

In the beginning, there was a Void, and from the Void came a living planet. Barrenness is a natural part of the cycle of life and the place where your journey begins. Desert Woman is your guide to this phase where you reflect on what is not fruitful and fertile in your life—and what you can let go of. Owning your inner emptiness, you make room for new ways of being. Shedding what is not working in your life, you create an opening for something new to enter.

Forest Woman: The Dark Womb

Forests are the lungs of the planet and a source of oxygen necessary for all life. They are also the verdant realms where an incredible diversity of life gestates and takes form. Forest Woman heralds a fecund period, rich in imagination and exploration. In her womb-like darkness, you plant the seeds of new dreams, of barely sensed possibilities. You must wait for the seeds to take root, and nurture them in the depths of your being. With patience, you will experience a quickening.

Ocean and River Woman: The Breaking Waters

Water covers more than seventy percent of the Earth's surface, and this element responds to the pull of the moon. Through Ocean and River Woman, you understand the tides of your own energy and emotions. The more you explore your depths, the greater your power to live from the heart of your longing. Like a rising river breaking through a dam, you feel an urgency to move past any resistance, ready to bring more of your wild self into the world.

Mountain Woman: Giving Birth

Mountains seem like they've been here forever—but they didn't start forming widely until two billion years ago, or halfway through the Earth's development, and they represent a huge new undertaking. Mountain Woman will show you how to initiate a new project, serve your community, spark a movement, or simply claim your own fury and fire. In touch with your inner agency, alive to your sacred dreams and desires, you emerge into the world as an authentic, unstoppable force.

Grassland Woman: Nurturing the New Life

In the open space of the grasslands, humans learned to walk, run, and create complex social structures. Now Grassland Woman welcomes you back into community, helping you to solidify your learnings, integrate them into daily life, and share your gifts. In her presence, you dance to the rhythms of nature and reap the blessings of your journey.

While I've laid this out as if it is a linear journey, it doesn't have to be. You may find yourself immersed in Forest Woman, only to realize that you need to relearn Desert Woman's lesson of letting go. Or as Mountain Woman rises in you, you may need to reclaim the loving presence of Ocean and River Woman. Each archetype balances the others. Circling back when you need to will allow you to deepen and broaden your experience of each, building a resilient inner matrix for your journey of growth and healing.

We will explore each Wild Soul Woman Archetype by considering how it can help you overcome a core wounding by the patriarchy (the Challenge). You'll learn how it empowers you to reach for a fuller, more creative life (the Shift). We'll look at how the archetype offers a process for opening to more wisdom (the Way). I'll discuss how to embody the archetype in the cells of your being and how the emotional tone of the archetype can release vital energy.

At each stage of initiation, I'll offer journal prompts, rituals, embodied exercises, poetry, and other explorations. These are invitations into greater aliveness, artistry, and activism, and into a way of living that arouses full participation with this precious Earth and your own wild depths. Throughout the book you will also find quotes from women who experienced the Wild Soul Woman's journey in our workshops. As you will see, the more you engage with archetypes, the greater access you will have to your authentic self, so I encourage you to take the time to respond to these invitations. But rest assured, simply reading about the archetypes is more than enough to awaken them within you.

Laying Bare the Shadow Wild

That numbing of mind and heart
is already upon us.

—JOANNA MACY

What happens when we are cut off from these archetypal energies? Separated from Earth and her power, we feel a terrible loss and lack of support. But the need for that connection does not go away, and so we keep searching for our Wild Soul even when we don't know what we are looking for or how to find it. It is then that our lives can take a wrong turn or a deadly detour. In our desire to feel alive and at one with the world about us, we reach for something, *anything*, to rid us of the numbness or the pain. This can lead down any number of bumpy roads: booze, drugs, drama, sex and love addiction, excessive shopping, gambling. Look about you, and you will see how our consumer society is riddled with addiction and other unworkable "solutions" to the pain of disconnection.

I call this the *shadow wild*, a path of rebellion that ultimately ends in utter self-abandonment. I spent the first many years of my life following it.

My own shadow wild journey involved alcohol. From the age of sixteen until I turned twenty-seven, I drank to the point of blackouts, shakes, and a disturbing heart arrhythmia. I grew up in an alcoholic family, and alcoholism was part my genetic birthright. But that doesn't begin to tell the tale.

I drank to feel alive. I drank so that I didn't have to care what others thought of me, or keep second-guessing myself, or censor my passionate nature. I drank to feel the spirit of Gaia, of life herself.

And for a while it worked. That's the thing—the shadow wild is deceptive because it serves a purpose at first, freeing us before it locks us back in a cage that is a small and dark and often very hard to escape.

I was an emotional, physical, and spiritual mess when I sobered up in 1983. But by that time, I lived in the San Francisco Bay Area, and even in my darkest days, the beauty of this place pierced my heart. So I turned first to nature to begin the healing process. I walked everywhere, including long hikes in the open hills of the Marin Headlands and the sanctuary of Muir Woods' soaring redwoods. Without my being conscious of it, some part of me knew I needed to feel life thrumming through my body. Sunlight. Air. Trees. Birdsong. The wild chorus of the Earth opened me to what I had always wanted to feel: oneness with the great spirit of life.

Looking back, I can see how even then the Wild Soul Woman Archetypes were acting on me. How they have always been here, helping me to find my way back to myself. As they are waiting for you, to help you find your way back, too.

In the chapters ahead, I tell my story of recovery and beyond through the lens of a Wild Soul Woman reborn through these archetypes. I have dug deep into my lessons in the hope that they provide an example of how the archetypes work to free us to be whole. While I tell other stories too, mine is one that I know best. It is also my hope that in the baring of my soul, you will find the courage to bare yours.

The cosmologist Brian Swimme once said, "This is the greatest discovery of the scientific enterprise: you take hydrogen gas, and you leave it alone, and it turns into rosebushes, giraffes, and humans."[3] When we reclaim our wild feminine nature, we can't know what will happen. That's the point. When we express from our wild souls—the part of us that recognizes we are one with mountains, rivers, and forests—we invite Earth's processes and evolutionary impulses to work their magic through us.

Prepare to be surprised, for this journey will take you places you have yet to imagine. But this, too: Whatever has brought you here—the desire to break free of a bad relationship or unhealthy dependency; the realization that your life is passing you by and you want more, and to *be* more; your fear and grief at what is happening to the Earth and her inhabitants; or a desire to feel a greater sense of aliveness, connection, and creativity—the journey set out in these pages will carry you home.

Shall we begin?

Opening to Desert Woman

As you prepare to take your first step towards becoming a Wild Soul Woman, take a deep breath. Come into your body, into the quiet, into the significance of this moment. You are about to leave the everyday world and cross the threshold into a land that is vast, arid, and silent. This is a thorny place to begin your journey. Desert Woman will challenge you to confront your barrenness—those areas where you no longer feel lush and fertile. She will urge you to stop your striving and make space in your life for something new to be conceived. Once you respond to her soul summons, nothing will be quite the same again. And so, take another deep breath. It is time to go and meet her.

1

Desert Woman

Soul of a Desert Woman

She walks in fire, through fire, treads cracked earth with bare feet.
Silence and spaciousness are her companions.
Born of sand, rock, dust, she needs no pool to see her own reflection.
Garbed in gold by day, at night she shimmers by starlight.
In her presence snakes curl up like kittens.
She defies plough and planter, knows she is enough.
A desire to let go of all that is not hers to carry has
fashioned in her something real.
Prickly as cactus, cracked and half-crazed,
her fierce tongue and sharp wit suffer no fools.
She is intensity and immensity.
She has seen through the mirage, all the way to the horizon.
To look into her eyes is to know the truth.

Stage of Initiation: Barren Worlds

Challenge: Knowing You Are Enough

The Shift: From Mirage to Vision

The Way: Releasing the Old

Embodied Dimensions: Space, silence, honesty, change, transience, death and re-birth, solitude, simplicity, stillness, grief

Guiding Question: What is the truth of my situation?

Barren Worlds:
The First Initiation

How could you become new if you had not first become ashes?

—Frederick Nietzsche

This is how it begins. Desert Woman arrives like a firestorm, burning through your life. With her, she brings sudden loss, fierce love, restlessness, exhaustion, and burnout—any number of things that uproot and unbalance you.

Thrown into exile, you enter her barren lands, caught between the known world and the one yet to be discerned.

This is the realm of emptiness and silence. Of non-doing. Of endless horizons and a sky as wide as your imagination. You are here to put enough space between you and the everyday so that you can bear witness to your life. Heeding Desert Woman's call, you come to embody what Carol P. Christ calls the "nothingness that precedes an awakening."[4]

Everything you thought was carved in stone shifts like sand beneath your feet. It is time to cease your constant striving—to do more, have more, be more. To stand where the air wavers in the heat, and the sun—high, sharp, clarifying—strips away to the bones. To seek answers to questions you have suppressed for far too long.

Who are you, really? For what do you thirst? What is real and true? These are questions that can only be answered when you sufficiently detach from the particulars of your life to be able to see it free from illusion. And yet for many of us, separating from the comforting details and demands of the everyday, feels like a kind of death.

Traditionally valued for our ability to connect with and care for others, we may ignore the call of Desert Woman for fear of losing others' approval. Or we may be terrified of looking inward, toward our own needs and desires. Then life shakes us loose. Something happens—death, loss, a burning passion—and we realize we barely know ourselves or what we want. We only sense that we are being urged to a wilder and more authentic existence.

Will you answer the call of Desert Woman? Her fierce independence has earned her many epithets over the centuries—crazy, misfit, recluse. Scorned as dust-dry and undesirable by a culture that values women who are lush, fertile, and endlessly accommodating, she lives on the margins. But she revels in being free of others' expectations. Her blood beats true as a snare drum. Nothing stands between her and the glittering night sky, the earthy fragrance of creosote bushes after rain.

Barrenness holds no fear for her. Emptiness, no terror. She is comfortable with non-doing, the void that precedes the conception, the blank page, the open territory. On her body, you will trace the first lines of your new story.

Alone in the vastness, silence slips into your being. You stop your rushing. Quiet down. Like the exposed rock, your very essence is laid bare.

Nothing may be harder for you than to walk away from your web of obligations and relationships, to encounter Desert Woman. But she will teach you how to make your way alone. How to leave, with the doors closing behind you and the wide horizon beckoning.

And so, as a Desert Woman, you take one last backward glance and turn toward the open land that awaits. Watch your footsteps vanish in the wind. You begin your journey alone, as you must. Lift your skirts and stride out, *determined to save / the only life that you could save.*[5] Your own.

Why Exile Is at the Heart of Initiation

> *Now you must go out into your heart*
> *as onto a vast plain. Now*
> *the immense loneliness begins.*
>
> —Rilke

Separation from community is the first step in any journey of transformation. To reclaim your true Self, you first need to retreat from the web of relationships, habits, and behaviors that keep you trapped in an inauthentic life. For women, who are naturally relational and collaborative, this can prove painful and challenging.

Many of us have a love–hate relationship with Desert Woman. We long for time and space to simply be, are angry we don't have enough of it, but when we have a few moments off, we often find ourselves feeling anxious and prickly. Some women I work with are affronted by my even suggesting they step back from their usual duties and responsibilities for a while and simply do less. Don't I understand the demands of their lives? Don't I realize that the world is falling apart, and we need to get on with it? And I do understand. But this I also know: Nothing will change—not our lives and not this world—unless we have the courage to withdraw and look inward, with honesty.

At this point, you may be screaming:

Are you asking me to abandon my children or leave my job or marriage?

How would I survive if I left? How would they?

I can't walk away—I've invested too much.

So let me say emphatically—you don't have to literally change everything to put distance between you and your life. Here, at the start of your journey, you are being tasked with claiming what Virginia Woolf, in her essay "*A Room of One's Own*," described as a psychic space in which you can withdraw your energy from the world and give it to yourself.

On a cold winter day in December of 1983, at the age of twenty-seven, I walked into an Alcoholics Anonymous meeting and said these words out loud, "My name is Mary, and I'm an alcoholic." After all the struggle and paralysis, after years of shame and trying to keep my drinking hidden, the truth was out. The words seemed to float in the air, to open doors I didn't even know were shut. I felt lighter, freer.

Everything that came afterwards was changed by speaking my truth. I had to separate from every drinking haunt and almost every person in my life. Nothing was stable during the early years of my sobriety. Like the sands of the desert, I was constantly forming and reforming as I tried to figure out what shape my life would take as a sober woman.

In owning the reality of my situation, I was set free to find myself. But I first had to withdraw from my old life, not only to protect my newfound sobriety, but to find out who I truly was, free from old influences and relationships. It was excruciatingly painful at times, especially when the old drinking crowd judged me as heartless or selfish.

Pushback is almost inevitable when a woman attempts to inhabit her own space. (After all, if enough women became self-actualized, we might topple the patriarchy and that would never do!) Even those who mean you well are likely to begrudge you time apart if they feel it takes something from them. But as you begin your journey, it is essential to make time to sit and be with yourself. For you cannot change what you cannot see. Your mission, for the moment, is to develop your awareness of who you are and the truth of your situation.

What does this look like, for you? It may mean getting up early to spend a few minutes journaling. Or taking a solo walk during your lunch break. It may look like turning off the TV or the car radio and tuning into a deep quiet or taking a meditation or yoga class. A friend of mine puts a sign on her door, *Writer at work: do not disturb.* Another uses a headset to tune out the noise of her kids and husband. These small acts of autonomy add up. Slowly, you begin to reconnect with your inner self.

If you were to tune into your inner Desert Woman right now, she might say: *I am that part of you that is untrammeled by others' opinions or demands. I am the spaciousness you seek. I am the wild empty lands where you can think and dream, free of worrying about everyone else. It is time to make space for yourself, to come to know your own truth. I ask you, what is it that you truly need?* Just take a moment to let those words sink in. Notice if you feel any resistance. Or perhaps you sense Desert Woman energy stirring in you? Don't judge, just pay attention.

A friend's husband recently left her. She tells me that she hurts all over, but with her husband gone, she has more time for herself. Into those spaces come thoughts of, *I get to decide when I am hungry, and what I want to eat. I get to choose when I go to sleep.* She's curious about where these questions might lead and—as painful as this time is for her—who she is becoming.

Sometimes, our journey begins by naming our own wants. Sometimes, it begins by looking at how we are betraying ourselves. For me, transformation would have been impossible without confronting my alcoholism. I required physical sobriety first. For you, it might be psychological or emotional sobriety, the realization that you need to drop the drama or release a toxic relationship. In any and all cases, becoming grounded in the realities of our situation has to be first and foremost.

Desert Woman asks you to name those things in your life that aren't working. Whatever is causing you pain, numbing your creativity, or eroding your self-worth—name it and own it. Let the words come. Desert Woman will not judge them or you. She is the one who has been called all the names, from bitter to misfit. She knows the pain of letting go. Of allowing the heat to burn away all that is false until she is deep in her bone-truth. How some decisions and realizations change the whole trajectory of a life. She knows the power of simply stepping back and allowing the truth to emerge, unadorned by old stories or fears.

She is the ache in the heart of the one who is leaving. But she is also the wide and beckoning arms of the new horizon.

Signs that Desert Woman Is Trying to Get Your Attention

Burnout—You are so exhausted by stress and overwork, or even ill health, you have nothing left to give.

Barrenness—Nothing you do is taking hold or bearing fruit.

Disillusionment—Nothing makes sense—not the culture, not your life; it all feels like a mirage.

Need for Solitude—You sense that something is happening within you that needs attention. Noise, chatter, even the company of good friends feel like distractions from a deep internal process.

The Dead Zone—A feeling of complete desolation that is a result of bottoming out on an addiction to love, sex, alcohol, drugs, shopping, etc.

Numbness and Depression—As the result of not expressing grief.

Irritability—Resentment towards loved ones, envy of others' creativity.

A Burning Passion—An idea or overwhelming passion seizes you and you feel yourself on fire, knowing your life is about to change, but not knowing how.

Robyn Davidson: A Natural Desert Woman

Robyn Davidson is just twenty-six years old when she sets off alone in 1977 to cross 1,700 miles of desert from Alice Springs to the Indian Ocean, a journey that will take nine months. For company, she has four camels and her dog, Diggerty. With her youthful, slender frame, she looks almost too fragile for the task.

Holed up in the remote town of Alice Springs in the Northern Territory, her departure point, Robyn works for a camel trainer. In return, he promises the camels to carry her supplies, but he never delivers and, half-crazed, threatens to kill her. A local guy tells her that she's been nominated to be the next "town case"—the next woman to be raped. "You shouldn't be so friendly," he admonishes. The message is clear: Free-spirited women deserve to be punished.

Despite all obstacles, Robyn will not surrender her dream. Told she is mad, that a girl shouldn't even try such a thing, she obstinately stays true to herself. And so, finally, after two years in Alice Springs, having acquired her camels from a different trainer, she sets off. She writes, "All around me was magnificence. Light, power, space, and sun. And I was walking into it. I was going to let it make me or break me. I felt like dancing and calling to the great spirit."[6]

Robyn had to fight for her right to embark on this adventure. And while your own quest is likely very different, perhaps you can relate to the challenge of not giving up on yourself, especially when the world is hell-bent in keeping you so small. Robyn's story demands that we imagine bigger, braver ways of being. She makes us wonder what would happen if we simply took that first step.[7]

The Karoo Desert of South Africa

Here, on this land that has been in my family since the 1800s, I call upon the vision and guidance of my ancestors. In her sun I am stripped of the inessential. The wind speaks clearly, and the natural rhythm of day surrenders me to the slow life—to the ceremony and art of living. A vast openness of time and space that once intimidated me now inspires. I raise my hands to the skies in gratitude and prayer.

This blessed, sacred life.
Beauty—my companion. Simplicity—my teacher.
In emptiness I dance, singing my soul into infinity.
Some call it nothingness. I call it everything.
Here, away from the incessant noise and busyness,
I can finally breathe.

—Gabrielle Alberts

Integration

Journal Reflection: Taking the First Step

As you contemplate Robyn Davidson's story, note your reaction to it. Do you admire her bravery? Do you think she was reckless or thoughtless to take such risks? Don't judge your reactions, simply pay attention to them.

Then quietly contemplate your own relationship to risk. Do you tend to take chances? If so, what kind? Do you like to feel secure? If so, what provides you with that feeling? How willing are you to negotiate between taking chances and playing safe?

How comfortable are you with the idea that women are also free to set off alone, in search of themselves?

What about women who have children and other responsibilities? What about you?

There are no right or wrong answers.

When you're ready, simply jot down any thoughts and ideas that come to you in your journal. Then ask, what first step am I willing to take?

Journal Reflection: Answering the Call

- ❋ I've been called to this journey because . . .
- ❋ I know I've been called, because . . .
- ❋ At this moment, I fear . . .
- ❋ At this moment, I am excited by . . .
- ❋ I hope to emerge from my time with Desert Woman with . . .

Space for Solitude

The desert is a natural extension of the inner silence of the body.

—JEAN BAUDRILLARD

Desert Woman embodies solitude and silence. At home in a sparse land, she craves the blessing of aloneness. The desert creosote bush puts down poisons so other plants—even her own offspring—which cannot grow in her vicinity. In the same way, Desert Woman fights for her own space. She needs it to survive and thrive.

To fit into family life or society, we often conceal our true sense of self. The natural solitude of Desert Woman is the antidote to that kind of estrangement. She gives us a space apart from the constant thrum of convention and the need to conform. With her, we come to know—and claim—the vivid reality of our own being. As Terry Tempest Williams writes, "Perhaps that is why every pilgrimage to the desert is a pilgrimage to the self. There is no place to hide and so we are found."[8]

There is a reason the Australian aborigines map every bush, sand hill, and water hole through music, along songlines, handed down from the Ancestors in the Dreamtime. This is the way to survive in the Outback, one of the harshest places on Earth. Similarly, a Desert Woman maps the vastness of her inner landscape. She comes to know it with a wild singing intimacy that allows her to navigate the toughest terrain without losing sight of who she is and of what she's capable.

That said, you may have a complicated relationship with solitude. Historically, women have been the ones to join in community, to work in groups in the fields or to gather at the river to do the washing. We needed company and laughter to keep the wild animals at bay and to support each other. Thus, deep in your DNA, solitude feels dangerous. It is as if when you are alone, you worry something might pounce and devour you. If solitude is new for you, it is only natural that it brings up such primal fears. Solitude is a practice. One you can approach in small increments at first.

The more you acclimate to Desert Woman, the less you will fear the silence. Away from the noise of the world, the emptiness at the center of your psyche is transformed into a realm of subtle vibrancy. There is at your core a deep aliveness. Like the desert's Joshua Tree, the creosote, the flowering shrubs, this vitality always remains, regardless of heartbreak or times of drought.

Some of the things you discover will fill you with awe. Others will terrify you. When a scorpion scuttles across your path, you draw back, fearing its poisonous tail and sharp pincers. A sidewinder snake slithers through the dunes at your feet, and you recoil. Your "fight or flight" reaction is activated. Behind this swift and instinctive response is a cultural fear of nature—and of all that is strange and primal in you.

Apart from community, in the vastness of your desert soul, you begin to bring the different parts of yourself together, learning to accept the prickly, the lowly, and the thirsty portions of your being. Through self-acceptance, you make peace with yourself. This is the long, soft exhale when you find yourself laid bare and unafraid.

Desert Woman celebrates all of you, even those aspects others have tried to eradicate as unworthy or unlovable. She makes room for those portions of your life you may have shut away. She teaches you to not bear just witness, but loving witness to the quirky, unaccepted, sometimes very terrifying and as yet unloved parts of you. Can you feel the spaciousness in that invitation?

Celebrating your uniqueness, you come to realize it is your strangeness that make you strong. You have been taught to dull your eccentricity in order to fit in. Desert Woman reminds you that all those that make their home in the desert—from tiny foxes with huge ears or lizards with horns—are wondrously weird and resilient. And it is those aspects we see as weird that enables them to thrive. If you remain a stranger to yourself, always trying to adjust yourself to others, you will never know how extraordinary you truly are.

What is the gift of freely chosen solitude? Deep authenticity. This is what places your journey of transformation on a solid footing. It is time to experience the magnificence of your inner being. Like Desert Woman, you are following your own songline.

Integration

Journal Reflection: Making Space and Time

How will you make space and time to be with yourself? One of the great mistakes is to believe you need hours and hours of time, and so you don't take advantage of the small openings in your life. But what if you did?

❋ Make a list of five things you could do to create a little bit more space and time for yourself, e.g., set a timer to limit Facebook or TV and schedule daily Desert Woman breaks.

❋ Make a list of five things you could do in five to fifteen minutes that would help you connect with yourself, such as meditating, taking a walk, or listening to a meaningful podcast.

❋ After you have read through your list, reflect on which ones you could start implementing, right now.

❋ Then put them into your calendar.

Forty-four years ago, my first marriage failed in the desert. The whole experience was buried, never spoken about. I moved on. Listening to the Desert Woman meditations, I saw that it was not failure that happened in the desert, but liberation. I wish I had had the courage to see that. To branch out and become someone new.

—Carol

In the desert of my soul, I stand still. I am alone, but I am not afraid.

—Camille B.

I am surprisingly but profoundly grateful to be awakening the Desert Woman archetype and feeling the deep rumble of liberation from constructs like *Nice* and *Good* that have been holding me hostage to cracking out the prickle and cackle— how terrifyingly marvelous!

—Jacquelin S.

Entering the Emptiness

They cannot scare me with their empty spaces
Between stars—on stars where no human race is.
I have it in me so much nearer home
To scare myself with my own desert places.

—ROBERT FROST

When I first got sober, had you asked me what I wanted or who I liked, I wouldn't have been able to answer. Caught between two powerful addictions—alcoholism and people pleasing—I had no idea who I was. Worse still, my shame for all the "crazy," "slutty" things I had done while drinking meant I couldn't stand my own company. Twelve-step meetings helped to keep me sober by offering community and support, but they didn't always help when I walked out of the rooms and faced myself, alone.

An added challenge was the constant anxiety I felt in early sobriety. My thoughts flitted everywhere, specs of dust in sunlight. Sometimes my anxiety was so acute my heartbeat would race, and I would gasp for air—a full blown panic attack that landed me in the emergency room struggling to breathe. A doctor prescribed Librium to calm me, but I knew, for me, a mood pill was a slippery path that could lead back to drinking. I was a bag of jumping anxieties and nervous tics. How could I even begin to slow down and turn inward?

Sitting quietly on a zafu to meditate for long stretches was not an option (way too advanced!). But as I walked the city to my 12-step meetings, my agitation lessened, and my breathing and pulse fell into a comfortable rhythm. As I walked, I found it much easier to observe myself without judgement. There was more room to simply be, and the world presented me with surprising delights—a hummingbird perched on a branch, a colorful rock, a shimmer of leaves. Nature was showing me how to open to what was present without and within.

Later, I learned of the Tuareg, a semi-nomadic people who have made their home in the Sahara for thousands of years. Their music, played by both men and women, follows the rhythm of a camel's walking. It is music that arises from setting out alone across a vast stretch of desert, traveling for miles in a trance-like state. It is a song of the soul, beautiful and haunting. This was what I felt as I walked the streets of San Francisco, slowly coming to know myself deep in the bone.

We can find the rhythm of aloneness in other ways, such as when we are washing dishes or making dinner or cleaning the house. These repetitive domestic tasks, so often delegated to women, are perfect opportunities for turning inward.

But historically, women have also taken radical steps to assure a path of solitude, away from the ceaseless demands of family. The desert mothership—early Christians—gave up worldly things and went into the wilderness to embrace the inner life. They sought to find themselves by getting closer to the divine and to their own inner worlds through contemplation and prayer. Silence was part of the fabric of their existence, as was the wild sweep of the desert where the sky burns with stars. They lived simply, honoring stillness and solitude and kindness. In their desert tradition, the primordial sin was the sin of forgetting that each life is a wondrous gift to be treasured. We, who have forgotten our own sacred depths, are also called to the desert to remember who we truly are.

For many years, however, I had "good reasons" not to look inward. What if I didn't like what I saw in myself? What if I wasn't a good person? Or even interesting? An existential sense of terror greeted me when I thought of solitude.

In this, I know I'm not alone. Perhaps you, like me, are worried that you will have to confront some level of guilt or self-loathing before you are comfortable with your own company. This is not a reflection of some personal failing, but a symptom of the way women have been shamed over millennia.

I have sat in groups of women who judge themselves without mercy. Their inner critic is so cruel, it tears into the soft flesh of their psyches until it draws blood. I have listened to the stories of abandonment and brokenness and unworthiness. And a sense that if they ever knew—or the world ever came to know—the truth of who they are, they would be destroyed. So many of us have been led to believe that we are deeply flawed. When we finally make space to be with ourselves, we may feel panic-stricken. The inner critic, let loose, begins to name everything in us that's "wrong": we are imposters, selfish, lazy, and on and on.

No wonder we may first find ourselves resisting the call of Desert Woman by distracting ourselves with romance, TV, shopping, or the addiction of our choice—anything to avoid the discomfort of being with ourselves. When I first got sober, I was told it was never good for anyone to get into a relationship their first year. I lasted three months. Romance, even with a man I wasn't particularly attracted to, offered a means of escape.

Or it can be that when you finally allow yourself to be alone, it feels as if you are standing in front of a locked door—your soul is on the other side, but you just can't get to it. That's when you experience the true terror of *terra nullius*, a term for the desert that means "the land of nothing." The experience is that of an overwhelming sense of kenophobia, from the Greek for fear of empty places. Even just thinking about the vastness of your inner self may trigger anxiety and nausea.

But know this too: Desert Woman has a genius for healing that aloneness. She burns with a passion that comes from deep within. She urges you to explore what is lost, neglected, or even discarded in your life. *Don't you know*, she asks, *there is no one like you in this entire universe?* With her help, you can start tracking down the unknown and startling aspects of your wild soul.

The word *abandonment* means to be without a destiny. We abandon ourselves when fear and hopelessness prevent us from knowing ourselves deeply, and apart from others' expectations and demands. The poet Anne Sexton writes of this despair: "Each night, I am nailed into place / and forget who I am."[9] What is that you have forgotten about yourself? What do you need to remember?

As a Desert Woman, you discover that you have a particular kind of soul. At first, this awareness may be just a spark, but if you remain constant, giving it air and space, it will grow. A flame of passion long denied will flare up, and you will rekindle your creative self.

The more time you spend with Desert Woman, the more you come to know every rock, gully, and sandhill of your own inner terrain, the more peace you will feel. And the more you know the ground of your being, the more secure the foundation upon which to build your life as a Wild Soul Woman.

The Far Away of Georgia O'Keeffe

In her early forties Georgia O'Keeffe left the orbit of her husband, New York photographer Alfred Stieglitz, to retreat into the Zen-like simplicity of life at Ghost Ranch in the high desert of New Mexico. Stieglitz, a charismatic, egotistical man, many years older than O'Keeffe, was often demanding and overwhelming. In New Mexico, O'Keeffe came into her own, developing her striking series of flowers and animal skulls, as well as the color palette that would make her famous. Everything was distilled to its essence in the desert, which O'Keeffe called her "Far Away." While Stieglitz was alive, she split her time between New York and New Mexico. Yet daringly, O'Keeffe decided to carve out her own life, to claim the space—literal and psychological—to pursue her art.

Integration

Meditation: Reclaiming the Hidden Life

I first came across cryptobiotics, a word that means hidden life, in the desert. It was on a sign, warning visitors to keep to the trail so as not to destroy the life we couldn't see: a delicate embroidery of lichens, mosses, and bacteria that held the fragile soil in place. In a similar way, we contain hidden and forgotten worlds that Desert Woman invites us to pay attention to. We, too, are looking for cryptobiotics—the hidden life in us.

For this practice, simply find a space where you feel safe and at ease. Settle down, light a candle, or play soft music—whatever allows you to consciously relax every muscle in your body.

Imagine your body as this beautiful desert place. Then, in this expansive, relaxed, and non-judgmental place, ask yourself:

What do I need to remember about who I am?

Allow any and all images to arise, and simply welcome them home, with compassion and love.

And again:

What do I need to remember about who I am?

Keep asking the question until you naturally feel that you have absorbed as many memories and images and insights about yourself as you can hold at this moment.

Know that you can return at any time and pick up where you left off. And then, slowly, allow your eyes to open and come present to yourself in the moment.

Take some time to reflect on what you've learned. And if you are moved to do so, take out your journal and record your experience.

Journal Reflection:
The Weird and the Wonderful

What are some of the weirdest desert animals and plants that you know about? If you are unfamiliar with any, do a little research, and you'll soon discover a wealth of information on some of the strangest and most well-adapted desert inhabitants. Choose one that piques your curiosity and write a character sketch about them. Have fun. A character sketch is a like a portrait in words, and you will want to bring this plant or creature alive on the page. When your character sketch is complete, take a moment to read it through. Then complete these sentence stems,

  ❋ Reading this, I notice . . .
  ❋ This [*name of creature or plant*] mirrors my . . .
  ❋ The [*name of creature or plant*] makes me feel . . .

Desert Woman speaks to me, reminding me I have the infinite space to be myself, to reach out beyond the endless dusty horizon unashamedly. To be bare bones, open, exposed, raw and real for the world to see. In the desert I can have the solitude and quietness to go within, experiencing both my darkest coldest nights and my warmest and sunniest of days.

—Tamara E.

The Wide-Open Space of Grief

You want psychoanalytic advice?
Go gather the bones.

—Clarissa Pinkola Estés

Unattended, grief can appear as endless as a desert with no water in sight. If it cannot be witnessed or shared, it spreads into every crack and gully, taking hold as depression, numbness, rage, or as a dust-dry ache that permeates every part of your being. Fatigue drags you down and makes action almost impossible. But grief expressed is like water in the desert, ushering in life.

And so, in the most inhospitable places, healing begins.

The desert is littered with bones that do not easily decompose in the dry air. To walk in the desert is to walk close to death. It is to feel the loss of all that has passed—of not living fully up until now, of past losses that haven't yet been grieved, of shedding and releasing the old self. The desert reminds us that life is a perilous adventure and loss is a part of it. You are here to gather the bones.

Do not fear what may arise. Though you may be parched, thirsty, desperately lonely in your pain, Desert Woman will help hold you in the space of grief.

What is it you need to mourn? What will never come to pass in your life? What hurts cut deep? There are things you cannot recover: perhaps your ability to bear a child, or to restore a relationship, or to recreate the past, or live in world where nature is pristine and unpolluted. As a Desert Woman you face harsh realities but, in doing so, summon the courage to feel, honor, and release your grief.

When your heart dries up, you naturally yearn for the release of rain. And even here, in the most parched places in your life, you may sense the drought will eventually be broken, and your heart will overflow again. As you come to know the desert you will learn that water exists even in the harshest places. And so, my sister, it is time to simply sit with your sorrows and griefs and let them come. This is the way of Desert Woman. You stay put, understanding that there are times when the best you can do is breathe. Or you dance out your agony under a merciless sun.

Desert Woman neither conceals nor coddles. In her, we confront the pains we have buried, the thirsts we have long suppressed. We own our grief, express it, learn from it; we discover its depth and its potency.

Desert Woman makes of grief an art, an ecstatic pain. Ecstasy is from the Greek *ekstasis*, which means both "insanity" and "removed from our proper place." And isn't acute sorrow just that? Doesn't it expel us from life? Derange us? Send us into exile? Here, in the desert of your heart, you learn to transform grief into something beautiful.

Patience will be required, as will trust that all is timed for your good. Wildflower seeds in the desert wait and wait until the rains are strong and the season right. The rain is intended not to just awaken them but to shift them, so that when they bloom it is in a different place. You, too, will find yourself standing on different ground when your tears finally flow.

My sister, it is time to howl your grief into this wide-open wasteland.

The Dance of Sorrow

The heart that breaks open can contain the whole universe.

—JOANNA MACY

Remember Robyn Davison's story of crossing the Outback alone, with her dog, Diggerty? One night, Diggerty eats bait, poisoned with strychnine, set out by trappers for the dingoes. He convulses and froths at the mouth, and Robyn can do nothing to help him. She picks up her gun and shoots him.

That day she walks thirty miles, barely eating or drinking. And again, the next day. And the next. Her grief so great at the loss of Diggerty, she barely knows where she is or where she is going. Her trance finally breaks in the claypans, an immense area consisting of hundreds of square miles of perfectly flat packed earth, without a blade of grass or a tree or any sign of life. Exhausted, heartbroken, she ties up her camels and strips down. On the vast, smooth packed earth, she begins to dance.

The sun flares. The silence surrounds her. In the broiling heat of the desert, on blood earth, naked, she howls and dances out her loss under the blank gaze of a white-hot sky. Finally, shaking from fatigue, she collapses into sleep.

Robyn is a young woman who has been literally and psychologically stripped bare. The depth of her vulnerability, her overwhelming grief, stirs me even now. She shows me what it is to lose control, to surrender completely to the agony and also the ecstasy of grief.

It's not the end of her journey. She still has 450 miles to cover, but it is in many ways the turning point. She experiences a relief from grief so deep, it transforms her. She describes it this way. "When I woke," she writes, "I felt healed, and weightless, and prepared for anything."[10]

The image of Robyn dancing out her grief is to me a profound gift. She is the embodiment of Desert Woman. We live in a culture that has no way of holding and helping us through our pain. I, like many, have long carried a deep source of grief inside that I didn't know how to heal from. Thanks to Robyn I had an image I could work with. I could literally see myself moving through my grief wordlessly and vulnerably. I saw myself stoking the fire of my grief, rather than trying to cool it or tamp it down.

Robyn's was the heat of grief, and it burned. I knew in my heart that I too needed to touch into something fiercely heartbroken, wildly sorrowful. My grief wasn't going to surrender gently. Like Robyn, I had to go and meet it at the fiery edge of the world.

I was just four years old when my brother, David, was sent off to boarding school, and I can still feel the heartbreak. I was left the only child in a large house with two alcoholic parents. My brother, three years older than me, was my best friend and protector. In his absence, I felt as if I had lost some part of myself. When he was just thirty-nine, David had his first heart attack. At age sixty, his heart gave out. Pain again wracked my body so that I could barely eat or think. But by then, I had come to approach grief with reverence. I knew to first sit in the silence and feel its burn. Then to move. So, when David died, I danced my grief, barefoot and wild, until my tears mingled with my sweat. *I am alive*, I would think. *I hurt; I am in pain. I miss him, but I am alive.*

One night, six months after his death, my brother appeared to me in a dream. I was following him down a long path when he turned to me and told me that I couldn't go beyond the point at which he stood. "It's okay," he said. "There will be plenty of time to talk later." I awoke sobbing. It was time to let my brother go.

Grief touches us all. We cannot be alive without losing the people and things we love. Grief is an expression of our humanity, our ability to feel the sorrows of a struggling world. And unlike depression, which settles upon us like ash, grief has energy and movement. It tears through us a raging sandstorm, shredding our dignity and defenses. It is mighty and at times violent. Opening to grief, we often feel a primal release, as if all the accumulated grief of the world is pouring through us. Our hearts blown wide open, we experience the widening circles of empathy and compassion we will need as we continue on our journey.

If you have ever cried your guts out, snot pouring out your nose, a keening rising from deep in your throat, then you know that grief rearranges every cell of your body. And when it is over, you feel washed clean. Grief, acknowledged, is a keystone emotion, restoring vitality and energy to every aspect of your life. To fulfill your destiny, you first need to feel. And in order to feel, you must make peace with grief.

When author Elizabeth Gilbert lost her lover and best friend to cancer, she wrote, "I am not depressed, in the wake of Rayya's death. I am DESTROYED, but I am not depressed—but that's only because I'm willing to be destroyed."[11]

Imagine if, rather than denying it, you finally allowed the knot of grief to uncoil, liberating you to feel more intensely and live more creatively. You are not a crybaby or weak. You are Desert Woman, your grief as necessary to the planet's healing as it is to your own. Deep ecologist Joanna Macy puts it this way, "as your heart breaks open there will be room for the world to heal."[12]

A friend, still healing from childhood trauma, asks, "Is there a timetable for grief?"

Desert Woman's endless horizon would suggest not. Here, grief is granted all the time and space it needs. Grief is neither a problem to be solved nor a riddle to be figured out. Grief enters our lives, and we are transformed. The parched and fissured landscape, the perfect mirror of our broken hearts.

Don't be a crybaby, You care too much, Don't let them see how much it hurts. These are all messages fed to us from childhood. New Age religions preach that if we focus on the negative, we'll create more suffering. This doesn't just silence us; it shames us. The message is brutally clear: if you focus on your heartbreak, you contribute to the world's suffering. Is it any wonder that we relegate our sorrows to some dusty corner of our hearts?

Which is why owning our anguish is one of the most radical acts we shall ever perform. Our culture would have us drive heartbreak underground, as if it is unworthy of us. But to not be in pain in a world of suffering is to not be alive. And aliveness is what Desert Woman wants from you. It is what the world needs from you. And it begins, here, my sister, by speaking the truths of your grieving heart, long silent, long buried, and no longer willing to remain hidden.

Integration

Journal Reflection: What Is Dying? What Is Being Born?

What grieves you? What hurts like hell? What are you mourning? Read the following poem by Kathy Kuser, out loud, several times.

Desert Soul

Somewhere burning
in the desert of my being
lies a deep inexplicable sadness.
My consciousness circles
like a vulture sensing
but not yet seeing
what it is that is
struggling
below.
There is nothing to do here
in this terrible place, but to

sit and breathe
and to pray to stay open
to that raw tenderness of life
that plays itself out
on the open stage that is
my desert soul.

One thing I can trust
is that all pilgrims must
come here at least once—
to learn how to die
with their eyes wide open.

When you are ready, begin writing your own poem or prose piece:

Somewhere burning
In the desert of my being . . .

Movement Prompt: The Dance of Grief

As we have been learning, dancing is a powerful means of moving grief through your body. As you prepare to dance your grief, you might want to think about the spaciousness of the desert, that wild expanse. Allow yourself to be extravagant in your movements at times, knowing that you can fully embody your expansive Desert Woman self as you dance.

What you will need: A free half hour. A candle or two to light your way. And music that draws out feelings of sadness and grief. I like to listen to classical music, but a sad song by your favorite singer or any music that evokes deep emotion is good. You may like something with a strong beat or something fluid and floaty. There's no right or wrong in your choice.

As you listen, allow grief to begin to fill you. Your thoughts might wander to certain losses, or you might simply feel grief grip you as a tightening in the throat or belly, or an ache in the heart. We don't have to know the particulars of grief to experience it.

Let the music sweep you up in emotion. Can you make room for your feelings without shutting them down? Allow grief to flow through you and, when you are ready, begin to move to the music in whatever way feels right to you. If tears come, welcome them. If images arise, welcome them. If old heartbreaks resurface, welcome them. Move the feelings through your body as you dance. If it feels right and comfortable, allow yourself to sing, howl, keen. And if you need to stop, stop. Take care of yourself.

After you dance, take a few moments for quiet contemplation. If you like, you can record your experience in your journal. Or simply relax, allowing yourself to fill with peace and calm.

Note: If you have a group of girlfriends to whom you feel deeply connected, this can be a powerful group experience. After dancing, share your experiences with each other. What did you release? How do you feel now? What have you made space for?

Emptied
I weep at the beauty.
Here, in the desert
I am nothing.
I am everything.

—Laurie Shade-Neff

I accept Desert Woman's wisdom
A thirst quenched in dryness
Sustained through silence.

—Meganne Older

The Challenge:
Knowing You Are Enough

I Want to Learn . . .

to speak the language of saguaro,
grow tall at my own pace, take my time,
put down one root deep into the Earth's belly
and swell with rainwater to see me through the drought times.
I want to learn to speak the language of slowness,
of learning to say . . . not now . . . later . . .
Of taking seventy years to offer my first bloom,
the bleached color of moonlight,
and watch bats cross miles of crystal night
to seek out my precious nectar.
I want to cultivate long bristles and a thick skin
to know, always, that in and of myself,
I am enough.

Everything about Desert Woman proclaims, *Take me as I am or don't
bother.* Her capacity to look after and please herself, stands at odds
with the message many women have internalized: that our value
is dependent on constantly giving to and caring for others. Desert
Woman reminds us we are not just a garden of delight supplying
endless nectar. We are thorny souls with minds and wants of our own.
And we don't need others to provide our sense of worth.

Imagine wrapping yourself in a thick cloak of protection. This cloak, like the spiny flesh of the saguaro cactus, is to declare yourself "off limits" for a while so that you can concentrate on your inner resources and needs. Even if you physically stay close to family, community, or a difficult situation, you must turn inward to seek your own truth and toughness. If you don't have healthy boundaries, how will you ever take a stand for your own life? If you are constantly striving for approval, status, or material possessions, how will you ever know yourself apart from others?

Many of us fear Desert Woman's capacity for self-interest, because we fear being thought of as selfish. It is as if we live in terror that the slightest shift of direction in the winds of approval will cause us to vanish, like footprints in the sand. If we stop doing for others, will we cease to matter? If we admit to our stress and exhaustion, will we be called weak?

These are not the imaginings of an overly fraught mind. Women have been taught we are expendable and replaceable. We have been written out of the books, our *herstory* neither recalled nor lauded. Is it any wonder if we sometimes struggle to recognize our own substance? Is it any wonder if there are days when we seem to exist only in our usefulness to others?

Just as the desert is described by its limitations—too dry, not enough vegetation, too hostile—so we as women define ourselves by our deficiencies: not strong enough, pretty enough, smart enough. Right from the get-go, we are taught that we must try harder, do more, simply to have the right to exist.

But here's the thing—we've been better. We've done more, given more, worked harder, and we still aren't where we want to be. Increasing our efforts is not the answer. Doing more won't change things.

In the desert, where life burns hot and you find yourself depleted, overdoing can kill you. If you cannot find it in yourself to say, "No," your body will eventually say it for you. This is how it happens that there are more women with chronic illnesses than ever before. Our systems are exhausted. We are literally dying from too much trying. It is time to pull back.

In the dry, parched landscape of Desert Woman, toads lie dormant for months, even years, waiting for the rains to burst forth so they can surface, sing, and mate. Foxes burrow underground until nighttime. Lizards sit as still as rocks. Nothing is demanded of you but your attention. Everything is present. The sun warms you, a sunset blazes across the horizon, and stars thicken across an impossibly vast sky. There is nothing to do, no one to impress. It is all perfect, just as it is. Just as you are.

The poet Joy Harjo, who has lived most of her life in the deserts of the Southwest, writes of her beloved landscape, "It doesn't need to be flattered by the rain. It certainly needs rain, but it does with what it has, and creates amazing beauty."[13]

If you listen inwardly to what Desert Woman has to say, she will tell you: *The deepest kind of self-care is when you can savor and protect what you have, without always striving for more.* Knowing you are enough brings a wild freedom to love your life as it is and yourself as you are, however quirky or unique. If you can learn to trust yourself, if you listen first and foremost to your own voice, then you, too, will reclaim something fierce and free within.

And it is this that makes the Desert Woman so important to you. You are here to learn how to resist being defined by others' needs. You are here to grow and to give, like the saguaro cactus, according to your own rhythms and wants.

The Art of Doing Less and Being More

I want my life to be a celebration of slowness.
—Terry Tempest Williams

If you feel overwhelmed, exhausted, and undervalued, I want you to understand this: the capitalist system you inhabit is built for burnout. It exploits women's desire to care for others and extracts from us every ounce of spare energy. The result? We are dying on our feet. This is not news. Women are paid less, wield less political power, and have fewer financial assets than men. We take on more responsibilities at home, regardless of our work situations, and are frequently the ones left caretaking both the kids and our aging parents. And while we know that this is changing, it is still our reality in the main.

Most women I know feel as if they are falling behind on almost every front. But if you blame yourself for not ever getting on top of your workload, your bills, your to-do list, then your sense of self-worth will eventually erode. The worse you feel about yourself, the more exhausted and powerless you will become. In this state, it is all too easy to fall into the role of pitiful victim. No blame here, either. I've done it many times.

Then Desert Woman shows up in the form of burnout, resentment, or envy. She exposes the false narrative of self-sacrifice. She doesn't overwork, and she doesn't require a lot of anything or anyone. *Imagine,* she says, *if you stopped comparing yourself to others, stopped trying to figure out how to manage everything and everyone, stopped over-giving and overdoing to feel better about yourself.*

This might be a good time to take a deep breath. It can be uncomfortable to confront all the ways we control and manage others, because we don't trust that we are enough. And, if we're really honest, we can see how lack of a belief in our own agency causes us to manipulate people and situations to make ourselves feel better.

It's as if we have a series of secret contracts that only we know about: *If I do this for you, then I expect you to do this for me.* And if they don't deliver, then we are back in victim mode again. *Isn't it enough,* we ask ourselves, *that we are working all kinds of hours to make everyone else feel good?* The whole process is exhausting. The fewer rewards we receive, the more insecure we feel, the harder we push.

Which is why, when you set out on your journey, you need Desert Woman with you—for she doesn't require you to prove anything, or to be anything, other than what you already are. Consider: everything about the patriarchal culture is designed to have you alter yourself in order to fit into a system not of your own creation. In stark contrast, Desert Woman asks only that you reveal more of who you are. This is how you learn to come home to yourself—not by shaping yourself to suit others, but by owning your true nature.

When I think of my addiction to alcohol, I know that it hid a deep inner emptiness—a gaping lack of belief and confidence in myself. In first getting sober, I remember attending a Christmas office party. Trying hard not to look at the line of wine bottles gleaming by candlelight, I felt a sense of emptiness in my solar plexus that almost brought me to my knees—the black hole that addicts and alcoholics refer to. There isn't enough food, sex, booze, admiration, or any other substance to fill that yawning chasm. I soon learned that you can never satisfy an inner need with an outer solution. It only leads to more misery, more exhaustion, and more emptiness.

A Desert Woman, however, is at peace with who she is and knows how to care for her own needs. She is less desirous of approval than most. She takes pride in her ability to support herself, to mend her own clothes, fix her own car, balance her own books, speak up for herself, make her own way. She acquires skills not to impress, but so that she can tend to her own needs, both emotional and material. For her, that's freedom.

At this stage of your journey, you are beginning to explore a sense of an autonomy. The more you lean into Desert Woman, the freer you are of the dictates of others. To paraphrase Brené Brown, the opposite of scarcity isn't abundance, it is *enough*. And you, my sister, are definitely, absolutely enough.

Marta Becket: No Need for Applause

In 1967, on a holiday from New York, ballerina Marta Becket's car broke down in an abandoned mining town in Death Valley Junction. As her husband sought to repair the vehicle, she wandered into an old hotel that had a stage. It came to her in a flash that she would perform on that stage for the rest of her life. And she did, writing music and plays and choreographing dances.

At first, no one came to her performances in this remote, unpopulated town. But applause wasn't what she craved. It was autonomy—being able to dance in her own way.

In time, the intensity of her work and the power of her vision sparked people's curiosity, and the seats filled. But that wasn't the point. She simply wanted to live her life and express her creativity authentically.

In a world that reduces creativity to a commodity, a Desert Woman is guided by her inner flame. She writes poetry, dances, and dreams, but never on demand. Desert Women have a purity that can be bewildering, even downright annoying to some—*I will not do this for money; I will not produce to a deadline; I will not alter my creativity to suit your needs.* When a Desert Woman is on fire with creativity, sparks fly. When her flame goes out, she simply walks away. She burns on her own terms.

Integration

Journal Reflection: What Would You Do?

- ✳ What would you do if you didn't care what others thought?
- ✳ If you freed yourself from practical considerations, what would you be inspired to create?
- ✳ What fuels you?

Journal Reflection: Knowing You Are Enough

Describe a time when you looked after yourself in some way. Perhaps you cooked a delicious meal for yourself when you needed to feel nourished. Or you learned a new skill. Or you extracted yourself from a challenging situation. Or you negotiated a better payment plan. These are not small things. But in overlooking them, we often neglect how resourceful we are.

Choose one memory, however insubstantial it may seem at first. Then simply write the story in your journal, using the third person "she," or "the girl," or "the woman," and present tense (is). By writing in the third person, you are practicing the Desert Woman skill of witnessing. In this case, you are bearing witness to your self-sufficiency. By using the present tense, you more easily conjure up the emotions and details of the situation.

When you have finished writing, take a moment to reflect on your story. Then ask:

- ✳ What have I discovered?
- ✳ What surprises me?
- ✳ What about that story is important for me to remember?

I can see how I won't let myself be enough and then the tears come.

—Katie K.

I am stripped to my bare bones, leaving only the true essence of myself as a scaffolding, in which to support the next phase of my growth. Like a Phoenix rising from the ashes, I can live again, in whatever form I choose. I can be myself, the true me that I have yet to meet.

—Pam W.

The Shift:
Mirage to Vision

I believe in walking in a landscape of mirages,
because you learn humility.

—Terry Tempest Williams

A Desert Woman knows what it is to live out others' dreams and to
find herself thirsty and dry as dust. Hers is a world of mirages. The
air shimmers and distorts. Rocks turn into ravens, Joshua trees into
prophets, the blue sky into a beckoning lake. Everything is suspect
and hard to pin down. Desert Woman's is trickster terrain, and she
is set to turn your world upside down.

Paradoxically, to know the substance of things, you must first
become dis-illusioned. You must come to see that your whole body is
clenched tight, thirsting for something and not getting what it needs.
Lover, job, religious community, home—you can project onto almost
anyone or anything the ability to slake your soul, but that doesn't
make them effective in satisfying those needs. Looking to have your
needs met in the wrong places is harmful. And you may burn out in
the most painful ways before you finally accept that you have been
living a falsehood. Only one thing is clear: if you continue to drink
from a mirage, your spirit will eventually die.

And so Desert Woman works on you, stripping you of your assumptions, scattering your fantasies to the wind until your sense of reality is blown wide open as the sky. She is teaching you to discern between what is false and what is not. The mirage from the true oasis.

To embody the wisdom of Desert Woman is to experience the world as ephemeral. All around, cathedrals and temples in the form of hoodoos and towering mesa make the desert stranger than fantasy—a place more of spirit than flesh. Nothing is set in stone. Everything is shifting, changing, immense, fantastic. What you think you see is constantly challenged.

It is here in this wild liminal land that you reclaim a Desert Woman's visionary capacity to see through the veil to the truth beyond. What currently surrounds you isn't sufficiently lush and liberating. You are still parched. Don't rationalize that away. Don't make excuses. Instead, go deeper into the desert and gaze beyond the mirage, and farther still.

You are seeking a dream of a future that doesn't exist yet, but that can be lived into reality. You will recognize it because it arises from out of your own vision and your own thirst. It is not a fantasy. It is not believing that an oasis will magically appear because you want it to. It is a vision powerful and compelling enough to draw forth your creativity and your dedication. In the desert, a spring suddenly appears, and every cell of your parched being can taste that cold clear water on your tongue. But you will have to dig deep inside yourself to discover that hidden wellspring—what brings you alive.

Living for too long in the world of illusions may make you doubt yourself, and even silence yourself. Perhaps you will feel a little crazy, too. And yet, every day, if you touch real things, walk on real earth in bare feet, you come closer to knowing what is true and what can be relied upon.

In claiming your right to your own vision, the ability to drink from your own inner spring, you are breaking the drought. The world of the desert is phantasmagorical, but as Desert Woman knows, it is also comprised of real earth. Desert Woman offers the capacity to simultaneously hold both worlds—your current reality and the dream of your greater self.

It is time, as a Desert Woman, to speak your vision out loud. And when your vision returns to you, echoing from the red rock chambers in the canyons, welcome it, as it resounds over the vast, sunbaked earth.

Integration

Journal Reflection:
Name It. Explore It. Transform It.

Desert Woman's deep commitment to radical honesty is a powerful force. When you claim that aspect within, you begin to reclaim authority over your life. This simple exercise is the beginning of a powerful partnership with truth that will create a strong foundation as you progress on your journey.

Before you begin, consider this: The truth will set you free, but first it might rattle your bones. Pace yourself, find your own rhythm, and take self-care breaks as you write truth, now and always.

Here are some examples to help you think of your own.

Name It:
My name is . . .
and I am an alcoholic
and I am in a toxic relationship
and I hate my body
and I am always angry
and I feel invisible
and I tell lies because I am afraid of hurting people
and I want to be loved but push people away.

Now it's your turn. Remember to hold yourself gently. You are beginning to develop a practice of bearing witness to your own life without judging yourself. What you are claiming doesn't make you bad, it makes you real. And being real is something rare and necessary in this increasingly truth-averse world.

Explore It:

Now that you've named some of the "truths" about yourself and your life, it's time to explore what impact these have on you. For example, say you wrote, *I feel invisible.* Simply get curious about what that affords you and how it affects you. How do you feel when you're invisible? When did you first feel invisible? What is the story you tell about your invisibility?

Transform It:

Having named it and explored it, what do you want to do about it? Do you want to let it go, simply own it and move on, or is there perhaps a gift in that truth? For example, if you feel invisible, might that allow you to move freely in the world, like Harry Potter with the invisibility cloak?

Developing Radical Honesty

We can't help being thirsty, moving toward the voice of water.

—Rumi

There is a transcendent clarity of vision described by the poet Rilke as a "conflagration of clear sight."[14] This term perfectly captures Desert Woman's ability to burn through the falsehoods that trap us in too-small lives. She urges you to recognize what is real. The question you carry into every situation is this: *What is the truth here?*

We live in a society rank with delusion. The media stokes false grievances while denying the reality of what is really going on. Told that people and planet are better off than ever, we look at the devastation to our ecosystems and communities and respond in disbelief. Told that women are now equals and we should just be grateful, we feel an urge to yell, "Not true!"

Bombarded by distortions, we question our own sanity. Nothing makes sense. Worse still, when we finally turn our attention inward, we realize that we have also been living with our own personal illusions. Why did we pour so much of ourselves into a stale, go-nowhere relationship? How was this job ever supposed to make us happy? How did we end up spending our life . . . (*fill in the blank*)?

As you proudly claim Desert Woman's status as an outsider who shatters societal illusions, you gain the ability to look at the system with clear eyes. As you burn away the layers of illusion, you enter a new place. It is like emerging out of a long blindness into the brilliant light of the desert. You can feel shockingly exposed and want to retreat to the safety of not knowing. Yet if you do, how will you get to the deeper meaning of your life?

Let me say this: our notion of reality has always been subjective. There is no one overriding truth. But there are layers of truths and deeper realities than we are now living. One of the greatest fallacies perpetrated by Western civilization is that it owns the truth, when in fact there are a multiplicity of perspectives. Now we stand before Goliath and dare to add our own visions and outlooks to the mix.

In 2018 my husband and I attended an exhibit of Indigenous Australian women's art at the Museum of Anthropology in British Columbia. The curator of the exhibit began telling us about the women artists whose work was on display. Many of them were elders, but each had only recently been permitted to paint. Indigenous

Australian women had historically been weavers and craftswomen. The men were the only ones allowed to call themselves artists and create images of the Dreamtime.

As I listened to the curator tell these women's stories, I wondered how they must have felt when they looked at that first empty canvas. I thought of their courage, picking up that brush, making that first mark. And I wondered, what if women's visions began to spread across the wider canvas of the world?

As we took in the women's work, I was drawn to two large paintings by the artist Angelina Pwerle, one with a background of sooty black, the other of pinkish red, and both composed of thousands upon thousands of tiny white dots. I was tumbling into the Universe through a swirl of milky galaxies and an infinity of stars. I later discovered, they were, in fact, the small white flowers of the bush plum, native to Pwerle's desert country, northeast of Alice Springs. They were part of her heritage as one of the Bush Plum clans. I remembered what the curator had also told us, "Don't look at these paintings, look into them."

This, I thought, is what we all need to do to heal our fractured world. We need to look more deeply. To see not only plum blossoms, but the deeper reality, not visible to the ordinary eye, of a cosmos that holds everything together. You, me, plum blossoms, and stars.

Developing your Desert Woman vision, you will recognize the larger reality of the world we live in. And as you engage in meditation, art, poetry, ritual, embodying the deep quiet of Desert Woman, you will move beyond subjective truths to experience the eternal ones.

You started on this journey because you sensed a truer vision waiting to be born. In quiet moments it steals upon you, this realization of what this world was intended to be. The rest is just a mirage.

Lynne Twist: A Vision in the Desert

In 1980, Lynne Twist, founder of the Hunger Project, traveled to Thies in Senegal, West Africa, a city on the edge of the Sahel Desert. Her destination was a group of seventeen villages deep in the Sahel where years of drought had resulted in hundreds of deaths, most of them children.

Lynne was invited to sit with the heads of the villages and the other men to discuss the situation, the women's voices excluded from the circle. But one woman kept trying to get her attention, and later Lynne sat down to hear what she and her friends had to say. For a long time, they had been dreaming of a huge underground lake. They knew the lake existed, but the men wouldn't listen to them.

Lynne arranged for the Hunger Project to supply simple tools—buckets, ladders, shovels—to help the women search for this hidden reservoir. The men stood by unwilling to participate. For a year, while caring for their children and tending to their farms, the women dug until, at last, they hit water—a deep and vast underground aquifer that stretched for miles.

The men saw only the drought. The women, who were barred from that inner circle, also saw the drought. But they saw something else—the water beneath. They dreamed it and had the courage to believe in their vision. In the harshest of conditions, in the driest of lands, they found a hidden oasis.[15]

Integration

Journal Reflection: Your Desert Woman Vision

Rest quietly for a moment and reflect on the state of the environment. You may feel pain or a sense of helplessness or anger rising in you. Just let those feelings be. Then take a deep breath, and another, and quietly ask yourself, *Is there a greater truth that I sense about the state of the world?*

Like the women of the Sahel, who dreamed of the water in the midst of drought, see what life-giving visions are rising in you. Begin writing, *As Desert Woman I see . . .* Allow the words to come freely, without censure. After you have written for five or ten minutes, read back through your words. What do you notice? What wellsprings of wisdom have bubbled forth?

Practice: Create a Vision Board

Collect a pile of old magazines, and as you leaf through them, cut out images and phrases that speak to your vision. When you are satisfied that you have what you need, take a piece of thick paper or board—the size is up to you—and play around with how you want to arrange the images and words. When you're ready, get out the glue and paste them down.

Write about what you notice as you gaze at your vision board. Do you see connections or themes that had eluded you before? Possibilities? Obstacles to overcome? Surprises?

Place your vision board where you can see it. Let it inspire your vision of what the world can be.

Note: Feel free to adapt this exercise and paint or draw your vision. The importance here, is not the medium you use to capture your vision, but that you have a tangible expression of it, so it will feel more real.

Practice: Speak Your Truth into the Circle

To begin, bring together two or more sisters to practice speaking up. We experience the power of truth most forcibly when it is spoken out loud and witnessed by those we trust—people who will be supportive and will listen to us without judgement. You might begin by asking each other:

What is the one illusion that you long to shatter?

What do you dream for yourself, your family, your culture, your world?

What does the desert mystic in you see beyond the mirage?

Give yourself permission to speak from a place of deep integrity about what you want and don't want, what you feel, sense, believe. Help each other move deeper into your truth. Don't feel you have to comment or give advice. Practice listening and non-judgment. Simply hold the space for each other in this time of discovery.

It can help to use a talking stick so that it's clear who is the storyteller in the moment. You might give each woman ten or fifteen minutes to speak, or whatever time feels right to you. Avoid cross-talk, by which I mean commenting, interpreting what you hear, or interrupting others to argue a point. This is not a debating society. Every woman's viewpoint is valid and needs space to be fully heard. Remember, this is a sacred space, where visions are emerging. After each person in the group has spoken, you may want to close the circle with a poem or a blessing.

The illusion I want to bust is that life is all about money, owning things, being successful, etc., and that there is no space for magic, fun, pleasure, and enjoyment. How did we get to this place where being busy, stressed, tired, unhappy, etc., is the norm? And people aren't even happy!

—Trina

The illusion I would like to bust is that my marriage is a happy one. I keep pretending but know that we have a lot to work to do, if this relationship is going to last. I want to let my husband know what I really feel.

—Louise R.

The Way:
Releasing the Old

Some day, if you are lucky,
you'll return from a thunderous journey
trailing snake scales

—Geneen Marie Haugen

Desert Woman's spirit animal is the snake, a powerful symbol of rebirth and transformation. When she uncoils in your being, you may feel a shock of Kundalini energy down your spine. This is an indication that you have arrived at a time in your life when you must shed an old skin and let some part of your being die.

Everything about this stage of your journey is set to strip you of what is not alive and growing. The dead weight that causes you to feel heavy of heart has to be surrendered if you are to inhabit your true self. Growth demands sacrifice. This is Desert Woman's way.

She asks: *What will it take to release the limiting stories and labels, to look deep into the patterns that can keep you stuck? What emotional baggage needs to be set down? What habits are constricting?*

Just as the snake rubs against something rough to make a tear in her skin and begin the shedding process, so restlessness and anxiety go to work, rending a hole in your denial. Is your situation really so perfect? Aren't you destined for a wider, more authentic life? Desert Woman's ally insinuates herself into your psyche, winding her way deeper into your core until every cell of your body yearns to let go and be transformed.

Betwixt and between selves, you may feel as blind as the desert snake before the scales fall from her eyes. As you begin to shed your old form, and enter this period of withdrawal, you will likely feel a bone-biting desire to return to the smaller life, the smaller you. And yet, for Desert Woman, security comes not from any value outside herself, but in a commitment to her own authenticity—and a willingness to go wherever that leads her.

The word crisis comes from the Greek *krino*, which means separation. One way or another, you will be separated from your old life. You will get sick, a new lover will challenge you, a friendship will fall apart. Nothing in the desert is permanent; wind and water constantly shift and scour the terrain. When Desert Woman enters your life, you can't cling to the way things were—not even if you try.

How can you embrace this process? Simply. Clearing the clutter from your environment and schedule, you create a spare, desert-like space as part of your shedding ritual. It may then become apparent that you are carrying things so heavy that they drag you down. You will never be able to cross this hot and thirsty landscape unless you set them aside or toss them out—things like guilt, addiction, or a deep-seated belief in your unworthiness.

What do you need to rid yourself of now? What is too great a burden to carry for even one more step? The snake sheds many times over her lifetime; you will also experience many initiations. But you must make a beginning.

Retreating into the desert, you may feel especially raw and vulnerable. Some people, including those you love most, may hover or try to cajole you out of this place—not understanding this is a necessary death and one that must be faced consciously. Others may discourage you, with the message that you have no right to grow and change. It's better for everyone, they'll say, if you just stay put. Here's what I have learned. As you embrace Desert Woman, all that has constrained you so far will rise up and try to pull you down. At times you may feel as if you are dying. But it is this intensity—the awareness that you stand at a point in your life fraught with danger—that gives you the energy to let things go.

Desert Woman has no time for docility and domestication. In her presence, you—the awakened, unapologetic you—rouses. You've outgrown your habitual life. You are partaking in the ancient ritual of death and rebirth.

Shedding Burdens

She woke knowing that if she was to cross the desert she must shed burdens.

—Doris Lessing

Each month a woman recalls her power of shedding as she releases her uterine lining. Her womb is cleansed, making space for the next reproductive cycle. The capacity to release the old is what makes new life possible. This is strong medicine, and it is *your* medicine, even when you are older and well beyond your moon bleeds.

This is how transformation begins—you let go of what no longer makes you feel alive, to make room for the new. In your undoing is your becoming.

Over the years I have shed many layers of skin, and many outworn beliefs. I know this process will continue until I die. Each shedding of some limiting attitude, hollow habit, or heavy shame, has helped me to grow and change, bringing more of who I am into the light. I claim the part of me that is creative, fierce at times, in my desire to protect what and whom I love. And I also claim the part of me that is restless and dissatisfied and sometimes crabby. As I grow older, and more at home in my own skin, I am learning to be with myself, exactly as I am.

Letting go requires that you drop the familiar and face the void. If you aren't this thing, then what are you? Does your life still have meaning if you abandon a spiritual belief or some deeply embedded perception of yourself? Shedding may bring up the fear of dying, of going mad, of entering a No-Woman's Land where there are no visible milestones. Even though you are not facing a physical death, you may fear this change as if you were. And that's the point: acknowledging that dying at some level is essential to valuing our lives.

A workshop participant is undergoing radiation for cancer. She knows she cannot escape the desert until she learns its lessons. Chemo is drying, and radiation a blast of heat, and she is aware there is something else she needs to let go of, along with her cancer cells. Each day, she identifies the things she doesn't want to carry into her life once her disease is in remission. She posts photos on Facebook, of herself, bald and beautiful and vulnerable. She shows us every bit of her pain and her fear. She sheds her armor in front of our eyes.

Another woman tells me that she is going to spend a year in her inner desert. In her daily life, surrounded by clutter, she struggles, amid all the chaos, to find a shirt to wear, or a pen to write in her journal. She feels the need to examine her overstuffed life. She tells me that "too many aspirations and hopes are the same as having none at all, because nothing gets done." Clearing out her material environment, she believes, will help clear out the internal clutter of ideas and enable her to sort through a host of unexamined desires.

Small acts of letting go can be just as transformative as big ones. This was the lesson I learned as a recovering alcoholic: to take it one day at a time. I also knew that all the good intentions in the world would come to nothing without my getting sober. As you think of making your desert crossing, ask yourself: What is the burden that is simply too heavy for you to carry? And are there other smaller burdens that Desert Woman is asking you to shed?

As you face the unknown, and this vast new world that awaits you, it is okay to feel afraid, to feel the desire to cling—to old attachments, to the old life. But know this: if you are to fulfill on your promise, you have to let go. In order to live fully, some part of you must die.

Integration

Journal Reflection: Let Go, Let Go, Let Go . . .

Begin by making a list of the things you want to let go of. Your list may contain just two or five things, or maybe twenty or more.

Here are some things that women have told me they are ready to release:

* Unhealthy relationships
* Shame
* Life-draining habits
* Making myself small
* Resentments and anger
* Disempowering beliefs—I am too this, not enough of that . . .
* People-pleasing
* Overeating
* Grown children

* Drugs and alcohol
* Hating my body
* Being ashamed to speak out
* Fear of losing youthful beauty
* Competing and comparing (especially among women)
* Stories that make me ashamed of myself
* The feeling that I should be doing more, better, greater things

Now it's your turn. Take a large sheet of paper and some bold big pens in different colors and start to make your list. You might even make it in the shape of a snake, letting it spread across the page.

Feel the energy of each thing you want to release and choose the color to represent it. As you write it down, allow your creative self to come forward. Notice how your body responds. Keep adding to the list until you feel it is complete.

When you look it over, do you see a pattern? Is low self-esteem an issue? Do you recognize any obsolescent beliefs your family instilled in you when you were a child? What about cultural pressures to conform in certain ways? Don't judge yourself. Just notice.

After you have made your list, spend some time reflecting on which habits, notions, or behaviors you are ready to let go of. Mark the ones that might be the easiest to release. If you practice letting go of the easier things first, in time it will be less challenging to tackle the larger things that no longer serve. And remember, this is a lifelong process.

Ritual: Desert Woman's Ritual of Release

This Desert Woman ritual focuses on the release of habits, beliefs, and behaviors you identified in the preceding exploration. This is a significant and important part of your process. Make sure to allow enough time for each step: preparation, the ceremony itself, and the bestowal of a symbolic gift.

Preparation:
Choose a dry or desert-like location for your ceremony, if you are able. Then create within it a sacred circle using whatever is at hand: twigs, stones, a stick to draw a circle on the ground. Then spend some time collecting things that nature has let go of—perhaps a dry leaf, branch, pebble, petal, or feather. These objects will stand in for things you are ready to release: a certain belief, relationship, job, fear, etc.

Once Situated:
Spend some time quietly with your inner Desert Woman. Feel where she resides in your body, how you sense her presence in you, and the strength she offers you.

Place each of your "dry things" one by one in the center of your sacred circle or altar, naming out loud what you are ready to release and let go of. Feel the energy of letting go. Let Desert Woman alchemize these offerings, turning them into new energy for you.

Set aside at least five minutes of quiet time and ask Desert Woman: *What gift is there in letting go? What am I making space for? What is the truth here?*

Take five minutes or more to journal Desert Woman's response, as you hear it. Then take a moment to read it back to yourself. *What surprises you? How do you feel? What is your body telling you?*

Complete this part of your ceremony by thanking Desert Woman for her wisdom.

Symbolizing the Gift:
In the days that follow look for something in nature that represents your discovery. Or create a drawing or collage that symbolizes the gift you have received from Desert Woman. The idea is to memorialize

this process of letting go of that which no longer serves. Be sure, as well, to include something that represents what you've learned and serves as an image of what is possible now that you are less encumbered.

Am I mad at how I am treated? Do I have an issue with the immigration policy? White society? Patriarchy? Yes. Whatever it is, I'm taking it all off in the desert, opening up to my anger and rage in order to burn away these feelings so I can get in touch with the strength and wisdom buried within.

—Estella

I wanted to rub up against rough rocks and slough off old habits, thoughts, and emotions. I wanted to hear the silence, to be pressed into the heat and the quiet so that the world tilts and the horizon I started with is not the one I have now. I wanted to crisp my skin so it would flake off, leaving pure bone.

—Caroline S.

I glide through the sand. I am a snake, feeling the coarse grains on my body. I start to shed my old skin, that which I do not need, that which does not serve me anymore. I am rebirthing, coming out. A new skin underneath glowing, moist, tender, ready to be seen in all my beauty and strength.

—Camille B.

Emerging as Desert Woman

A Fully Embodied Desert Woman

You value solitude and silence, shun superficial chatter or any exchange that feels gratuitous or unnecessary. You are drawn to what is essential, vital, real. Sensitive and intense, you require space and silence to process your feelings.

Your creativity can never be bought or dictated to: you bloom in your own way and time. Long, parched periods between new stages of growth aren't unusual, but you have learned to be comfortable with this. You may resist arbitrary deadlines or producing on demand. Your interests are becoming more focused. Even your sense of the divine may be sharpened in this stage, to its essence.

Though you feel deeply, you can also struggle to show your emotions. Self-reliance, self-sufficiency, and self-restraint are the languages of your soul. Like the cactus, you can appear prickly and sharp-tongued at times, but those that know you love you for your nourishing depths.

You are poetic, quirky, a non-joiner, but you are also deeply dependable and loyal to those you love and to what you believe. A truth-teller, you can offend some, but your honesty and lack of demands helps those around you be themselves. You give everyone plenty of space and expect them to return the favor.

Your sexuality, like your creative passions, tends to have a fierce focus. You are more at home with a single partner, or an erotic relationship with self. Your sexuality is born from urgency and a heat so intense it can turn your lovers to ashes. Your challenge is to tend to the embers without being engulfed by the flames. But you may also choose a solitary path. Celibacy, to you, isn't bland and cool; it is self-aroused, self-kindled.

A Desert Woman Caught in the Shadow

What happens when you aren't conscious of Desert Woman's energy? Like many passionate women perceived as too sexual, too fierce, too aggressive, you learn to turn your fire down, resulting in depression and burnout. At this point, you experience the shadow side of this archetype.

With the spark extinguished, you tend to isolate and become hermit-like. You enter the void. You become reluctant to engage with life. Your prickliness punishes and pushes away even those you would draw close. This is a recipe for despair.

When disappointment shuts you down, you start to resent those who can express their joy or passion. You grow adept at taking the air out of the room in order to tamp down others' enthusiasm. You judge people harshly. Become sparing with your affections. A Desert Woman who is disappointed is hard to be around.

And yet, the flame you carry cannot be entirely extinguished. If you give it the slightest bit of light and air, it will glow again. And you will see the sands shift to make a place around you, where you can again embrace life.

Desert Woman and the Planet

You are an example of how to make do, and even thrive, with very little. You live within your means and savor what you have. You mend things, build things, make things last. This simple, spare way of being is a gift to the planet.

You understand the limitations of the physical world. Enough is enough, in your book. You don't need ten pairs of shoes, another car, or even more money in the bank! You recognize when a body, planetary or human, is being pushed beyond its capacity to give, how a river can only irrigate so many acres before it begins to dry up. How a woman can only take care of so many before she burns out.

Equally, you understand that spirit is infinite—that this is where true growth occurs.

You are more comfortable living by your principles and leaving others alone, rather than joining movements and leading the charge. But if a cause sears itself into your soul, watch out world, for you will find a way to turn a spark of a movement into a conflagration of protest.

You don't like standing in the spotlight, and you're not here to convert others. Even so, you know what's right. You know what's needed. You lead by example. And sometimes, you blaze new paths.

Some Final Reflections on Desert Woman

What is Desert Woman's greatest gift to you?

What aspects of Desert Woman challenge you the most?

How do you see yourself embodying Desert Woman's wisdom in the future?

Which areas of your life could most benefit from Desert Woman's presence?

If you were to fully embrace your Desert Woman self, what would change?

How will you express thanks to Desert Woman?

Opening to Forest Woman

You have faced some hard truths, shed some outmoded beliefs, made room for something new. Still, moving from Desert Woman's bare landscape into the lush realm of Forest Woman may feel overwhelming at first. But feel how the forest beckons: this shadowy realm of nourishing dreams and images where you will incubate fresh possibilities for your life. This is not the time for urging your dreams into the light of day. You must wait until the new life takes hold, nurtured in the depth of your being.

Be patient: It may take a while to accustom your eyes to the darkness.

But then, so many wonders await.

2

Forest Woman

Soul of a Forest Woman

*She spins and spirals, expresses herself
in a thousand shades of green.
She is magic, mystery,
a whirl of wonder in a world made plain by literalism.
In leafy tongues she calls you to join her
in the land of enchantment.
Her crown is a tangle of branches,
her feet are rooted in moist earth.
She makes her home in shadows beyond
the unrelenting light of rationality.
She knows everything is birthed from darkness.*

Stage of Initiation: The Dark Womb

The Challenge: Rising from the Ashes

The Shift: Linear to Spiral Path

The Way: Cocooning

Embodied Dimensions: Rootedness, patience, intuition, presence, curiosity, imagination, body wisdom

Guiding Question: How will I face the dark unknown and trust my own instincts?

The Dark Womb:
The Second Initiation

Pathmaker, there is no path, you make the path by walking.

—Antonio Machado

Forest Woman stops you in your tracks. The dark, impenetrable aspect of her realm beckons, but she doesn't present you with a clear or easy-to-follow path. There are myriad slender trails to explore—and sometimes there are none at all.

You cannot change if you forever skirt the edges of the forest. Deep change means going deep within, into the dark womb of Forest Woman who knows how to be with the night and the magic. Her message: *Refuse to follow the well-worn path. Learn how to make your own way through this lush and overgrown domain by trusting your inner compass.*

Ancient as a gnarled oak, majestic as a redwood, Forest Woman is a virgin forest, intact and inviolable. She cannot be controlled. She is the dark feminine that has for so long terrified the establishment. For her herbal lore and healing arts she has been reviled as witch, shrew, harridan, and hag. Western culture has long feared her ability to conjure life out of her own body and imagination.

As you seek to create a life that serves your soul you must bravely engage the heart of Forest Woman. Everything about her leans toward what cannot be domesticated or reduced to a simple equation. She is not interested in your "enlightened" answers or superficial responses. And as much as you might want to describe a deep shift in your being, this is not the time for literal thinking or pinning these changes down with words.

Forest Woman communicates in images. She demands you pay attention to your loamy depths. She asks that you gather symbols from your dreams. She calls you to listen to that knowing shiver down your spine. This is the language of the dark feminine, and it lives in your flesh and bones.

There is no clear-cut path on the Forest Woman journey. Your trail of breadcrumbs can vanish in a moment. Navigating the shadowy forest, there are times when you will fear for your life and long to return to the world of reason and its clear map.

But know this: Forest Woman offers you the most beautiful of sanctuaries. If you persist, you will find a sacred grove within, filled with your own personal magic and mystery. She will connect you with an ancient wisdom and awaken your creative desires. She will help you to discover your inner sight (in-sight) and give you the confidence to gestate your dreams.

When you feel her presence, the time of reverie is upon you. Symbols and images flutter in the moonlight; there are messages to be found in her stippled leaves. You are learning to read and trust the signs. The direction moss grows on trees, the muddy footprints of raven—everything has meaning.

Forest Woman knows the hoot of the amber-eyed owl, the pearly sinew of the spider web, the sensuous shifts in light or temperature— all the subtleties of life are, for her, paths for transformation. *Anything is possible*, she says, *when you lose yourself in me.*

The Realm of Dreams

No longer who we were, we know not who we may become.

—MARION WOODMAN

There is a time, after one door closes and another has yet to open, when you reside in the realm of the in-between—neither who you once were, nor yet who you will become. This is Forest Woman's world. A place made for exploring, dreaming, experimenting. And it marks the next stage of your journey.

Early in my sobriety, I had this dream.

> *I am standing on a balcony, high up on a tall building in New York City, slowly unscrewing the bolts that hold the balcony up. A wizened old woman, like a figure from a fairytale, stands before me. "I'm here to help you," she says. I tell her to go away, I don't need any help, and keep unscrewing the bolts.*

That dream summed up those early years of not drinking, where I continued to reject the wise crone in me. I was determined to keep pressing forward, even if it meant falling hard and fast. I made a lot of mistakes because I couldn't bear the uncertainty as I waited for my sober life to take hold. I rushed into things, forced solutions, never trusting in a greater plan.

Like all people in 12-step programs, I was counseled not to make any major life decisions the first year of recovery. I clearly didn't get the message. Nine months later, I married a cocaine addict. Nine months after that, we divorced. I was blundering from one disaster of my own making to another, pretending that it wasn't my fault.

One day while hiking in the woods, I heard a voice in my head: *Aren't you exhausted from all your pushing and striving?* The question stopped me in my tracks. Lacking trust in both myself and the unknown, I had barreled ahead recklessly. I was constantly exerting my will. But self-will, I was to learn, does not equal self-authority. It was time to slow down.

I began to spend hours among the soaring redwoods close to home, cocooned among their feathered branches, walking on their soft needles, listening to the stirrings of my own soul. I wrote down my dreams, practiced patience, and learned a new approach to life. I would be less reactive, taking a deep breath before responding to a situation. I would take time to check in with my body. *How was I feeling? Were my muscles clenched tight or relaxed? Was I excited or afraid?*

Slowing down, I discovered, has its own power. Non-action, its own intelligence. Waiting, its own grace. By not rushing into things, I learned to pay attention to my senses and to what was happening in the world around me. Synchronicities began to occur more often— those moments when you feel you have been given a sign that you are on the right path. And potent dreams stalked me, often concerning my relationship to my creativity. In touch with Forest Woman, I felt the whole sentient world helping me to find my true path.

Then, in 2001, I had a dream that would dramatically change my life. In August of that year, I drove with Bruce, my husband of many years now, to the Island of Cortes in Desolation Sound, British Columbia. We were attending a workshop on the fifth chakra. Along the way, we camped in the Olympic National Park temperate rainforest, took one ferry after another, and finally arrived at the retreat center.

We set up our tent in the old growth forest, sleeping under twining spruces, listening to the crackle of insects in the fragrant earth, the soft showering of needles like raindrops.

One night, this dream came to me:

I am inside a large white tent filled with children dressed in wool coats, cloth hats, and stout boots. One by one, they move to the center of the tent and begin to dance, each tap of their feet adding colorful dots, in the style of an Aboriginal painting, until they each have created a unique and beautiful mandala.

As another child begins to dance, I look at my wristwatch and say, "We don't have time for this." That's when I see the First Nation elders. They encircle the tent; long, white hair falling almost to the floor, heads thrown back in pure joy at observing the rich patterns each dancer is making. A yellow dog appears in front of me, his face inches from mine. We lock eyes. He has a wide red stripe down his face. In that moment, I get it: there is nothing more important than doing our unique dance.

Shortly after returning home, browsing in a local bookstore, a book literally fell off a shelf and into my hands. *The Circle is Sacred: A Medicine Book for Women* described my dream in detail. The author Scout Cloud Lee notes, "Linear people cannot understand medicine teachings." I blush thinking about my watch! Then she says, "Always at women's circles, it is important to post dog soldiers to divert meddlesome spirits. One who is sensitive to energies, or who is a seer, will serve as a good dog soldier."[16]

Mandalas, I was to learn, represent the feminine—the roundness of our wombs, our cycles. They ground and center us and bring us back to the heart of who we are. This dream was bringing me back to a non-linear way of thinking and being, far removed from the fast-paced corporate world I was accustomed to. This was life in the round—vibrant and celebratory.

I had come to the retreat center looking for answers about a change in career. My dream with the image of the mandala and dog soldier was the first step toward a shift from copywriting to life coaching, and eventually to poetry therapy and the work of the wild soul.

The path was not a straight one; it took many years to unfold. Yet I had been commanded by the forest to guard the beauty and diversity of life. The dream, I should also tell you, came just months after I had a partial hysterectomy and was coming to terms with the fact that I would never bear children. Now I was called to protect life in a different way. But how?

At that point, I didn't have a path or plan. I only had this profound image of a mandala, and the fierce gaze of a yellow dog to guide me.

"If we allow the images that arise from the organs of our own body to shape us, we incubate our own body-soul. If we allow ourselves to be twisted by society's images, we become sick." So writes Jungian psychologist Marion Woodman, who counsels us to "wait for the body to know its truth."[17]

What would it be like to root yourself in your own innate images and metaphors, distinct from those imposed by the culture? As a woman, you have a special ability to navigate this world on both an embodied and intuitive level. As you learn to take your wild dreaming seriously, to burrow into the forest, far away from the scorching glare of patriarchy, you meet the creative ground of your own being. While society strips you of meaning, and thereby denies your imagination and innate wisdom, Forest Woman insists that you regain your sovereignty and conjure a greater vision for your life.

As a Forest Woman, you are curious. You stalk the images and ideas that intrigue you like a wild animal moving through the woods. Every walk can offer up insights: A fallen branch speaks to you of what is lost; a squirrel hoarding nuts of the need to prepare for a long, dark winter. The world is a chorus of concern and guidance, if only you pay attention.

The images that resonate on these walks and the dreams that come to us at night reveal our hidden gifts. As we take them seriously, we take responsibility for who we are becoming. These living images work deep within us, like seeds buried in our womb. In the forest, we gestate our new lives.

A woman unready to meet her forest Self may struggle to connect with the deeper wisdom of her psyche. It is as though she is locked in the rational realm and kept there under a spell. Some of us skirt the edges of the forest but never give ourselves fully to it. We know we can encounter wild wolves and demonic creatures if we step too far off the path. And we fear the messages of our dreams and wonder where they might lead us.

Yes, the forest is dark and dangerous at times.

But if you want to re-imagine your life and the world, you must confront these fears. To turn back at this point, is to sacrifice some part of yourself.

And so, you enter Forest Woman's domain and move slowly at first, trying not to force your pace. You feel a presence that flows in and out of you, a deepening of your own interior world, now full of life. You spend time alone wandering the forest floor or a quiet tree-lined street. You pay attention to your dreams. You dance them, paint them, explore them.

You listen. You receive. You gestate.

You begin to unearth original insights, surprising images, fresh responses to age-old problems as you are drawn deeper and deeper into the mystery that is your life.

Wangari Maathai: A Natural Forest Woman

When Professor Wangari Maathai, the Kenyan activist, died at the age of seventy-one, a colleague said, "If no one applauds this great woman of Africa, the trees will clap."[18]

Wangari founded the Green Belt Movement in 1977 to mobilize Kenyans, most of them women, to plant trees across the country. She saw the connection between environmental degradation and poverty and conflict. More than that, she understood that the trees the British had cut down to fuel their colonial ambitions stole shade from women and their families who sometimes had to walk for miles to collect water. Deforestation also threatened the water itself, for trees reduce the amount of run off after rain and stabilize the riverbed. And all this impacted the land and lives of the people.

In her fight against environmental degradation and her efforts to raise up women and children, Wangari faced incredible opposition. Her own husband divorced her because she was "too strong-minded for a woman." She was beaten by state police, thrown into jail, called crazy, corrupt, and incompetent by men who were threatened by her strength and vision. Yet she continued to care for the land, the trees, her sisters.

Over the past fifty years, the Green Belt Movement has planted more than eleven billion trees worldwide. Like the ancient fig tree she stood in awe of in her childhood, Wangari stands unbowed, and her generous spirit has transformed her people. In 2004 she became the first Black African woman to win a Nobel Prize, and the first environmentalist to win the Peace Prize.

Signs that Forest Woman Is Trying to Get Your Attention

Disenchantment—You feel your life lacks in magic and meaning.

Disorientation—You have strayed from the straight path and lost your way.

Rebelliousness—You are tired of following in others' footsteps and long to follow your own intuition and instinct.

Creativity—You feel a need to turn inward, away from the world, toward your own creative being.

Expectancy—You sense an inner quickening, a feeling of excitement and possibility.

Dreaming—Your life takes on a dream-like quality where symbols and synchronicities invite you into uncharted terrain.

Integration

Journal Reflection: The Period of Incubation

* ❋ I am called to this stage of the journey in order to learn . . .
* ❋ I know that this is my Forest Woman time because . . .
* ❋ At this moment, I fear . . .
* ❋ At this moment, I am excited by . . .
* ❋ I hope to emerge from my time with Forest Woman with . . .

Practice: Breathing with the Trees

This is a simple practice. Spend at least five minutes a day focusing on your breath. Settle somewhere comfortable outside and nestle close to some trees. Allow your breath to find its natural rhythm. As you breathe in, thank the trees for their gift of oxygen; as you breathe out, thank the trees for absorbing your carbon dioxide. Feel the relationship between your lungs and the trees. Notice how Forest Woman and you breathe together.

After you have completed your breath session, simply write down your answers to these three short prompts: *How do I feel right now? What am I aware of right now? How do I want to be right now?*

Journal Reflection: Unbowed

What makes a tree strong? What makes a woman strong? Spend some time contemplating these questions. Then make two lists, one naming what makes a tree strong, then what makes a woman strong. Combine those lists in interesting ways in a poem or prose piece beginning with the words, *A Forest Woman is . . .* Let the words come.

I am ready to stalk my dreams again.

—Sarah K.

Forest Woman is a temptress into my new untamed self.

—Anna

Rooted in Stillness

In the stillness I hear my own voice again.
—Mary Reynolds Thompson

If you've ever stood by an ancient tree, you have experienced a rooted being—calm, aware, present. These trees mirror our desire to be fully alive to ourselves—grounded, Earth-connected, secure in our own bodies. Forest Woman invites you to be similarly rooted. She assures you the seeds of your new life will not fall from the sky; they will rise up in you from the deep, dark soil, if only you tend to them.

Over millennia, patriarchal cultures have attempted to separate women from our instinctual body wisdom. Stifled by tight corsets and underwires, we struggle to breathe. Shoved into spiky heels, we teeter anxiously above the Earth. Fragranced, waxed, deodorized, powdered, and smoothed until we are more marble statues than flesh and blood, we are left dangerously ungrounded. And yet, we rebel. Our roots run deep into the Earth.

A Forest Woman knows that to live only in the light of rationality and reason is to live superficially, uprooted from the wisdom that rises in our bodies and comes to us in dreams. Still, women's interiority, like the numinous quality of the Earth, is doubted. Overly valued for our surface charms, we often ignore our feral, somatic wisdom. Or perhaps it just feels easier to do so. Can we trust our instinctual selves, after all? We may long to, but we are out of practice, our dark and leafy knowing, foreign and unfamiliar to us. If the signs are hidden, and we no longer have the code, perhaps it is not so surprising that we rush past, disregarding the insights available to us if only we slowed down.

Moving too quickly in a forest can cause you to become disoriented. But stand still, and you will become aware of the tendrils that reach down into the dark recesses of your being. You will feel the energy rise as you draw a deep breath from the soles of your feet into your legs, your cunt (a word that comes from the Irish *cunna,* a cleft in the Earth), up into your heart. Creativity surges in you, green and alive, as you tap into this force.

Reconnecting to your primal power, you are no longer domesticated but attuned to the greater wisdom of the forest. It is the way of walking in the woods when everything goes quiet. A deep hush descends, and you become still and alert, every cell awakened and aware. No longer seeing just with your eyes, but with your entire being, you sense what lives in the margins and the shadows.

Knowledge for a Forest Woman has never been about the simple acquisition of information. It is a lived experience. Your body is a massive labyrinth of nerves and neurons that communicate with each other via electrical signals, just as trees communicate with each other through chemistry and signals that travel over a wide network of roots. Forest wisdom moves, makes connections, invites you into a whole, living, breathing ecology.

Every part of you holds medicine for your life. If you see someone coming toward you on the trail and a shiver of fear makes you want to turn back, listen to it! As a Forest Woman, you will be able to quickly assess people's energy and intentions—to sense if they mean good or ill. You trust your instincts and then you act upon them.

You also learn to trust images, dreams, and wild urgings that come from your unconscious. In signals subtle as breath, Forest Woman speaks to you. You may intuit that a child or beloved family member needs your help. You may dream that a friend is sick before they say a word or show a symptom. A tug in your belly warns you that something is not right. This kind of wisdom lives deep in your DNA. For as surely as certain trees know just how far to spread their canopies to make space between them and the crowns of other trees, so you are able to naturally attune to the world and react accordingly.

The orientation of a Forest Woman is downward, inward. To get in touch with this terrain, you take off your shoes and plant your bare feet on the ground. Feel how much of you still lives deep below the surface in the dark, rich earth. How your stability rises from this attachment and so, too, your unshakable wisdom. The more you root yourself in this kind of knowing, the more contact you will have with the part of you that is connected to everything in your environment, seen and unseen.

As you step away from chasing after knowledge, you begin to see and sense like Forest Woman. What rises in you now is ancient and wild. At first you may tremble like a quaking aspen to be this present to yourself and to the spirit of life. Yet in time, you will stand there strong, secure, trusting that your roots run far and deep.

Clare Hedin's Story: Going Down to the Root-Voice

Attending a "rewilding" retreat, Clare and the other participants were led into the woods by their forest guides. They were each given a spade and told to dig a two-foot hole. Then they took off their

Wellies and socks, rolled up their trouser legs, and stood in the holes, while the guides packed the earth tightly around their lower legs and feet planting each person in the ground. They then left, without telling the group when they would return. "At first," Clare told me, "I panicked. I wanted to run. I thought, *How do I get out of here?* I struggled to lift my feet, but soon realized I couldn't move. I wasn't going anywhere."

Then she stopped resisting, "I took a deep breath and relaxed. A quiet stillness came into me. I became a human tree, experiencing, like my tree relatives around me, the wind, the dappled light, the moist air. I could hear the birds singing and hopping about in the canopy above my head. The musty fragrance of earth rose to meet me. In shafts of sunlight, little wisps of steam rose from the ground. I looked at my companions and saw how majestic they were. An unbroken silence held as we swayed back and forth. I found that I could move my arms without falling. I allowed myself to dance in the breeze. It was beautiful. Thirty minutes later, when our guides returned and dug us out, I was reluctant to leave."

I think of Clare's pale pink limbs buried deep in the earth, and how surrender must have felt like a deep exhale. Our animal bodies are calmed when our feet touch the earth, while walking on concrete has been shown to raise our stress levels. Our roots run deep into the Earth. And eventually, we find our way back to them.

Clare, who is a sound healer, tells me that when she prepares to sing, she remembers that experience of being a tree. She plants her feet firmly on the floor and brings her voice up from the soles of her feet, into her legs, belly, chest, and out into the air, filling such places as Grace Cathedral in San Francisco with her mellifluous sound. She reaches down to what John O'Donohue calls the "root-voice."[19] This is where our power resides. This is how we learn to sing out loud.

Integration

Practice: Rootedness

This practice can be done outdoors among the trees, or if that is not possible, indoors. The important thing is to imagine your own body as a tree, rooted deeply in the earth. It's also important that you feel safe, wherever you choose to do this exercise.

Plant your bare feet firmly on the ground, hip-width apart. Feel roots extending from the soles of your feet down into the earth, so that even if you find yourself swaying a little, you are still able to stand tall and strong.

Then close your eyes, and tune into your other senses. *What can you hear? What can you smell? What does the air feel like against your skin?*

Then tune inwards. *What do you sense? What are your instincts telling you? What do you feel and where in your body do you feel it?*

When your body signals that it's time, relax and move to a comfortable place to reflect and journal about your experience.

The Wisdom of the Body

The body always leads us home . . . if we can simply learn to trust sensation and stay with it long enough for it to reveal appropriate action, movement, insight, or feeling.

—Pat Ogden

After attending the retreat on Cortes Island where I had my "Yellow Dog" forest dream, I returned to a society shaken by the terrorist attacks of 9/11. Everything and everyone was unsettled.

The landscape of Manhattan was changed but so, too, was the state of the world. Wars ensued. Regimes toppled. Fears were fanned. Many felt unsafe.

My urgent need to move beyond the confines of the corporate world and copywriting no longer seemed about just me. I was becoming increasingly aware how my life energy was being poured into feeding the consumer culture that was at the heart of so much suffering. Agitated, anxious, I felt ready for something new.

A friend told me about life coaching, and I began training, even naming my first coaching practice Yellow Dog. Then, in a synchronous turn of events, which came about because I was thinking of coaching women in second stage recovery, I attended a conference put on by Hazelden, an organization that publishes 12-step literature.

It was there I was introduced to poetry therapy in the form of one Kay Adams, founder of the Center for Journal Therapy and by then a registered poetry/journal therapist. During her presentation, Kay turned to the women present and asked them to write a poem structured around the alphabet, what she called an AlphaPoem, using the word RECOVERY written vertically down the page. Each letter in RECOVERY would begin a new word and line of a poem.

I then heard a sound that still sends shivers down my spine— hundreds of women writing in notepads and journals. As many stood up and shared their poems, my whole body vibrated. I thought: *That's what I want to do. I want to help people to write in this way, a way that serves their souls.*

After the session, I went up to Kay and asked, "Can you teach me to do what you do?" "Well," she replied, "it just so happens that I am running a poetry therapy training beginning next month. It will take you two years or more to complete it. Are you still interested?"

Thrumming with excitement, not even thinking of the time or the cost, I said, "Yes." Instinct told me that this was my new path. Another breadcrumb had dropped on the ground.

Gradually my work with Kay evolved to focus on the Earth archetypes and into the book *Reclaiming the Wild Soul.* I awoke each morning with a sense of purpose and quickening in my blood. I was also in the first phase of menopause, after my partial hysterectomy. I had lost an ovary to an ectopic pregnancy in my early thirties, and my remaining one seemed to be working overtime.

To gauge my hormone levels, I saw a renowned holistic doctor who ran a battery of tests. The results took a couple of weeks to come back, and I continued to burn hot and crotchety. Two weeks after my blood was drawn, I returned to the doctor's office. He looked at the sheet of paper in front of him, and looked again, and then up at me. "Strange," he said. "I have never seen hormones levels like these other than in a woman who is pregnant." If he'd been a woman, or perhaps more approachable, I would have told him what I sensed instantly: I was gestating a book. And this book would be my legacy, as much as any child. (I didn't know it back then, but this project would take nearly a decade to complete. It was a long pregnancy!)

Ideas, I discovered, don't just live in our brains as abstractions, they live deep inside our body, changing our chemistry in profound ways. It was as if the Earth was offering an embodied positive feedback loop, supporting me in knowing that I had found my path.

One of the most radical things you can do is to root yourself in your own body. The origin of the word radical comes from Latin *radic-*, *radix*, meaning "root." A woman rooted in her flesh and bones has begun to find her way back to her inner Forest Woman—earthy, instinctual, sensual. And in this knowing, she becomes radicalized, unwilling to settle for anything less than being her own wild and authentic self.

Forest Woman reminds you that to access your inner wisdom you must sink below the mind, into your sensing animal being. You can breathe to release your everyday tension, then practice dropping down to the roots. Here, you will recognize the feelings and sensations that come with another kind of knowing.

It may take time to trust your instincts. To interpret what the signs mean. To get comfortable with that tug in your gut or that shiver down your spine. To get used to speaking from this place of wisdom—sharing what you know to be true, even if you have been told you are too sensitive, are imagining things, or are overreacting.

The wordless knowing of the body isn't treated kindly in our unduly semantic culture. And we often try to stay in safe, familiar territory by censoring ourselves—shutting down, numbing out, denying our sensations, or only partially expressing them. But as you access your body wisdom you build a foundation, a way of seeing that can guide your path through the darkest of woods.

What would it be like, as Ruth Falk writes, "To live our lives as travelers with roots in ourselves"?[20] When I consider that line, I feel a deep sense of wonder that when I am rooted, I am most free to roam.

And yet we may fear exploring the dark woods of our own bodies. This is the realm we have been warned not to enter. We are told there is too much danger here. But what if the danger is really to the patriarchy, to those who want us to stay in the light of reason clinging to Truth with a capital T, to an "objective" reality that can never be challenged? This kind of Truth is supposed to make us safe. And yet, it acts as a bludgeon, denying myriad voices and shutting out people who see things in other ways.

Forest Woman is interested in truth that is intimate, subjective, rooted, and reflective of our individual experience, ethnicity, age, and sense of place. She celebrates diversity, encouraging each of us to add our intelligence and perception to the whole.

For many, the way into this kind of wisdom is through meditation. But meditation, as it is practiced within a patriarchal culture, often points us toward transcendence. We are supposed to rise above our earthly desires rather than enter more deeply into them. We are taught to quiet and suppress ourselves, to seek distance from those feelings that are trying to get our attention, to strive to overcome the body and control those energies that emanate from deep within us. But then Forest Woman asks us to enter her glorious labyrinth to feel and sense our way along her many paths.

The poet Mary Oliver advocates in "Wild Geese" that you *let the soft animal of your body / love what it loves.*[21] Your body is feral and ferociously intelligent. As you learn to joyfully reunite with it, let the sensations rise like sap. Learn from them. Feel them. Celebrate them.

Stillness doesn't require that you overcome your body or quiet your mind. It can be attained if you let yourself sink deeper into the mystery of life, following Forest Woman to her sanctuary and listening to the flesh and bone that houses your soul.

Integration

Journal Reflection: The Body's Wisdom

Write of a time when you realized something important, even though you couldn't prove it by reason or rationality.

Where did this wisdom reside in your body? How did you feel the truth of what was going on? How strong or subtle was the feeling? Where were you? Who was present with you?

Did you trust what your body was saying to you? Or did you ignore it? The reality is, sometimes we act, and we realize that we misread a signal. Other times, not sure we can trust to the message, we aren't willing to risk acting on it and can regret it later. The point here is simply to explore the consequences—good, bad, or mixed—of listening and acting upon your deeper wisdom, or not listening or acting.

After you've written down your experience, read it back and write a reflection. You may find these starter-questions helpful:

What has this taught me about my own body wisdom?

How would I treat a similar feeling or sixth sense in the future?

What is my deepest learning from this story?

I want to learn the language of roots so I can understand more about our Mother Earth. About the trees, those towering temples of wisdom, and all the knowing they have gained over the decades and centuries of being, of sitting still, and staying where they are rooted.

—Kate

Holding the Creative Tension

What's ahead of me and what's behind me
are nothing compared to what's inside me.

—JEAN SHAPIRO

Under dense cover, tender saplings bide their time, often for many decades, waiting for a break in the canopy. Only when the canopy opens and light pours down on them do they begin to rise and reach their branches to a beckoning sky.

You, on the other hand, may be impatient to get on with your life. Inaction is a challenge for many of us. Our culture values expediency over natural timing, pushing us ever onward: *Act now, get it done, don't hesitate.* You may feel that you've already put your dreams on hold for too long. After all, haven't women spent centuries waiting for our gifts to be recognized? It's hard to stand still. And yet when you stop rushing, you may realize that waiting strengthens you.

As young trees hunker down in the darkness, their wood becomes stronger and more flexible. All the while, the mother trees feed them sugar and other nutrients to help them thrive. In your willingness to sit in the unknown, you, too, will be gaining strength.

For a Forest Woman, waiting is part of actively learning, discovering, and engaging your creativity. This inner work is preparing you to take advantage of an opening when it arises. You are pregnant with possibilities, but you must nurture these before they bear fruit.

Forest plantations, prized for their quick growth and return on investment, are more fragile and less abundant than slow-growth forests. Progress overrides our sense of natural readiness. Fertilizers and other fast-growth methods pressure the land to produce. In a similar way, you may be pressured to realize your potential prematurely. If so, your most powerful ideas and wildest enthusiasms may miscarry. When we force life to fit an artificial timetable, we impede our natural progress and threaten the deep dreams of the soul.

As a Forest Woman, you have faith in your future. You trust that you will move instinctually when the moment arises. But first, you bide your time and wait for the right conditions to act. When you see a clearer path forward, you will be ready.

In the meantime, your job is to tend to your basic needs, acquire a needed skill, and give yourself a safe refuge. You are learning to balance the desire to act with the need to wait. To dance in the space between being and becoming.

Forest Woman is strong enough to hold opposites, to embrace shadow and sunlight, Earth and sky. She does not feel fragmented or forced to choose between her possibilities. She holds her center.

So much depends on right timing and the ability to hold the tension without opting for superficial answers or falling back on your old ways. Living with uncertainty, paradox, chaos, isn't easy. But tension is integral to transformation. You have to be willing to sit in the unknown long enough for something new to emerge.

So, I ask you: Can you find a quiet place to stand between your outgrown past and your unseeable future? Can you make space for what is yet unnamed, even unthought of, to emerge? This is how you begin to incubate a new life, a new world. One day, like an old growth forest, you will evolve into your magnificence.

Your destiny is already contained within you, as the mighty oak is contained within the acorn. Hold still. Bide your time. Heed Forest Woman's wisdom. Your authentic strength comes from waiting until action naturally arises from the depths of your being. Your time will come. And when it does, even the most frightened, vulnerable part of you will rise up and reach for the light.

Integration

Forest Woman Ritual: Living into the Mystery

What you will need: Your journal and a felt pen soft enough to write on a leaf, with a point heavy enough to inscribe a word on a piece of bark or wood.

Spend some time in a forest, a park, or any place with trees. If you have no access to nature, spend some time looking at photos of trees or old growth forests in magazines. Or download an app with forest sounds. Then close your eyes and imagine yourself in this place.

As you walk among the trees, think about a question you hold in your heart. It may have been seeded in you long ago, or you may only just have become aware of it. Make sure the question is a big, open-ended question, not one with a simple *yes* or *no* answer. You are living into a mystery.

What am I being called to?

What is it that I cannot see?

What is the most important thing for me to recognize, now?

Take a moment to settle down. Record your answers in your journal. Then write down the question that you can feel rooting itself in you, right now. Sit with this for a bit, then read it out loud. Ask yourself: Is it worded in the most powerful way? Does it feel like the right question? Keep checking in with yourself, until you have your question.

Write your question on a piece of bark or a single leaf. If you don't have the right pen, simply write it with your finger. Then place that question into the heart of the forest, or the hollow of a tree, or by a great root. You are entrusting your question (and its answer) to Forest Woman, *your wisest forest self.* If you are working with an image from a magazine, write your question on the page, then save it, and keep it somewhere that feels sacred.

Ask Forest Woman to hold your question for you, trusting that when the time is right, she will grant you the answer your soul is seeking.

Journal Reflection

Take a moment to reflect on your experience of handing over your question to the forest. *What do you notice? What do you fear? What do you hope for?* Write your response in your journal.

Keep coming back to your question and listening for the answer. When it comes, as it will in time (days, or even months, or longer) thank Forest Woman for her wisdom.

Find Your Own Rhythm

Rhythm is our universal mother tongue.
It's the language of the soul.

—Gabrielle Roth

Every time, I watch a woman make a snap decision I can sense her fear. A fear I recognize in myself: *If I don't act now, someone else will. If I wait, I will lose what I have and nothing else will come along.* We have lost our trust in life's natural processes and in our own life's unfolding. This is how we are driven to distraction. This is how we struggle to be present and patient. This is how we find ourselves always rushing: to finish a sentence, to finish a task, to get ahead. Never taking a moment to dream, to breathe, to think about anything but the next thing on our to do list—and then the next. And the next.

In 2017 I sat on a panel, "Breaking the Glass Ceiling," with a woman who, for twenty-five years, served as the Principal Horn at the Metropolitan Opera—the very first female in this position. The panel also consisted of female business leaders, each in their own way remarkable. They had essentially the same message to share on how to succeed as a woman. "Be better than the men."

When it came to my turn to speak, I questioned the metaphor of breaking a glass ceiling. Shattering glass is violent. It is painful. I recalled my own corporate years in the 1980s, when the fashion for massive shoulder pads made women look like football players ready to "tackle" the day. I recalled how competitive the world of advertising was, and how I constantly needed to keep proving myself by writing top-selling copy.

I wondered if we needed new metaphors for how women can take their rightful place. What if we didn't have to be better than the men, but simply truer to ourselves? What if instead of breaking glass ceilings, we simply moved outside where there are no ceilings? What if we shifted the model of hierarchy based on a pyramid—with a single leader at the top whose authority rests on widening tiers of less powerful people below—to a circle, even a sacred hoop, where everyone had a voice? I then offered up the image of an old-growth forest, in which every tree has a vital role to play in keeping the ecosystem resilient and strong.

A crowd of students in attendance thanked me for my words, and many who came to speak to me afterward were young men. The old system was brutal on them, too, they said. They wanted workplaces with more shared responsibility, more diversity, and equity.

It can feel easier in some ways to play around the edges and think, for instance, of shattering a glass ceiling rather than creating a renewed culture of change that includes all voices. It can feel easier to follow the path made by others than to bushwhack our own way through the wilderness. It can feel easier to roll up our sleeves and steamroll ahead rather than stepping into the unknown. But if we just keep on doing the same things, only more so, what changes? And at what cost to our souls?

What if in this dizzyingly fast world, the most powerful message is to slow down? As workshop participant Laura Salisbury noted, "The pulse and pace of the universe is love, and there is no rushing that." So, I ask you: What if the greatest power you possess is your ability to tap into a rhythm, as ancient as a mature forest, and formed by nature?

Chronological time is sequential and linear, and it rules our Western world. Everything points forward—no circles, spirals, or respite. But Kairos time is different—it is that magical time, that opportune time, when, after perhaps waiting for days or even years, an opening is perceived and taken. The word *Kairos* can be traced back to the loom and the moment when a gap appears in the warp of the cloth and the thread can be passed through. It is a moment born of patience, attention, and wisdom. And it is Forest Woman's genius to be able to judge that perfect timing, however long she has to wait.

Our fast way of living is dangerous, and technology doesn't help. We are ruthlessly impatient if a webpage doesn't load immediately or if we can't get through to someone or access the information we need in seconds. I know this feeling. I know I am being trained to want everything on demand. But this is a destructive way to live. Like a bulldozer tearing down a forest, we leave devastation in our wake.

I once heard Eve Ensler, author of *The Vagina Monologues,* say in an interview, "Slowness is the antidote to rape." Her statement struck me to the core. I began to think about how this applies to our treatment of nature. On the trails by my home, I have long noticed that electric bikes cause more damage than regular bicycles, runners more damage than hikers. The faster you move through life, the easier it is to run over a lizard, or a precious orchid, or crush an anthill—and not even notice. It is also easier to hurt a friend, destroy a relationship or ecosystem, or cut down a sister.

Speed equals destruction. Slowness is the antidote to rape.

So much of today's emphasis on transformation treats our own psychological eco-systems as we do the Earth, demanding we impose order on them, right away. We force change on ourselves without fully engaging our whole being. And there are consequences. Without waiting to see what naturally wants to emerge, we end up burned out and back to square one. In so many ways, we need to slow down. After all, if we paused to look at each other, could we then harm each other so easily? If a man really looked into the soul of a woman, could he rape her? If we had conversations with trees, would we view them just as timber?

Perhaps more than anything, we need to trust the organic nature of life, to live by the awareness that each being, each idea, each creative concept has its own natural rhythm and right timing. There is a rock cycle like a water cycle, but it takes millions of years to complete. Some insects live just one day, while some trees can live hundreds or even thousands of years. You must find your own timing as you hold the tension, trusting that in the pause, in the sacred slowing down, something long-dormant will finally burst through.

Integration

Practice: The Slow Walk

Workshop participant Jo Smith writes me, "I went for another slow walk today undertaking to do the whole walk carefully, as mindfully as possible. I discovered I was using a whole new set of muscles, and I had to take care where I put my feet. The thought then arose, what if I tried this in my day-to-day living? Caring about what my next step is, deeply concentrating on what I am doing?"

So often, we head out of doors with our running shoes on, ready to get some brisk exercise. People are increasingly wearing devices that measure their number of steps, heart rate, etc., in the desire to maximize their exercise time. This is all well and good, but if you don't slow down and pay attention, much will be lost on you.

So, each week, try to take at least one slow walk. If you have a toddler, this is a natural for you. For they will stop to splash in puddles and watch the march of ants. You might apprentice to their way of being that day. But it's also good to do this exercise alone, taking note of your own rhythms and the flow of your perceptions. Allow yourself to saunter, to see, to feel, to stop and reflect: how does the sun feel on your skin, what is your shadow passing over, how do the birds react to your presence, what about the grasses, the wind? Take some time to sit in one place and listen to the world around you, unfolding at its own pace.

After taking your slow walk, reflect:

> *How do you feel?*
> *What did you notice?*
> *What did you learn?*

Take a few minutes to record your answers in your journal. Read over your responses, then write a reflection.

The Challenge:
Rising from the Ashes

I have been woman
for a long time
beware my smile
I am treacherous with old magic
and the noon's new fury . . .

—Audre Lorde

In the heart of every Forest Woman lies circle upon circle that tells the story of her life. This is an ancient history. Her ancestral past is part of her cellular makeup, her complexity. The history of forests, like the history of women, is rife with trauma—and this trauma is passed down from generation to generation. A Forest Woman knows what it is to be silenced, to be cut down, to be burned. She carries this knowledge in the depth of her being.

Just as the forests have been clear-cut, so women accused of being witches have been razed. Just as we set fire to forests to domesticate the land, we attempt to domesticate women by punishing them for their wild, intuitive natures. From the 15th to the 17th centuries, hundreds of thousands—perhaps even millions—of women throughout Europe were killed.

No monuments are built to these women. And yet, six generations of children watched their mothers die.

Witches. Medicine women. Midwives. Healers. Herbalists. Crones. Hags. Gone.

If you dressed or spoke in a suggestive manner, if you had a mole or freckle or wart (a sign that you had been kissed by the devil), if you showed any creativity or curiosity, if you incited men's lust, if you honored seasonal rhythms and rituals, if you communed with trees and stars, if you knew about crops and animals and medicinal herbs, if you dared to believe in the oneness of all life and direct connection to spirit, you could be burned.

Women's wisdom, ancient, nature-based, handed down from one generation to the next, was not written down, but stored in our bodies and in our intimacy with the land. Yet it disappeared almost overnight. In some villages there was barely a woman left alive. In their place was a void as brutal as a clear-cut forest.

Today, women continue to be de-wilded by being driven into loveless marriages and overly domesticated lives. This de-naturing is an intentional disempowerment. The witch burnings were meant to take control of women's reproduction, sexuality, productivity, and life force. For centuries, the dominant culture has cut us off from our true power and blocked our economic independence. The witch hunts are just one example of how women from all over the world, throughout modern history, continue to be persecuted and disenfranchised.

For every tree that is felled, a community of life suffers. Nests, shade, shelter, wild foods are lost. For every woman who was burned at the stake, silenced, or forced to submit, a legacy is lost. But Forest Woman is still strong within you. Like an ancient grandmother tree, her wide roots reach out to feed you. Her ancestral wisdom lives in every part of you. You are witch woman, wise beyond belief.

And still, there is that hesitation born of history. Every time you long to speak the truth and find yourself tongue-tied, you relive that trauma. Every time you ignore a gut feeling, the call to create, to dance, write poetry, sing out loud, lead a protest march and you say to yourself, *It's not worth the price I'll have to pay* or ask, *Who am I to do this?* you are rekindling that trauma. And you are not alone. There are places in every woman that feel like dead wood, so calcified are they with hurt.

Knowing that you carry this trauma in the heartwood of your being is the first step to remembering who you are. If you root yourself firmly and take the time to examine your pain and fear, you will no longer be lost to yourself. You will come alive again, to all your possibilities. Remember, Forest Woman's thick bark provides a layer of protection. She will wrap her limbs around you and give you access to immense reserves of strength and knowledge. You may be hurt, but you will rise.

Not even fire can harm you. When the landscape burns, Forest Woman flings her seeds into the world where they have the power to regenerate. She can survive the worst of times. The same is true for you. However hard things get, you will rise.

Integration

Journal Reflection: Dialoguing with Forest Woman

For this practice try to give yourself an hour of uninterrupted time. You may want to settle into a comfortable nook in your home or head into the woods to write. The choice is yours and obviously also dependent on weather and circumstances. But don't forget your journal.

To begin: Mark your threshold.

If you are at home, you can symbolize the crossing from ordinary life into a magical state by lighting a candle. Close your eyes and imagine yourself in an ancient forest. One tree in the forest, in particular, represents your Inner Forest Woman, or wisest self. Make your way to her.

If outdoors, note when you have crossed a boundary—a road, a creek—or entered a copse of trees. Wander until you find the tree that most seems to represent your Inner Forest Woman. Once found, spend time breathing with this being. Notice everything you can about her. Notice how you feel in her presence. Notice why you are drawn to her.

Then, begin a dialogue with this tree, who holds so much magic and wisdom for you. And reach for your journal so that you can record every word.

You might begin this exercise like this:

You: I open myself to the wisdom you have to share with me. Will you help me to see where my own magic lies and what this means for my life?

Forest Woman: . . . . . . (answers)

You: . . . .

You will intuitively know when this conversation has borne fruit. As it comes to an end, thank this being for her time and wisdom. Know that you can return at any time and continue your dialogue. Know that this being *is* you. You hold the same ancient knowing within your depths.

Reclaiming Your Magic

In Witchcraft, the first thing a woman learns to visualize and bring to birth in the world is herself.

—Naomi Goldenberg

Once, a workshop participant asked, "Don't we just re-victimize ourselves when we bring up The Burning Times and revisit our traumatic history?"

The question unsettled me for a moment. *Does it?* I wondered. Should we just move on and look to the future? *No,* I thought. Remembering is part of Forest Woman wisdom. Just think about the rings inside a tree that record her whole history, often going back hundreds of years. We also carry the past with us, deep in our being, and there is no use pretending it isn't there.

The pace of modern life does not encourage retrospection. But what if by not reckoning with the past, we damage our future? What if by not examining the roots of racism, misogyny, or other inequities, we keep perpetuating the injustices we claim to abhor?

I have often been asked why, after decades of recovery, I still refer to myself as an alcoholic. It's because it is an important aspect of who I am, though I haven't had a drink in almost forty years. I know this propensity to addiction still lives in me. I have no qualm about admitting that, nor do I feel "less than" for calling myself an alcoholic. It is simply part of me, my story, my history. It is in the forgetting that I risk my present happiness.

In a similar way, when I first learned of the witch hunts, I reacted viscerally. My first thought, *Ah! This is why I am sometimes terrified to speak. This is why my body responds as if my life is under threat when I stick my neck out.* I didn't feel victimized by learning of the witch burnings, I felt vindicated. Something, call it sap or sass, rose in me, along with a fierce desire to reclaim my own magic. Not out of ego, anger, or revenge, but because I knew that if women's power had been consciously and deliberately taken from us, it could be consciously and deliberately taken back.

The English word blessing comes from the French, *blessé* for wound. Your wounds are a gift for as you heal them you grow strong. Reclaiming your stories and magic from a history fraught with danger and disempowerment takes courage. Even so, the process of mending some broken part of you has its own beauty. And behind you stand a lineage of women who have survived all manner of injustices and setbacks. Women who want you to succeed, to heal, to carry on. Like the ancient grandmother trees in the forest, your ancestors' wisdom and nurturance are always with you. This you can trust.

Much of my heritage is a blur—though I know I am mainly of Celtic descent and have a great, great grandmother who was a Romany gypsy. She settled in a small village in Yorkshire, in the North of England, where she became the local midwife. She also had the skill to foresee death, and the villagers both revered and feared her.

Growing up, my mother fed me morsels of her tale as if they were banned confectionary. I wasn't supposed to tell—it wasn't "nice" to have gypsy blood, after all, and people wouldn't understand. Romanies had been persecuted across Europe, most violently during World War II, and weren't welcome anywhere. But my mother must have wanted me to own some part of my Romany heritage, for she was quick to point out that due to my complexion, darker than hers and my father's, I was a throwback. And I was, for it turned out that I also had "abilities." From an early age I saw images in my mind's eye that told me what others were thinking. When I was six, my brother brought home a pack of cards and we played a game where you had to guess what card the other picked. There was a trick to it, of course, but I didn't know it. I could just see in my mind the cards he or one of our friends held.

I believe we are all born with psychic abilities. And while in the West we are no longer burned at the stake for this, we are often ridiculed or ostracized for them so that we still get burned. Consequently, I hid my gifts and then forgot them as I grew older. I began to drink when I didn't know what to do with all those other ways of knowing. My relationship was then to the shadow wild, the kind of wild you find in a bottle, or a crazy love affair, or any drug or habit that takes you out of yourself—that allows you to forget this "inner sight" and escape who you really are. Sometimes I felt quite mad. But the voice of enchantment was not entirely banished.

Over the years I reclaimed the Romany part of myself, learning to listen to my intuitions, to trust my way of seeing. Other women, too, are learning again the ways of the wise woman as we reclaim our sensitivities as the strengths they are, rather than seeing them as flaws or vulnerabilities. Accepting the mantle of witch, harridan, crone, and hag, we free ourselves from the old stereotypes. No, witches aren't warty, evil, ugly specimens of womanhood. They are women who know the world is enchanted, who honor the cycles of the moon and the rhythms of Earth, and who praise their own feminine life-force.

You are not bound at the stake; you are able to walk this Earth with your whole being. You can plant your feet on the ground, place your hands in the soil, gather herbs, gather with other women, sing the praises of the forest, raise your voices and dance naked. Oh yes, that too, for nothing rattles the patriarchy more than celebrating your own sensual beauty in community with nature and your sisters as the moon rises and your body becomes silvered and sylvan. As you honor the generations of wise women who have come before you, you reclaim your wise, fierce self.

Today, in the West, we have lost the practice of honoring our ancestors. Yet their wild and earthy wisdom still flows through you. We may use DNA tests to find our ethnicity, but DNA will not tell you how your grandmothers lived, whom they loved, and what they long to share with you. And so, you must reach back in time through your intuition and imagination, the knowing in your body, to make that connection.

As I walk among the towering redwoods, I say a prayer to my grandmother and her ancestors. I note how the trees have been marked by fire, their thick bark blackened in places, and yet they still flourish and grow green. At my feet lie cones small as my thumbprint, filled with tiny seeds. I wonder: How can these soaring beings grow from something so small? And then: How can the seeds of ancient wisdom, when tended, become a majestic presence in our lives?

Back at home, I light a candle, and recall the flickering warmth of a campfire. I imagine a long line of women, going back in time, each with powerful gifts to offer, with some magic healing for the world. I feel the power and pulse of each one of them as a blessing. They tell me, *We are there to heal each other.*

It may take time to work through the trauma and legacy of pain you hold in your body. Don't rush this process. Be gentle but firm. And remember to breathe. For in that breath, you will absorb the life-giving oxygen of the trees. Forest Woman feeds you, as she takes your exhale into her own body, giving you back everything you need to flourish, inviting you deeper into intimacy with all life.

Isla Macleod's Story: Returning to the Trees

After boarding school and university, my colleague Isla went to live by herself in the woods. Her friends thought her mad. Her family worried. The logical thing was for her to buckle down and get a job. But she chose to live alone in an ancient Sussex woodland, apprenticing herself to the trees, and one tree in particular, the Yew. This grandmother tree became her mentor. She writes, "It was here that I re-wilded myself. Here that I came back into a conscious and alive relationship with the Earth and stars, moon and sun, stones and streams, the plant, tree, and fungi kingdoms, and my indigenous ancestors."[22]

Isla is one of many women who are returning to ancient rituals and practices. We are forming sacred groves with our sisters, listening to the wisdom of plants, reclaiming our power as healers and wise women.

When you stand in the presence of an old-growth tree or a true Forest Woman, something moves between you. An idea takes root, branches out, and flows through your whole being. You stand taller and stronger. You are more willing to trust in the wisdom that lies not with others, but deep in your own heartwood.

Becoming an Elder: Polly Paton-Brown's Story

When Polly attended a sacred body painting weekend convened by a Druid Order, she was terrified as it involved being painted naked or nearly so. "Scared though I was," she writes, "my 61-year-old body had experienced so much abuse, physical pain, and surgery, it was crying out to be healed.

"The Chief of the Order painted a horse on my back, and he sang 'The Lady of the Woods.' That I could allow myself to be so vulnerable, not just with all my sisters, but also with a male I trusted completely, was transformative. We went deeper into the woods where I danced and drummed. The forest held me and gave me courage to shed years with an evangelical cult that demeaned and dominated women and that thought nature had no soul. Forest Woman met me and showed me that I AM her and she is me. There, I was broken open."

Integration

Journal Reflection: Reclaiming Your Personal Magic

How will you reclaim your own personal magic? You can do so with a ritual that honors the ancestors by naming them and talking with them, learning where you came from and honoring your herstory. Other ways to do this include:

- ❋ taking a risk and speaking out, refusing to keep silent about some harm that has been done to you or others
- ❋ awakening a childlike sense of wonder and learning how to cast some spells
- ❋ making a list of all your gifts
- ❋ painting or writing your wildest dreams

✳ remembering, as Robin Morgan suggests, that "We are the myths. We are the Amazons, the Furies, the Witches. We have never not been here, this exact sliver of time, this precise place."[23]

Your legacy of women's wisdom can never be extinguished. You know this. I know it, too. And so, I offer you this Forest Woman Blessing:

We are relearning the language of leaf and bark.

We are seeing what it is to stand strong, roots entwined, in the way of the ancient ones.

We are not just planting forests; we are rising as forests.

Now, I suggest you write your own blessing. Begin with these words, *I am relearning the language of leaf and bark.* Explore the ways you want to reclaim your personal magic. There is no wrong way. Simply allow Forest Woman to guide you.

I went into the woods to find my soul, caught in a magical web of my own choosing. I have never been so lost, and never so found.

—Becky

Forest Woman greets me, ancient wild and free. I cry for having left her. I thought I have not left. She is. I am.

—Meg

I am dark, complex. Mossy, grand, and old. The demise of the wild forest landscapes echoing my feeling of the loss of the verdant places in me.

—Sonia

I crave what was lost to me and all women. I bury myself at the base of an ancient tree to listen and learn. I smell the rich earth in its aliveness, soaking in its nourishment for the journey is long and arduous.

—Deborah

The Shift: Linear to Spiral Path

Nothing moves in a straight line,
But in arcs, epicycles, spirals, and gyres.
Nothing living grows in cubes, cones, or rhomboids . . .

—MARGE PIERCY

Many a woman walks a path that has been chosen for us by others. We forfeit our wild wisdom and intuitive understanding for a promise that if we stick to the straight and narrow, we will be rewarded. We make bargains, fantasize about riches and love, only to find we have lost touch with something fierce and true within ourselves. We ache with this loss. Giving up on our own dreams, we realize how dislocated we have become, how uprooted from our own destiny and inner nature.

After years of traveling a linear track laid down by others, you know in your soul that there is more to life than straightaways measured out with guard rails and acreage bounded by fence lines. The linear path is not suited to a woman's nature; its shape does not match your curvy body and meandering curiosity, your desire to explore and experience. You must learn the way of the feminine soul—the labyrinth path with all its twists and turns.

Deep in the woods, Forest Woman spins you about, inviting you to set aside the cultural compass and navigate by intuition, and with your animal body. Her energy rises in you like sap, making you feel more alert and alive. As a fresh breeze awakens your skin, you note the scent of wet leaves, the cool afternoon shadows. Everything in the forest is guiding you, showing you the way back to yourself.

In Forest Woman's contoured body, in ferns, pinecones, snail shells, circular trunks, spider webs, in the way leaves spin around branches, in cycles and seasons of renewal, you discover that the body of the forest is your own. And it is not made of straight lines and right angles, but entwined with possibilities, offering labyrinthine paths that weave their way into places barely dreamed of.

To walk the spiral path is to surrender to nature's rhythms. You co-create with the world, rather than pushing your way through. You let everything around you inform your next step. Forest Woman's realm is one of ever-widening circles of awareness.

Dropping certainty in favor of curiosity, you begin to embody the instinctual power of a Forest Woman. You respond to your surroundings the way a wild bird in the forest cocks its head at the snap of a twig. Or in the way a tree will bend, if needed, to serve its own unfolding. There are no rules here, no rigid regulations. Each being is different. Your way, your own.

The deeper you go into the forest, the more overgrown and trackless it becomes. Forest Woman calls you to leave the deadening ruts of your predictable life and discover the spontaneity and surprise of living from your senses. At any moment you can come across a fawn in the underbrush, or see a fish jump in a wild creek, or stumble upon an ancient spirit in a hidden grove—something that wakes you up and hints at what it is you long for.

Forest Woman encourages you to lose your way in order to find your own true path. No shortcut can lead you there. There are no signs posted on this route. As Rebecca Solnit explains, "That thing, the nature of which is totally unknown to you, is usually what you need to find, and finding it is a matter of getting lost."[24]

Integration

Journal Reflection: There Are Many Ways to Be Lost

We sometimes find ourselves off the well-worn path, not knowing where we are headed. We feel lost because we no longer believe in the life we've been living. And so, we wonder: How did we end up in such a place? Or perhaps we have lost some aspect of ourselves, and don't know how to find it. Here are three questions that will help you to accept this situation and find some wisdom in it:

> *How do you know you are lost?*
> *What quality does your lostness take?*
> *What do you sense will help you find your way again?*

The Spiral Dance

> *Linearity does not come naturally to me.*
> *It kills my imagination. Nothing happens.*
>
> —MARION WOODMAN

You cannot obediently follow a well-marked path and live a conscious, mythic life. Whatever your ambition or passion, you will, at some point, need to summon the courage to veer off track. The word ambition derives from the Latin, *ambire*, "to go around." Meandering is an essential Forest Woman skill.

The path of progress is one of the great myths of patriarchy. It tells us that life is a logical progression: education, job, marriage, children, house, retirement. Based on cause and effect, it argues: If you do this, then you will achieve this. Of course, the rules are skewed to white males, but we all have to keep to the path, don't we? And if it doesn't work out? Then it is our fault. We just didn't try hard enough. This is a ruthless judgement and an impossible way to live.

Walk into a forest, and you will notice how the tree trunks sway and branches bend, and the canopy swirls and arcs above you. Everything in nature bends and curves. This is the truth of Forest Woman. For a branch to grow straight it must be rigid and inflexible. Yet if it doesn't adapt and grow around an obstacle, there will come a point when it snaps. This is your truth as well. If you never explore the swirling possibilities of life, something in you will eventually break—your heart, your courage, your curiosity.

Uncertainty is the fertile ground of a life of renewal and resiliency. It requires you step fully into the moment of now with all its myriad unknowns. Every step you take brings you to a new place, and fresh prospects. To dance the spiral dance of Forest Woman, you become curious and playful, willing to experiment and discover new things. In this way, life becomes spontaneous and ever-surprising—an unfolding and evolving drama in which you are both walking the path as the path is also shaping you.

As a Forest Woman you forgo the fast-laned freeway for an obscure and twisty backroad. There, turning a corner, you discover a hidden village, or a sweet-smelling field of wildflowers, or a view that makes your heart stop with its loveliness. You may encounter someone who changes your life, or find the cottage of your dreams, and before you know it, one thing has led to another, and you are in a quite different place.

Where shall I go today? What calls to me? Which path shall I take? What are the trees and the clouds telling me? Like a heroine in a fairy tale who wanders off course, often in pursuit of a magical butterfly or stag, following your passion—what enchants you—is a powerful way to reclaim your own path in life. The journey, you realize, is more important than any goal you have set your heart on.

When I first got sober, I knew I couldn't walk past that familiar wine store or bar without being tempted. So, I tried new routes. I walked past churches where AA meetings were taking place, and joined in. Weekends, I walked in Marin County, across the Bay, soaking in the beauty of redwood forests and the thundering waves of the Pacific. I began to explore different neighborhoods in the city, ones that didn't remind me of my old drinking haunts and crazy behaviors. I began to hike longer and wilder trails, then began camping out, then backpacking—each adventure taking me further and farther away from my old life.

A friend has chosen to follow her own path as a poet. All her life she had been urged by her father to find a proper job, but she supports herself, not extravagantly but sufficiently, with her craft. Shortly before his death, she confronted him, "Daddy, I love you, but I neither regret nor apologize for following the path of an artist." He didn't respond. And yet she had spoken her truth. She needed to offer her creativity to the world, and nothing less would suffice.

This is how you enter the dark forest and begin to spin and sway on the spiral path. The kingdom—the existing culture—threatens your life. To remain is to be locked in a tower or married to an ogre or to have some vital and life-giving aspect taken from you—your hair cut, your hands severed, your gifts destroyed. Forest Woman puts you at a crossroads. A place of choice. You can continue to be held hostage to a path not of your own making. Or you can enter the dark forest and discover your own way.

When you move through the forest, you are no longer a path follower but a path maker. As one of my workshop participants wrote, "We shape the world by the steps we take." Her words ring true. On the linear path we are blind to so much beauty and miss so much information, but when we leave it behind, we encounter opportunities we never imagined. The more women who find the courage to veer from the linear path to make their own, the more options and diversity and possibilities will open up for all of us.

As a Forest Woman, you know how to leave linear, rational, reductionist thinking behind. You enter the wild woods, allow yourself to be led somewhere mysterious. You turn your back on a way of being that doesn't serve your soul.

The day of the linear path, my sisters, is nearing its end—and the spiral dance of the forest awaits!

Clare Dubois, Founder of TreeSisters: Life is an Experiment

Clare was literally knocked off her path when her car careened off an icy road in England and smashed into a tree. She was on her way to deliver a smart and orderly presentation on the topic of economics and biodiversity. Instead, she crashed into a tree and saw a blinding light. In this trance, she heard two words: *The Experiment.* Then a voice told her that humanity was running out of time. We could turn things around if we let go of our fear of failing. And that was the experiment. *You can't fail at an experiment,* the voice reminded her, *you can only learn from it.*

In shock and trembling, Clare asked, *What's my experiment?* Loud and clear, the voice responded: *To reforest the tropics within ten years.*

In that moment Clare gleaned what that would entail: setting up a non-profit, learning about technology, assembling a team, becoming a public figure, fundraising. She knew nothing about any of these things. She liked her quiet life. Now she had been called, and the voice, which she believed to be the voice of the tree, wouldn't let her go back to sleep.

The road that Clare was taking to that meeting wasn't a bad one. But it wasn't hers. She was literally flung from it and told her purpose lay in a different direction.

How many of us have realized that the first path we take in life isn't the one that will lead us to our true purpose? How many of us are flung from the straight and narrow, through an accident or loss, being laid off, or through illness, family responsibilities, or divorce? It happens. And it happens because life wants us to awaken to our greater consciousness. It wants us to hear that other voice—the voice of The Call.

For Clare, that meant several years incubating TreeSisters, a non-profit with a dual mission to reforest the tropics and teach feminine Nature-based leadership. TreeSisters didn't spring up immediately after Clare heard the tree speaking to her. But she now carried this beautiful, life-giving seed. And when the time was right, TreeSisters was born.

In you, too, there is a seed. Perhaps it is one you are not even aware of right now. But if the path you are on, at present, doesn't feel right, or you are confused about what you are supposed to do, remember Clare's story. One way or another, life will try and get your attention. So right now, make a promise to yourself to quiet down and start listening.

Wendy Wallbridge's Story: A Wolf Comes Knocking

At the age of twenty-four, and just a few years out of college, Wendy thought she had it made. She had started a successful company in San Francisco with two physicians, one of whom wanted to marry her. She was living in a mansion. Her life on the outside glittered. But she was running on ego and a fair bit of drugs and alcohol. Then, one morning, she awoke unable to move, her body screaming in pain.

Within hours she was sitting in the examining room of a noted rheumatologist. She had lupus, a dangerous and unpredictable autoimmune disease that would eventually destroy her kidneys and require a life-saving transplant.

The diagnosis stripped Wendy not only of her health but of all the things she had formerly relied on to make her feel good about herself: her ability to run a cutting-edge organization, to earn money, her relationship with her doctor boyfriend. Now she was stopped in her tracks. She didn't know who she was or where her life was headed. Her brutal inner taskmaster was deeply unhappy with her.

In the years that followed her diagnosis, Wendy watched friends achieve her former worldly success while she felt like she'd lost her chance. Having absorbed the patriarchal message that productivity is the measure of success, she felt worthless. *Who was she if she couldn't produce? And was it her fault she was sick? Had her hard living brought this on?* She thought if she could just get back some of the outer, situational stuff, she could put her life back together.

Meanwhile, Wendy's illness meant she had to return and live with her parents. Unfinished business with her mother began to surface. "I had to walk deeper into the forest, to find myself," Wendy told me. "I had to go back and revisit all the old Mother wounds in order to reclaim my own healthy feminine. In doing so, I discovered a source of authentic power I had never experienced before."

Wendy was being urged by life to heal her separation with the feminine—to come to know that side of herself. Not as someone who needed to climb the ladder of success, but as a woman walking the spiral path, learning more and more about the beauty and wholeness of her soul.

When Wendy first told me her story, I was fascinated by the fact that in Latin, *lupus* means wolf. The disease causes a rash on the face that creates a wolfish appearance. I thought immediately of *Women Who Run with the Wolves*, where Clarissa Pinkola Estés describes women's affinity with these wild creatures who are naturally playful, relational, with a heightened capacity for devotion.[25]

Wendy's autoimmune disease caused her body to misread its own tissues and attack itself. Was it possible that the wolf in her, the wild, instinctual, and feminine one, was trying to get her attention? Was it telling her, *Start loving yourself, become part of a pack, howl, play, and learn to foster your sensing and sensual animal body?*

Eventually, Wendy received a kidney transplant. Her body healed. But something else happened. Wendy was still ambitious, but now she approached her work differently. Her ability to push through no matter what, had proven useless in the face of lupus. Perhaps there was a different path for success, based on a less driven, more receptive, and intuitive model.

With this insight, Wendy created the Spiral Up path for women in positions of leadership who did not want to abandon their feminine wisdom and own needs for self-care and nourishment. This innovative approach was a rebuke of the linear path Wendy had been barreling down until she got sick. Now, instead of a fast track, there was a spiral path, one that allowed women to rise to their full potential while living and working according to their own truths.[26]

Integration

Practice: Dancing the Spiral

Trained to take the linear path, we tend to become impatient when our lives don't move fast enough, or we don't reach our goals in a single direct thrust. We want to know it all, now! On the linear path, uncertainty breeds discontent rather than opportunity. Severed from our dark, intuitive being, our willingness diminishes to let life unfold, organically and authentically. So how do we reclaim our more feminine, instinctual way of navigating the world? By understanding the archetype of Forest Woman and her insistence that we meander off the beaten path.

What follows is an embodied practice with two parts. This can be done alone, or with a circle of friends with whom you can spin and move and dance.

Walk the Straight line: Simply find a space or place where you can walk back and forth in a straight line. As you walk, notice how it feels to focus on a goal, and walk directly toward it, never veering off or paying attention to anything on either side of you. Do this for at least five minutes. Then ask yourself these questions and journal your answers.

> *How do I feel emotionally?*
> *How do I feel physically?*
> *How connected to my intuition am I right now?*

Dance the Spiral Path: Now find a place—it could be an actual forest or woodland, or anywhere you feel safe and can move freely. Take five full minutes to explore where your instinct and intuition lead you, with no set agenda.

You might want to dance or move spontaneously, swirling and circling to your own rhythm. Or simply walk with no set destination, guided by your inner knowing. When you are ready, ask yourself these questions and write your answers in your journal.

> *How do I feel emotionally?*
> *How do I feel physically?*
> *How connected to my intuition am I right now?*

Reflect: How do my feelings, body, and intuition respond to this different way of navigating the world? Which path feels more alive to me?

Journal Reflection: Two Paths Diverged in the Woods

Set aside at least twenty minutes for this exploration.

We can't always shift from one path to another in an instant. The linear path may offer the security and paycheck you need right now. It's okay. This isn't about bad or good. It's about evaluating the rewards and sacrifices on each path. For some women, living a domestic life (raising children, cultivating a garden, taking care of the home) might go against the linear path of "being a success," i.e., attaining wealth and status. For others, the long hours required to work their way to the top may feel sterile and punishing. Or they may feel just wonderful.

Take a page and draw a line vertically down the middle.

On one side, list the ways that you have followed the linear path, the expected route, the well-trodden path.

On the other side, list the ways that you have followed the spiral path, walking with curiosity, leaving the prescribed route, exploring your own inclinations.

As you look at your lists:

What do you notice?

How has each path rewarded you?

Or hurt you?

Capture your observations in your journal.

The trees are alive with growth. Petals are all around me. I am dancing with petals filling my hands. Dancing to the music of Forest Woman.

—Snezana

The forest feels playful, ripe for exploring.

—Camille

The Way: Cocooning

So there was no going back: she had to fight
for survival among the mysteries of life.

—CLARICE LISPECTOR

Just as the acorn contains the oak tree, so do you carry the unique imprint of your soul. Some call this your daimon, or genius, or true nature. By whatever name, it holds the essence of who you are. This seed cannot be rushed prematurely into the bright light of day. It grows in the depths of your being, cocooned in the darkness.

As seeds planted in the dark of winter grow stronger roots to survive, so the choice to burrow deep inside in search of your authentic self is what makes you strong. If it were easy to find your true identity, how would you ever evolve, learn, grow? You wouldn't need those deep, strong roots. You would be born full-grown and fully formed, yet without the deep wisdom that comes from consciously seeking out your true self.

Thus, nature conspires to have you forget who you are born to be, in order that you learn how to become wise and conscious enough to hold your greater vision and particular genius.

At your most vulnerable, when you feel the thread of your story slip from your fingers, Forest Woman acts within you like the force of gravity, drawing you down into the dark until you surrender some rigid notion of yourself. Like the caterpillar within the chrysalis, for a while you completely dissolve, and your ego vanishes. Cocooned, you remember: You are pure potential. You are a dream waiting to be lived into existence.

The ego may crave the spotlight, but it is the fecund darkness that first cradled you in your mother's womb, where you begin to emerge into your fullness. In awakening to Forest Woman, you are learning to build a container strong enough and flexible enough to hold your greater self. This is a dark, wild, and often tension-filled psychic space where you begin to ask the kind of questions that can make or break a life.

Who are you becoming? What is your path and purpose? What enduring images are rising up unbidden from your deep unconscious?

Visions that emerge from such a deep place are not linear or predictable. They are radical, astonishing, seemingly irrational. Forest Woman wants more than surface transformation; she is calling you forth to live from your essential self.

Our bright and superficial civilization denigrates the life-giving dark. We have banished the Earth goddess who understands the power of the underworld. In her stead, we have a sky god who views the dark feminine as satanic and sinful. He is pure; she is sullied. He is "enlightened," she is not. Given this, how can we not fear the shadowy realms where the soul makes its home?

Under the influence of Forest Woman, you embrace the lunar cycles, the wild stirrings of the earthy feminine, to reclaim the life that is yours. Crowded in by towering trunks and generous branches, you are held in the here and now—the future unseen, the past hidden from view. There is nothing to reach for or to attain. You hold all you need—all that you are—in the womb of your being.

In the dark, in the dreaming, you begin to detach from the frantic tasks of the "upperworld." Competing for the job, finishing that project, finding the perfect mate—all the surface desires fall away. The deeper into the forest you go, the more you sense your soul's immensity, its uniqueness. Everything is singing and speaking to you in this realm of deep imagination, where the dream of your life is seeded.

Listen, Forest Woman says, *honor your dreams, explore the repeating patterns of your soul, spend time in meditation.* In exploring your inner world, you are reclaiming your depths. Forest Woman, fully embraced, awakens in you a creative response to the deep knowing self, the one within.

In her shadowy realm, long dormant images rise that hold the key to your destiny or special purpose. Life begins rooting, in the darkness. This is the natural beginning of transformation and growth.

Integration

Journal Reflection: Keeping A Dream Journal

Every night we dream, but in not paying attention to those dreams we often lose them. But what if you kept a dream journal? By simply recording your dreams on waking, you will be amazed by how many more dreams you remember. Always date your journal entry and, if possible, give your dream a title, as I did my "Yellow Dog" dream.

As you will discover, there are certain dreams that require your full presence and attention. They hold the images and symbols central to unlocking the mystery of your life. You may want to take these dreams into collages, paintings, poems. In other words, explore them through different means, so that their full wisdom can slowly reveal itself to you.

Embracing the Dark Feminine

During the darkest times, the uterine unconscious,
Nature, feeds a woman's soul.

—CLARISSA PINKOLA ESTÉS

"Enlightenment (a noun) is a metaphor that skewers us firmly back into the story of duality," writes ecofeminist Starhawk. "It negates the dark, the earth, the body, the dark cunt, the dark womb, the night."

Over and over again, this split of dark from light is mirrored in the severing of Earth from body, body from mind, spirit from nature. In the process, we diminish the power of darkness. We ignore the all-important reality that ninety-five percent of the Universe is comprised of dark matter and energy, which we know almost nothing about. But at the center of cosmology—and of every woman's truth—is this one truth: Everything is birthed in darkness.

Today we seek the light of the spirit without any sense of how our lives are rooted, like trees, in the pitch-black earth. Darkness—associated with sin, the dark arts, the dark angel, the demonic—is mostly exiled to the margins. Yet, without darkness, without deep dark roots, we, like the trees, lack the ability to grow and flourish. As Starhawk again writes, it is time to "speak of deepening, of getting down as well as getting high."[27]

Women have been made to fear the dark. The threat of rape keeps us from walking dark trails or the streets of our neighborhoods after nightfall. I heard one woman describe this sensation as being excluded from the nighttime. It hurt me to hear her words, for I fully understood them. You too may feel vulnerable, tremble like prey, in the darkness. Even so, darkness is your birthright.

Similarly, we have come to fear the dark of the unconscious and our own wild nature. We are afraid that if we spend time in the gloaming of our imaginations, we may realize that the safe path we have been traveling is actually deadly. That it dulls our creativity and steals from our sense of purpose. We may also be afraid of what may happen when we pay attention to our dreams. What if we do go in search of those slender trails and inner inklings? Where might they lead?

Awakening to our Forest Woman Selves, we confront both the dark forest and the life-giving womb, the parts of ourselves that we fear and the parts of ourselves that are longing to be brought into the world. This tension between fear and hope, destruction and regeneration, is always present when we are ready to give birth to our own lives. If we are to grow, into the darkness we must go.

The longer you spend in the dark—walking in the woods, stepping into the garden at night, or sleeping beneath the night sky—the more you will see that darkness is full of life and even offers a form of illumination. Our ancestors knew this, for as darkness fell onto a wintering land, they gazed at the stars in the heavens and the moon silvering the distant hills. Like owls that can spy a mouse in the dead of night, they learned to see in the dark. You too can be guided by muted lights and fiercer insights. When darkness wraps around you, you learn to see beyond the known world into something infinitely vaster and more mysterious.

As the poet Rilke writes:

> *But darkness embraces everything:*
> *shapes and shadows, creatures and me,*
> *peoples, nations—just as they are.*[28]

Rilke tells us that light fences in the world. There are things inside the light that you can see, and things outside the light that you cannot. This is a bit like shining a spotlight in a forest at night. You see only what is illuminated by the beam. But turn off the light, and the darkness expands around you to hold everything.

The trouble with reductionist, enlightened thinking is that it doesn't recognize anything that falls outside its beam. That's why an enlightened, scientific attitude has little to say about consciousness or love. Rationality is a searchlight, illuminating only the smallest portion of our reality and dismissing the existence of anything that lies beyond the fence.

I learned this at a very young age.

As a child I was given a magic locket by a woman with flame red hair who lived in a hut in the mountains of Positano in Southern Italy with her Romany husband and a host of dogs, cats, hens, sheep, and goats. Vali and Rudy had a sow called Ramona I rode over the dusty mountain trails. My family spent holidays in Positano from the time I was a baby until I was ten years old.

It was Vali who taught me to dance when I was a chubby six-year-old, taking me by the hand, saying, "Imagine you are dancing with the animals. Listen to the music, then feel your arm rise to stroke the neck of a giraffe or sweep across the back of a donkey. Dance with all the wild creatures." And suddenly, my body, infused with enchantment, knew what it needed to do.

Vali was born in Sydney, Australia in 1930 and went to Paris at age nineteen to study dance. She lived for a time on the streets and later befriended Django Reinhardt, Jean Cocteau, Jean Paul Sartre. Her small ink drawings of women, created with a goose feather while lying in bed, were praised by Salvador Dali and Andy Warhol and purchased by Mick Jagger.

But I remember her bare white feet fluttering like doves across the dance floor. How she read my tea leaves, danced with me on the dusty earth outside her home to the music of the cicada and the barking of dogs. How she smelled of herbs, essential oils, and animals.

How my brother and I thrilled to spend nights in a cave near her hut. Known as The Witch of Positano for her free spirit and wild ways, Vali filled my own heart with wonder.

Our last summer in Positano, Vali gave me a lucky charm she had made from green silk and old-fashioned lace the color of parchment. It was about two-and-a-half inches square, with some objects inside that she told me she had carefully chosen but that could never be revealed, or they would lose their power.

I carried that charm with me everywhere, stroking the silk until it wore thin. That was when the need to know what was inside grew irresistible. I went to sleep one night, with the magic charm under my pillow, knowing that in the morning I would look at what was inside. After all, wasn't the fabric falling apart anyway?

The next morning, I reached for the charm, and it wasn't there. I tore off the sheets, moved the bed, searched endlessly, but never found it. All those years I had wondered what magic it contained, and now it was gone.

Years later, and by then in my late teens, I ran into Vali and Rudy at a London carnival and told Vali the story of the disappearing charm. "Of course, darling," she responded. "You were never meant to know what it held."

Over half a century later that charm still carries totemic power for me. Its disappearance remains a profound and tantalizing mystery. Yet it taught me that there is something invisible in this world—something unnamable, unknowable, and unseeable that we should trust.

To honor the mystery, to embody the wisdom of Forest Woman, you must learn to move through a dappled world, embracing both light and shadow. You don't turn your back on intellect or reason entirely, but you learn to make room for the mystery. You enter a cocoon where you are held by the darkness, and some ineffable force that sees and knows you for who you truly are. Like Vali's charm, the realm of Forest Woman is magical, mysterious, powerful.

Integration

Ritual: The Dark Womb Circle

Gather a circle of women friends, preferably outdoors, and at night. If that's not feasible, any living room with the lights turned low will do.

The purpose of the ritual is to create a safe womb-like circle, then hold each other in the dark. This is a way to welcome each woman into the world, honoring her native genius and making sure that she feels fully witnessed, loved, and embraced by her community.

Create the space: Together, with your sisters, create a central focus like an altar. You might lay down a beautiful piece of fabric and have each woman place a talisman on it or bring in some elements from nature. Co-create it together, just as you like, knowing that this represents the womb. Allow enough space at the center of the circle for a woman to stand comfortably.

Share about an object: Ask each member to bring an object that symbolizes some aspect of who they are that they ordinarily do not share with others. For example, a piece of bark could embody their need for protection while they grow strong. After they have shared, invite them to place the object in the circle.

Settle in: Deepen this sacred space by reading a poem or playing some meditative music.

Hold the center: Each woman will take a turn standing in the center of the circle as the other women each take a minute or two to welcome her into the world. Tell her that she is loved, welcomed, needed, and that her gifts and her heart make the circle whole. Energetically, beam your love and welcome.

Return to take your place in the circle: As each woman returns to sit in the circle, in unison, chant: *You are loved, you matter, you are needed.*

When everyone in the group has had her turn, each woman will retrieve their object offering a few words about what has shifted for them after being welcomed by the circle and held in the group womb.

Close the circle with a poem, a song, drumming, or however you choose to honor what has just taken place.

A Forest Woman knows every moment is unfurling exactly as it is meant to, fed by the rich darkness and the soft black soil.

—Claire

What I give birth to will come naturally, from what I have and what I am and what I am becoming.

—Yvonne

Emerging as Forest Woman

A Fully Embodied Forest Woman

You are creative, curious, and attuned to your own inner compass. Rebelling against traditional roles and male structures, you have developed a way of knowing, navigating, and responding to the world that is deeply feminine and wholly original.

Imagination is your touchstone. You need time in the dark womb in order to seed your creative life. You love to explore, experiment, try new things. You are most deeply connected to yourself when in the act of dreaming up some new approach to life, some creative project.

Relationships for you work best when they also hold an element of surprise. If something doesn't feel fertile and alive, you know to gently release it. In any relationship, you need to feel your own person and have room to explore your own ways and creative callings.

Attuned to nature's rhythms and impulses, especially to the waxing and waning of the moon, you have a love of ritual and ceremony and often invite others to join you in these celebrations. Your spirituality is grounded in the cycles of nature and a deep appreciation for the spirit world of animals and plants. You honor patience and the slowness that sometimes is necessary to align with your own rhythm and the rhythm of life.

You naturally attract to you those who long to live more authentically and explore their talents. You encourage those around you to take appropriate risks, to discover their own paths in life. You are a natural mentor and inspiratrix, and children, in particular, love your spontaneous, playful side.

A Forest Woman Caught in Her Shadow

Any time you fail to trust the natural rhythms of life and are pushing through life in a slash-and-burn manner, the shadow side of Forest Woman has you in her grip. Too afraid or impatient to surrender to nature's timing, you are also cut off from your innate wisdom. At such times, you may sacrifice those around you in your desire to get ahead.

The shadow of a Forest Woman can show up in other ways, too. You may become so enamored of the many creative paths, the swirling possibilities, you never fulfill on any of them. You continue to wander the labyrinthine paths of the forest, without anything to show for all your creative ideas. You may even become envious of other creative women who manifest their talents. *I could have written that! I could have come up with that plan! I thought of that first!*

The answer is always to slow down and take time to be present. A deep breath can interrupt a manic need to keep rushing ahead. As you become present to yourself in an embodied way, you have an opportunity to make different choices.

Forest Woman and the Planet:

As a fully conscious Forest Woman, you inspire new ways of being through your creative way of living and your refusal to keep walking the punishing, predictable path of patriarchy. Listening to your inner wisdom, you invite others to question the sanity of our modern world with its emphasis on workaholism and consumerism. You know that to change things, we need new stories, new options, new images, and fresh metaphors.

As a woman who embodies patience, you realize true social and environmental transformation is a collaborative effort, taking place across generations.

Creative rebellion is your forte. You know how to take art to the streets, how a poem can change hearts and minds. You understand the importance of replacing old symbols with new, life-giving ones. You celebrate the decolonizing of power and the redistribution of creative means to every being.

You are found in protest songs and songs of praise. You, at your best, show us how we can all rise strong and effect change.

Some Final Reflections on Forest Woman

What is Forest Woman's greatest gift to you?

What aspects of Forest Woman challenge you the most?

How do you see yourself embodying Forest Woman's wisdom in the future?

Which areas of your life could most benefit from Forest Woman's presence?

If you were to fully embrace your Forest Woman self, what would change?

How will you express thanks to Forest Woman?

Opening to Ocean and River Woman

Forest Woman provided you with an enclosed womblike space, an inward-looking structure in which to safely explore your imagination. In the process, some fresh things stirred in you: ideas, dreams, images— and perhaps an inkling, however vague, of the direction your life wants to take. As you move to meet Ocean and River Woman, prepare to feel a rush of energy to pursue your passions. Like a river breaking through a dam, you are readying yourself to move past any resistance in order to bring more of your fierce, loving self into the world.

The journey is about to get wilder, freer. Can you feel the difference in your body as the waters of the Earth begin to welcome you?

3

Ocean and River Woman

Soul of an Ocean and River Woman

She is flow and feeling, the flood of sexual desire.
Shapeshifter and Earth-scriber so powerful,
stone gives way beneath her touch.
In time she moves mountains.
She is the blue stream of veins, the wild wave, the still lake.
From her oceanic womb life arises.
Moonlight tugs at her swaying body.
Her hair is the white of mountain snow.
She is thirst quencher and tide dancer, full-throated and still as ice.
She is the stream of consciousness, the sacred fountain.
In her gentleness, we are lulled.
In the face of her fury, we are humbled.
In the full force of her passions, we are unstoppable.
When we surrender to her flow, we come fully alive.

Stage of Initiation: The Waters Break

The Challenge: Learning to Love Ourselves

The Shift: Dam/ned to Flowing

The Way: Shapeshifting

Embodied Dimensions: Love, passion, forcefulness, expressiveness, ebullience, sexuality, playfulness, depth, flow

Guiding Question: What brings me fully alive?

The Waters Break:
The Third Initiation

. . . we are vertical rivers, walking watersheds . . .

—Ruth Gendler

Each one of us carries within, like a vast body of water, an ever-changing cycle of emotions. At times, we may experience this internal system as a still lake, a cheerful stream, or a raging river. We may churn like the surf, working away at the edges of our problems, or we may feel like an ocean current that travels incredible distances, turning up deep upwellings of nutrients.

How you dance with your emotions determines the course of your life. Beyond your own experience, it shapes the landscape around you. Like the flow of a river that over time carves the canyon, every droplet of desire, every droplet of love and wanting, shapes the contours of your existence and even the world's.

And yet in so many ways our emotions and desires have been polluted, diverted, and dam/ned by a culture terrified of feeling. After all, if our emotions were taken seriously, what changes would be required? It is easier to call women hysterical, a word that comes from the Greek *hyster*, meaning "of the womb." Easier to condemn us as unhinged: too frail to be told the bad news, too erratic to hold power, too emotional for our own good.

Society judges harshly those women who express their emotional needs. It prefers women to be docile and sublimate their own desires—including sexual desires—to serve those of others. How quick we are to condemn a woman who rages or breaks down or possesses a buoyant sexuality! No surprise, then, that many of us keep tight control of our feelings or culvert them, creating deep underground trenches to hold those "unacceptable" emotions.

Thus, you may make the deadliest of agreements. You may decide to stem the flow of your own feelings in order to fit in. But emotions aren't meant to be static. The very word *emotion* holds the need for motion. Feelings, like water, need to circulate.

Ocean and River Woman invites you to welcome the rising tides of your longings. Even if they feel muddied, or out of control, or reduced to a trickle, one day your waters will break, and you will embark upon your own rebirth.

The question you must ask is this: *Am I willing to risk losing things—relationships, regard, status—in order to ride the wild river of my wanting?*

To live according to your passions, you must dismantle the dam that holds you back. You must open yourself to being moved and changed by life. Claiming your Ocean and River Self, you will discover that you can never be broken. You are immense and powerful, like the waters of the Earth.

Put your hand on your heart. Feel its beat, like the pounding of waves, and know that the work that follows is deep work, as the oceans are deep.

Ocean and River Woman is already streaming through every vein of your body, waiting to carry you in the direction of your wild and wanting heart. Will you step into the flow?

Surrendering to the Flow of Desire

To trace the history of a river or a raindrop ...
is also to trace the history of the soul.

—GRETEL EHRLICH

To fully embrace your life purpose, you must reclaim your ability to feel fully and passionately. In this, the third stage of your journey, your task is to become fluent in the language of emotion. And it begins with plunging into deep waters in search of your true self.

The Latin derivative for the word emotion, *motus*, literally means energy in motion. When you are in touch with your feelings, you unleash a powerful current—one that can help you to find your true direction in life. As mystic and dreamworker Toko-Pa Turner writes, "At the heart of exile, we must finally encounter the longing we have hidden in our own hearts. Longing is an impulse, born out of what is missing from us which we ache to return to, even if we've never known it directly. It aches too, for our homecoming."[29]

But how do we get in touch with our longing in a culture that sublimates feelings, especially those considered outside the norm: mystical experiences, a playful sense of embodiment, sexual passion, any yearning that sweeps us up and tears us from our usual moorings? It is, after all, all too easy to deny our natural depth and vivacity. But when the dull predictability of an emotionally constrained life drains us of our vitality, Ocean and River Woman challenges us to find other currents of possibility. Like a river that moves mountains to unite with the ocean, our longing will lead us home.

We cannot live without water. If you have ever been thirsty for a few hours, let alone a whole day, you know that water is essential for your own survival. Now, as Ocean and River Woman stirs in you, you come to realize that emotions—long associated with water—are the source of your own aliveness. Whereas Forest Woman provided you with an enclosed womblike space, an inward-looking structure in which to safely explore your imagination, as you move into this next stage, the journey gets wilder, freer.

Women and water have a long partnership. Our bodies are attuned to moon cycles and tidal surges in an ancient, wordless rhythm that structures our experiences in profound ways. We are deeply affected by the amniotic oceans that fill our bellies in pregnancy and the welling of our breast milk. Through our watery bodies, we experience the flowing rhythms of Earth and Cosmos. Our bodies know that we are part of the great river of life. Like an underground stream, our emotions are always present. But will we trust them and allow them to guide us?

I grew up in England, a cold country for emotions. Tucked away in a convent boarding school, I felt stifled. Emotion wasn't part of our lexicon. As some are drawn to learn French or Spanish, I set out to learn the language of feeling. At every chance, I'd sneak away to read the lush and lilting poetry of Kahlil Gibran, "Love one another, but make not a bond of love: Let it rather be a moving sea between the shores of your souls."[30] Poetry was sensual, exciting, and reading these verses was like holding a secret meeting with a lover. In poetry, my longing for meaning and depth was mirrored back to me. It showed me what was in my own yearning heart.

In the early 2000s, I attended a workshop by Joanna Macy after the release of her new translation of Rilke's *Book of Hours*, with her collaborator Anita Barrows. Macy's work in the field of deep ecology had greatly affected me, and in listening to her read Rilke's poetry, I was stirred. Something began to move inside of me—a current of energy, a quickening of my pulse.

After the workshop, I told Joanna about my work with the Wild Soul. At the time I was still searching for my own voice as a writer. I hoped to receive some guidance from this amazing woman. She smiled at me and asked me to search for the following line in Rilke's poems: *Go to the limits of your longing.*

Back at home, I lay on the sofa, opened her book, and began reading. Rilke's language cascaded through me, summoning me into my own fierce feelings. Encouraging my love of emotional language, constrained by years of copywriting, it was as if Rilke was whispering in my ear, asking me to love this Earth and to love it through my words. By the time I reached page 119, and read: *You, sent out beyond your recall / go to the limits of your longing,*[31] I was ready to write again—not from my head—but in a state of flow, my words like a wellspring, emerging directly from my body.

Ocean and River Woman had spoken to me. This deep thirst, this passion for the Wild Soul, for the poetry of nature and spirit, is what drives my work today. When I am disconnected from that longing, I end up in a stagnant pool, stuck and small. My passion restores and sustains me. It is an energetic wave that carries me beyond any self-imposed limits into something far greater and more alive.

And so, I say to you, make that commitment to "go to the limits of your longing." You can start simply by naming something or someone you love. Allow yourself to focus on that love. Follow the energy of your longing. Let it build in your heart. Let love and longing melt you so that you can merge into a greater consciousness. You won't be in control, and that's okay. Passion is a powerful current. You don't have to know what to do with it. All you have to do is let go.

Signs that Ocean and River Woman Is Trying to Get Your Attention

Longing—You fall in love with a person, a cause, an artistic pursuit that pulls you out beyond your comfort zone. Or you simply yearn for something you cannot yet name.

Turbulence—Passion, rage, and joy seem to spring out of you at unexpected times and inexplicable ways.

Addiction—You find yourself using outside stimulus (drugs, alcohol, shopping, food, etc.) in order to feel alive.

Blockage—You suddenly feel drained or held back and can't see a way through.

Readiness—You feel as if something is about to change. Excitement bubbles up inside.

Diana Nyad's Story: A Natural Ocean and River Woman

Diana Nyad dreamed of swimming the unpredictable waters from Cuba to Florida, one of the most dangerous stretches of sea in the world: shark-infested, full of treacherous eddies and oddities like the box jelly fish which has the deadliest venom in the ocean. No one had ever done it. She tried to swim this part of the ocean in her twenties and failed.

At sixty-four, her desire was much greater. Everyone said it was foolish for a woman of her age to imagine she could do such a thing. But she didn't want to look back in regret. So, she told herself, *Find a way. You have a dream. Find a way.*

When I heard her say those words in a TED Talk,[32] I thought, this is what water does. It finds a way, moving under rocks and over them, slipping underground and through small cracks in its quest for freedom. It pounds city pavements, surges as moon-lit waves.

It meanders through valleys, rises as mist on moors and in sleepy hollows. As long as you are willing to surrender to the currents of your deepest desires, you, too, will find your way.

Diana's quest was about much more than becoming the first person to swim those wild waters. It was about not giving a dam/n—not listening to all those who would hold her back. When she was fourteen, Diana's swim coach sexually assaulted her. Such abuse might have stopped any woman, no matter how strong or talented, from fulfilling her dreams. But while her life was dramatically altered, she refused to be held back.

So, having read Diana's story, I ask you: Will you accept the emotional limitations society imposes on you? Or will you keep moving in the direction of your own passionate heart?

Integration

Journal Reflection: The Call to Surrender

* I am called to this stage of the journey in order to learn . . .
* I know that this is my Ocean and River Woman time because . . .
* At this moment, I fear . . .
* At this moment, I am excited by . . .
* I hope to emerge from my time with Ocean and River Woman with . . .

Practice: Go to the Limits of Your Longing

Focus on something or someone you love, and simply stay with your feelings. How does this emotion change you? Don't judge what arises. Simply notice how this rush of longing is connected to your mind, body, and spirit.

I long for freedom...to feel...to express pure emotions without restraint...like the sea...to ebb and flow with love, joy, exuberance, joy, joy, joy...where is my joy? I long for joy.

— Eileen

Born from rivers of forgiveness,
flowing golden through pine trees
of ancient memories,
rounded softly by whale song
and ocean tides of moon magic.

—Signe

Depth

*I must be a mermaid; I have no fear of depths
and a great fear of shallow living.*

—Anaïs Nin

There are places in the ocean so deep and dark, we have only the slightest notion of what life may exist down there. The Mariana Trench, the deepest oceanic trench on Earth, plunges to a staggering 36,201 feet below the ocean surface and stretches for 1,580 miles. This abyss reminds us that nature—and our own nature—contains unfathomable depths. This is the realm of Ocean and River Woman, the one who has the courage to dive deep.

Ocean and River Woman can playfully splash on the surface of life or plunge into its churning depths. We, as well, are made to live in both worlds. The trouble is that many of us are more comfortable skimming the surface while ignoring the vast waters of our unconscious. And it's no accident. Many traditional religions and New Age practices preach transcendence at the expense of exploring what lies below the surface. It will take boldness and an inward dive to discover your instinctive resources. But it is toward depth and meaning that our wild souls are drawn.

Ocean and River Woman beckons you to explore the sea-caverns of your soul. In these dark and mysterious places, you will encounter your own monsters, muses, and motivations. How did they help you get here? What is it you came here for? What is still waiting to be discovered in the depths?

To live a life of significance, to be truly responsive to the plight of the planet and your own wild soul, you must break from the surface world and dive deep.

Once you drop down, you will know yourself as part of the whole. As the ancients tell us, we are more than a drop in the ocean, we are also the ocean herself. We were all birthed from these same deep waters—from a place of silence, deeper than words, deeper than intellect or ego can fathom.

And yet, distracted by the pace of modern life, how easy it is to stay trapped in the shallows. Flashing computer and TV screens, the scintillation of social media, constant web-surfing—all have us skim the surface of things, so that we move from one activity to the next, barely touched by our experience.

Ocean and River Woman provides an antidote to all of this, drawing you into the dark interiority of the soul. This is where the real meaning of your life can be found. Her message: *There is more to life than the obvious. To experience the greatest fulfillment, you must enter the abyss.*

Integration

Journal Reflection: Go Deeper!

As you get ready for sleep, take a few minutes to do this journal exercise. On the left-hand page, write down all the main activities you engaged in during the day. You might want to call this list your "surface self" list. On the opposite page, let your deeper Self respond to the way you've spent your time.

Here are some of the questions you might review:

How are your surface activities keeping you from discovering the deeper currents?

What do you sense lies beneath their surface?

What are the currents you are barely acknowledging?

If you were to dive deeper, what would you find?

Making a practice of this before bedtime, will feed your dream self, helping you to explore what is going on in your unconscious. In the morning, write down any images or messages that came to you in the night.

Then reflect:

What are these images, dreams, or messages telling you about the deeper currents of your life?

Taking the Plunge

*The river needs to take the risk of entering the ocean
because only then will fear disappear*

—KAHLIL GIBRAN

Life on Earth emerged out of the oceans 300 million years ago, just as we emerged out of our mother's watery wombs, each birth a reenactment of our evolutionary journey. Water is part of our origin story and frequently the first element in creation myths across the world. Primordial waters, also known as the cosmic ocean, gave birth to life. Your body retains your oceanic history. Before you had fingers you had fins.

Ocean and River Woman calls us to remember who we are. She urges us to reclaim our depths, and within them, rediscover our wild desires and profound and numinous connection to life. It is here, after all, in the shadowy depths of our oceanic selves that we will find our greatest treasures, the key to our own souls.

Writes Adrienne Rich: "At twenty-two [poetry] called me out of a kind of sleepwalking. I knew, even then, that for me poetry . . . could be a fierce, destabilizing force, a wave pulling you further out than you thought you wanted to be." Its message, she said, was "You have to change your life."[33]

What is it that pulls you out of your depths? Love for this world? A swirling anger? A grand passion? When we begin to meet something deep and true within ourselves, we often feel swept up, lost at sea at first. But then we begin to re-member who we are.

As I shifted from the world of advertising and marketing to the world of poetry and journal therapy, I had the following dream:

I am in a large warehouse. Bad men have brought me here, but now they have gone. I am free to leave before a demolition crew torches the place to the ground. I approach a smartly dressed businesswoman and tell her that I must speak with the demolition crew. I have left valuable things inside! I go back to collect gray and white pearl earrings and a pink heart pendant without a chain that my mother gave me.

I find a workman and tell him that pieces of me are lying under a blue tarp—pieces that my abductors have hacked off. I glance down at my hands, and I realize that bits of me have been stuck on, but if you look carefully, you can see they don't match.

A man who is very ambitious and money-focused offers to help. But the worker says, "No problem" and pitches in. He is big and burly and kind. As he lifts my sawn-off parts, still under the blue tarp, a clear liquid gushes out and onto the floor. I lean against the wall, with the businesswoman on one side and the ambitious man the other, and we all begin to weep.

The dream was calling me to re-member and recover my lush, feminine aspects—the pearls, those lustrous jewels of the depths; the pink heart my mother gave me. For so long I had rejected my passionate feminine nature, choosing instead the dysfunctional masculine path of feigned achievement and cut-throat competition. The result? I am living with parts that have somehow been applied, or artificially stuck on. When the waters break and those lost parts of me come tumbling out, I weep with joy and relief. I recognize all that I have given up in order to become that fake person, that non-woman, striving to succeed in a Warehouse World. I, too, receive the message: *You have to change your life.*

Civilization has spent the last few thousand years trying to pull us out of the unconscious matrix, into a realm of pure rationality. From this islet of reason, we view ourselves as separate from nature's depths and vastness. But sooner or later, Ocean and River Woman will call us from the tidy, safe plain of rationality, into our depths. Waves will come in the form of larger-than-life emotions or turbulent dreams, and we will find ourselves submerged. But we know how to be with the unconscious. Our first home was floating in an ancient sea of amniotic fluid in our mother's wombs. We have never separated from the water or from the vast oceanic consciousness that is our origin.

In 1983, just two weeks after I had quit drinking, I was hiking the Marin Headlands on a stormy day. The Pacific Ocean was pounding the rocks below. I was a churning mess of insecurities, wondering how I was going to stay sober. But looking at the roiling ocean, a thought entered me— the ocean was also churned up, yet it was still immensely powerful and strong. I tasted salt in my mouth and couldn't tell if it was my tears or the ocean's spray. I felt completely at one with this great body of water. In that moment, I claimed the strength of the ocean and knew I was going to be alright.

Other friends have had similar insights. Gazing into her newborn niece's eyes, Kay was utterly overcome. She witnessed an aspect of God in this tiny being, fresh from a watery womb. A therapist for many years, Kay said this moment forever changed her perception of who we are and our potential as human beings. She perceived a deeper truth: we are divine, immense, fathomless.

The women I know who are changing the world, providing for their kids, protesting wrongs, standing up for justice and inequality, and trying to save the planet, all draw their strength from the same place. They have shed the husk of superficiality. Through generative and generous exchanges, they dive deep and come up with new solutions to our social and environmental problems. They don't just speak deeply, they see deeply, looking into one another's hearts. They know we are all connected to something greater than ourselves.

Psychologist Abraham Maslow described peak experiences, but an Ocean and River Woman draws from the depths. She knows that whatever we are not conscious of has power over us. Even depression, even our submerged drives that feel monstrous and scary, are all part of our soul journey. Women are often encouraged to medicate those monsters. But what if they are our teachers? If we are willing to experience the waves of feeling engulfing us, we can surely learn to dive beneath the surface and discover what needs to be brought back into the light of day.

Consider the legendary female free divers of Japan and Korea. For the last 2,000 years these women dived to extraordinary depths, naked as mermaids, their bodies completely at home in freezing waters as they fished for scallops, abalone, and pearls. Now, more often clad in wetsuits, they can make up to two hundred dives a day, holding their breath for minutes at a time. These women live long because they have remarkably slow heart rates and unusually clear arteries. They remind us that we also gain in strength as we plumb our depths, again and again.

The Japanese divers are called *Ama*, meaning "women of the sea." And in Korea they are known as *Haenyo*, meaning "women of independent spirit." Like them, we are called to dive deep to bring back treasure.

Elizabeth Dougherty: For Love of a River

Elizabeth is the Director of Wholly H2O, a non-profit that educates people about their local watersheds. As she puts it, "If people aren't emotionally connected to their source of water, they won't protect it." Elizabeth's own journey has been like a meandering river.

Elizabeth grew up in Rhode Island in a house with a lawn that sloped down to Narragansett Bay, her playground. Later, living in the San Francisco Bay Area, she explored the river basins out West and became a frequent traveler to Nevada City where she would sit for hours beside the Yuba River, which she describes as kindhearted.

Her young nephew would often join her and tell people, "Don't talk to her, she's listening to the river." Elizabeth came to think of the Yuba as her mother river.

In 2007, after a major earthquake in Peru, Elizabeth, who has a Ph.D. in anthropology and ethnography, went to South America to work in disaster relief. The sanitation systems in the coastal town of Pisco had been crippled by the quake, and Elizabeth and her team worked to replace them with sustainable systems. She also worked on a water filtration project in the Andes of Peru.

Back in the United States, Elizabeth studied rainwater harvesting and greywater reuse. Given her previous work in energy efficiency, it was a natural step to connect municipalities to the idea of using rainwater and greywater, in addition to rivers and groundwater, as primary water sources.

Then, during a sacred journey, she had an experience that changed her life. In a vision, the Yuba River asked her to start an organization with the mission to protect water sources. She had no idea of what this meant or would entail. But currents were already flowing beneath the surface, carrying her toward her dream. In another sacred ritual, the name of her educational organization came to her: Wholly H2O. A name that speaks to wholeness, the whole, and to the sacredness of the water.

Elizabeth also honors water through the arts. After the devastating 2013 Rim Fire along the Tuolumne River, the source of water for San Francisco and Silicon Valley, she produced several art exhibits including, "Standing with the Watershed," featuring sculptures and images from multiple artists. Working with non-profits, governmental water agencies, businesses, schools, and individuals, Elizabeth continues to draw our attention to the importance of water.

It has taken many years to evolve her non-profit into a thriving organization. Elizabeth tells me, "Just because a river sends you a powerful message, doesn't mean everything just flows together."

"But in time," she says, "if you really give your heart to the water, you don't just *feel* water flowing through you. You *become* the river."

Integration

Practice: Diving Deep

As Jung wrote, "Wisdom dwells in the depths." To dive deep, it helps to develop a practice that liberates us from the ego, which ignores our unconscious drives and desires. It doesn't really matter what the practice is—running, swimming, art, poetry, dance, song, music, yoga, meditation. Anything that allows you to move beyond the small *I* and embrace your deepest self will suffice. The common thread with these practices, is that they disengage the controlling mind. We enter a deeper flow state where all kinds of ideas and emotions rise to the surface.

After your practice, write down any images, sensations, or ideas that you experienced. What did you notice? What surprised you?

I want to dive farther down, to be at one with the teeming life force.

—Sharon

I am surprised at the stillness of the lake. It is dark, deep. What lies beneath?

—Eileen

Aliveness

. . . what I want in my life, is to be willing, to be dazzled . . .
—MARY OLIVER

Like setting off down a rushing river as the sun rises, Ocean and River Woman stirs in you fresher and more compelling desires. Though on the surface you may shiver with fear, you sense a responding surge of playfulness and passion deep inside. What would it be like to sacrifice the safety of certainty for the wild promise of fulfillment?

Ocean and River Woman reminds you that life follows energy. You can trust what brings you alive. Elemental and life-giving, Ocean and River Woman exposes the hollow heart of a mechanistic society that functions on the principles of expediency and productivity at the expense of wonder and joy. Who are you when you stop absorbing the messages of the culture and start listening to the urgings of your own soul? The purpose of your life, she reminds you, has always been to seek your own aliveness and then to gift it back to the world.

Your wild soul is, after all, oceanic. Connecting to that deep and free part of yourself, as each river longs to, as each woman must, your life starts to possess a buoyancy that is beautiful to behold. Feeling acts in you like water, moving you toward health (a word that shares its root with wholeness).

Over time, aliveness becomes a crescendo, building on itself until it begins to invigorate your life. Spontaneity starts to override security, and true purpose your neatly constructed plans. Carried away by a groundswell of vitality, you find yourself able to take risks, create, play.

A polluted river causes everything it touches to wither: the vegetation on the banks, the salmon in the shallows, the waterfowl who can no longer feed from it. There are cascading effects to toxicity. Similarly, if you turn away from your true desires, expect your life to stagnate and your longings to slow to sludge. But there is a deeper current that runs through you, that is your destiny, and that holds the hidden purity of your own wild heart.

If you have ever drunk water fresh from the source, then you know how a single sip can wake up every cell of your being. You know how your heart sings with gladness to taste such deliciousness. You know how after drinking from it you feel reenergized. This is the sacred water that brings you playfully, joyously, unabashedly alive. Life, you realize, is not some dreary march to some brutal end, but an adventure filled with beauty and purpose.

Like the salmon, you may strain against the prevailing current, yet you can also leap over obstacles, muscle your way through on fin and faith.

As an Ocean and River Woman, you are iridescent as you return to the clean, clear waters of your own soul.

Integration

Journal and Art Prompt: My River of Creativity

For this exploration you will need a big sheet of paper and lots of colored pens. You are going to create your own watershed. A watershed is the land that contains all the streams and every drop of rainfall that nourishes a given region. It may contain mountains and ridges, as well as waterways.

Review the questions below to start your creative juices flowing and to make tangible not just your River of Creativity, but how everything that borders it helps either feed it or drain it. Create the surrounding topography, complete with mountains and meadows.

❉ What feeds your creativity? Where are its headwaters?

❉ What dam/ns it?

❉ What releases it?

❉ Where does it flow fast? Where does it pool and slow?

❉ What course does it take?

❉ What ocean of longing does it feed?

Mark these things on your map. Chart your river visually, then give names to what you are depicting, i.e., The Dam of Self-Doubt, the Joyful Creek, the Waterfall of Wanting. Next, give your River of Creativity a name that best captures its essence.

Then take a moment to reflect in your journal:

❉ What did you notice about the lay of the land?

❉ What hems in your creativity?

❉ What allows it to flow?

❉ What places do you feel comfortable?

❉ Which areas needs more rain or nourishment?

❉ What part of your watershed would you like to change?

The Sacred Gift of Life

Any world is a valid world if it's alive.

—Joseph Campbell

In baptism, in sacred wells, in the metaphors of cleansing and purity, we equate water with healing and even holiness. To bathe in the Ganges is to be blessed by the Goddess Ganga. To drink from the holy wells of Ireland is to be healed and purified. All over the world, in different cultures, throughout different mythologies, water expresses the idea of sacredness because we depend on it for life. In a similar way, Ocean and River Woman is calling you to reconnect with your own sacred and loving center.

Joseph Campbell, the great scholar, suggested that we follow our bliss and take that as our inner compass. He knew that we long "to feel the rapture of being alive."[34] And yet the pull of the mainstream culture is hard to resist. But when going with the flow of the collective is leading to disaster, as we see in our unwillingness to confront climate change or care for the vulnerable in our society, it may require a great effort to shift course. It is then we need to swim upstream in order to find a fresher current and tap into the wellsprings of life.

From the moment you are born, your life begins to flow in a certain direction. The tides of convention are quick to sweep you up. But look back to what you loved to do as child. Recall hours floating by, almost in a dream, as you played certain games, or built tree houses, or talked to flowers, or played with friends, or wrote, as I did, plays and stories. Or perhaps you loved to read, curled up like a nautilus on the windowsill, lost in your imagination. These loves didn't vanish, they still dwell inside of you.

This certainly was true for Joey Heusler, a docent for the National Point Reyes Seashore.

Every summer, Joey's family would pack up the camping gear and leave their home in Cologne, Germany for the West Frisian Islands off the Dutch coast. They lived near the beach for weeks. During those days, Joey, who suffered from severe and debilitating bouts of bronchitis, was never sick. Not once.

Tiny for her age, she'd run in and out of the waves, even the big ones that she was afraid of and that sometimes pulled her under. "I came to life in the water," she says. Her mother called her "Little Water Rat," a term of endearment for her wild child.

Many years later, Joey moved to the San Francisco Bay Area and fell in love with the gray whales that migrate past its shores. While working full time as a physical education teacher, Joey began to guide kayaking groups out in Richardson Bay for an organization that also ran guided treks to Baja, the breeding lagoons of the gray whale.

And so, it happened that she was invited to watch the grays in their spawning grounds. Before going out into the lagoons, her guide warned her, "People who experience the whales are forever changed." Joey wasn't convinced. She knew change wasn't always good. She'd just dissolved a twenty-year domestic partnership and was raising a nine-year-old daughter on her own.

The mother whales ushered their calves towards the boats. One particular calf came so close to Joey, she could touch its face. The calf slowly turned, and they gazed at each other. "And there is the world before and there is the world after this happened," she told me, tearing up at the memory. "I looked into the face of wisdom, the universe, endless time. And the mother just allowed this to happen. It was almost as if she said, *Go, baby.*"

Later that evening, Joey stood at the edge of the ocean, knowing that something was about to shift. "I had a great job I loved in physical education. But there and then, I knew I needed to be in the ocean. I needed to bring people into the experience of this place—this outside place that changes our insides."

A couple of years later, she quit her fulltime job and sold her house to fund her own business, Explore in Nature, to guide people into connection with water, nature, whales. "I had this connection to the sea when I was little. The ocean has always been home to me, and this work feels like my soul journey."

In her poem "The Thread," Denise Levertov refers to an invisible filament that runs through our lives. She describes the stirring of wonder we feel at its tug, the energizing nature of our true calling. We may lose touch with it at times, but when we feel it again, we are filled with a sense of our own destiny. And so it is that Ocean and River Woman calls us to think of survival in a new way. She knows it is a matter of living according to our essential nature—doing, as Joey discovered and Levertov describes—what we were born to do.

But is this easy? And how often do we get distracted? Certain desires flash by. We buy a new "toy" and feel a surge of endorphins. A minute later, we need another diversion. After that, another fix.

Early in my drinking years, I realized that one drink was never going to be enough. But there is a big difference between craving and longing. Chasing after fleeting satisfactions isn't the same as sating a soul hunger. And yet our motivation is often similar. In truth, I thirsted for spirit. Messy and ugly though my drinking was, it arose out of a desire to connect with something greater than myself. Something I could not tame. Something as wild and sacred as life itself.

Robin Wall Kimmerer, a professor of environmental biology and member of the Citizen Potawatomi Nation, writes, "I want to stand by the river in my finest dress. I want to sing, strong and hard, and stomp my feet with a hundred others so that the waters hum with our happiness. I want to dance for the renewal of the world."[35] All I can say to that, is *yes!* I wanted, and I still want, that too.

The Mississippi River runs 2,340 miles through ten states, from Minnesota to Louisiana. Thanks to cartographers, we can track how this amazing body of water has meandered over time. It has jumped its banks and changed its course, sometimes dramatically. Even the walls and levees built in the 1940s by the Army Corps of Engineers couldn't keep the Mississippi from moving according to its own inclinations.

Elizabeth Gilbert writes of the Mississippi's "meander map"—its ever-shifting course: "This map could be a portrait of my heart's own journey."[36] In her wonderful Elizabeth Gilbert way, she is saying that if we don't like our present course, it is okay to change it. It's okay to change our minds, to say, *this didn't work out as I had planned.* Or *this isn't working for me.* Or *I've fallen in love with someone else.* It's okay to begin again. To start over. To try something new.

For an Ocean and River Woman, all emotions, like the wild forms of water, are a natural part of our own personal watershed. You get to celebrate them and recalibrate them. Emotions are made to drift and shift. The only question is: how will you express them in healthy ways? It is important both to honor your feelings *and* take responsibility for them.

We live in uncertain times as one crisis after another crashes over us. If we keep doing the same thing, choosing superficial solutions, we will only have to paddle harder. The mainstream culture is contaminated, and its outmoded views won't carry us through. We need new streams and fresh waters. We need to sparkle with so much pure life, others are swept up in our passion to renew this Earth and be kinder to each other. As Ocean and River women, we can begin to fashion a truly relational, revitalized world.

Lisa Turner's Story: My Name Is River

Lisa Turner stood in a sacred circle of women. As they introduced themselves, she surprised herself by saying, "I want to be known as River." The name felt sacred and somehow appropriate for this phase of her life.

Soon after, Lisa learned she had breast cancer, and water became her talisman. It reminded her the flow of life is sometimes fast and chaotic, sometimes slow and gentle. Immersing herself in water also helped wash away her deep grief for the loss of her imagined future and for the physical and mental challenges she was experiencing.

The afternoon she was told that she might lose her breast, Lisa attended a woman's retreat and shared her breast "bucket list." Whatever was to come, she wanted to have lived wildly and freely.

And she wanted to honor this part of her that had nurtured her two children and had given her such extraordinary pleasure.

It was a cold winter day. In the presence of her circle sisters, she walked across the ice and snow and knelt by a small stream. She placed her breasts and face into the water. The water felt like a thousand needles on her skin. Then it felt like fire. The women around her sang, as the river sang—and she allowed the voices of the women and river to flow and weave through her until she experienced "complete surrender." She wasn't giving up, she told me. This was a deep prayer that she would live.

When Lisa talks about this experience, her eyes shine like the river. Now, three years after lumpectomy surgery and chemotherapy, swimming keeps her connected to her wild and precious body. She often swims with other women and loves the pure, raucous, gut-spilling joy of splashing in icy rivers. "Just being in the water," she says, "keeps me sane, keeps me present, keeps me happy. Water keeps me alive."

Integration

Practice: Water Blessing

You are more than seventy percent water. You were birthed from ancient seas of amniotic fluid. Given all this, what blessing could you perform to give thanks to this amazing element, water?

Will you write a poem? Or dance a water dance? Or say a prayer? Or sit in silence and gratitude? Or immerse yourself in a river, lake, or ocean? Or will you volunteer to help clean up your local watershed? As long as it comes from the depth of your heart, it will be a true blessing.

Practice: Cleaning Up the Waters

Poisoned desires are like toxic water. They won't revitalize the Earth or help us heal ourselves. This exercise is a powerful practice to embody the aliveness of fresh water.

Your own community likely has a group that monitors local streams and keeps them free of debris and toxins. You might want to join them. Or you can make a practice of cleaning up trash on the shores of a river or beach.

You also might reflect on how you are treating water in your own home. Are you using too much when you brush your teeth or wash the dishes? Are you avoiding dangerous fertilizers in the garden that can pollute the watershed? Are you taking outdated medications back to the pharmacy to be safely disposed of, so they don't get tossed in the landfill and taint the groundwater?

Next, think about how you would like to clean up your own inner waters.

What debris would you like to be free of? What toxins would you like to eliminate both from your body and your heart? What is the number one pollutant you are ready to clean up?

I am cosmos turned over and over, tumbled by water, spun into the nebulae of the cosmos—weaving from water to space. Atomic, cosmic, deep, and vast, free from the sharp edges of want, but still in the spacious liquidity of desire.

—Pollyanna Darling

Let the roar of waterfalls be my laughter.

—Bettina

The Challenge: Learning to Love Ourselves

A Woman in harmony with her spirit is like a river flowing.
She goes where she will without pretense and arrives at her destination
prepared to be herself and only herself.
—Maya Angelou

One of the hardest things we women have to face is how we have fallen out of love with ourselves. So much of our natural libido has been misdirected or, worse still, poisoned by a culture that sneers at our emotional effusions and ebullient joys. As our sexuality is censored and natural buoyancy denied us, we can lose not just our love of life but our love of self.

Self-love may sound trivial, even problematic. But there is danger in *not* loving yourself. In the absence of self-love, you may lose yourself in others, merging so intensely with them that you can't find your way back. Without a healthy self-love you may never experience the passion needed to fulfill on your dreams. Self-love can be a powerful, life-giving force. I am not talking about the shallow, self-centered love of Narcissus, but the kind of love that nurtures everything and everyone around it. A love that is reciprocal, radiant, radical. A woman who loves herself sends ripples of love out into the world. This is the gift of Ocean and River Woman.

Love, like water, needs boundaries. With boundaries, you possess a healthy self-regard. Consider how a river moves with a kind of reciprocity. It carves the banks, and the banks cradle the river. Sometimes the river breaches its own boundaries. At times, you will test and overspill your own.

This entire process is a delicious dialogue. In the act of lovemaking, you mingle your salty oceans with your beloved, then return to yourself, the way that the ocean falls back with the ebbing tide. You merge, and then flow back into your own being.

To merge with the other in an act of love is a worthy quest for wholeness, but you also need to know yourself as whole. During passionate lovemaking you create an ecotone (a word that describes the blending of two bioregions). Two bodies and souls converge and out of that something miraculous and fresh arises. It is a moment of rich and fertile communion. But this depth of connection is only possible if you love yourself. Otherwise, you cling.

And water doesn't cling. It moves. It flows. It returns to itself.

Love, in full flow, is the most powerful force in the world. It demands our respect. It also demands our courage, from the old French, *coeur*, for heart. For the path of love sometimes runs through a tsunami of pain and hurt. Ocean and River Woman does not demean love by sentimentalizing it or implying it is easy. She challenges you to your very depths.

Ocean and River Woman is also the gentlest of mothers. Water was your first home. You were rocked and cradled first in the womb. And once you embrace your Ocean and River nature, you will feel truly supported. Like a little girl learning to swim, you realize that once you stop struggling, you begin to float. Even if the seas are rough and your feelings in turmoil, as an Ocean and River Woman you are carried on a current of love.

Integration

Ritual: Being Cradled by the Waters of Mother Earth

Take yourself off to a body of water and immerse yourself in it. Or simply sit in a warm bath. The important thing here is to allow the water to hold you. Cradle you. Rock you.

As you feel the water gently holding you up, imagine yourself being held in the womb of Mother Earth, your first home. Feel yourself floating in an ancient sea, the home of all life on this planet. Allow yourself to feel the love that is yours by birthright. Give yourself to that love. Allow it to seep into every pore and cell of your being.

Then ask yourself: If you could swim in love each day, what would be different?

Learning We Are Love

To enter stone, be water.

—Linda Hogan

Love, like water, spills into every gully and cavern, every channel and hollow. It therefore follows that in the places you feel most wounded or worthless, love wants to pour in. Yet, somehow, in some way, at some time, you may have closed down and shut out love. You may have learned only to think of loving others but never of loving yourself. For many women the notion of self-love is hard to grasp. It seems an indulgence. Yet all human beings have inherent worth. Why do we doubt ours?

Violence, anger, or abuse, whether it occurs in childhood or adulthood, can erode the boundaries that hold you safe. Like a river with crumbling banks, you may become vulnerable to others' toxic beliefs about who you need to be and what you need to do in order to be loved. In time, this may lead to an inability to distinguish between what you want and what someone wants from you.

Mixed messages, especially around your sexuality, can cause love and desire to become clouded with confusion. Dress more attractively, but not to elicit unwanted attention. Care for your body, but don't preen. Be pleasing, but don't give anyone the wrong idea. Conform to heterosexual "norms," otherwise it's your fault if you get hurt.

This is how your sense of self-worth is eroded. Then every time you set a boundary—*this is what I need; don't touch me that way; you cannot say that to me*—you may doubt yourself. *Did that really happen? Am I overreacting? Is it my fault?*

A couple of years into sobriety I began to sponsor other women in AA, guiding them through the 12-step program. I soon realized that one of the biggest challenges to getting and staying sober was learning to love ourselves again. Many of the women I sponsored felt something I recognized from my own experience: a sense of being unworthy of love, not only because of things we'd done while drunk, but also, sadly, because of things that had been done to us. Breaking free of an addiction is the ultimate act of self-care. But how do you commit to recovery if you don't think you are worthy of love?

I would hear my sponsees' 5th Step outdoors. A 5th Step is when a woman shares her "personal moral inventory" with her sponsor—an accounting of the patterns of behaviors that have led to this point. I liked to meet with each woman in a garden, or a meadow, or by a creek. I would sit beside her feeling the support of nature and listening with my heart. And soon her words would come, first as a trickle, then tumbling out, all the hurt, shame, and guilt, the self-hate, and the pain.

As a woman in the depth of her vulnerability honored me with her truth, I felt such love for her. I was moved beyond words by this incredibly brave, beautiful soul. Nothing she had done—nothing she told me—could take away from her essential purity. She may have behaved selfishly or recklessly, or even committed serious crimes in the past, but that didn't mean she wasn't loveable. This is how compassion rose in me, not just for all the women I sponsored, but for myself.

Under patriarchy, women are viewed as seducers—sirens who dash men's bodies against the rocks. We are not only guilty of our own sins, therefore, but responsible for men's as well. And more so when we are "cursed" with our bleeding times and our bodies become lush and fertile and arousing. It is this myth of our sinfulness, particularly the sinfulness of our bodies, that we must cleanse ourselves of. Ocean and River Woman washes our "sins" away. You receive her baptism when you know you are made of love.

When you come to absorb this central message, you realize that your job isn't to spend your life overcoming your authentic nature but to align with it. This is a profound shift in direction: You begin to trust your inner flow and ability to live from the truth of who you are. Imagine if we all loved ourselves and carried our creativity, our sexuality, our longings, and desires confidently into the world, unpolluted by misogynistic messages and untainted by self-hate? But first, we need to design a culture that encourages us to become strong and confident women. And for that, we need rites of passage that honor the ripening of our bodies and souls.

For women, after all, rites of passage are inherent in our biology. Our menarche, our first bleed, is one of the most significant, marking the transition from girlhood to womanhood. For each of us, the story of our menarche will differ. Yet given the disregard with which our culture holds this threshold experience, it is important to acknowledge how painful—and even shaming—these stories may be. And how frequently they are at odds with loving ourselves. This was certainly true of my experience.

I was among the first in my class at boarding school to begin menstruating. It was nighttime when I discovered I was bleeding, and we were gathered in the long dormitory preparing for bed. Torn between wanting everyone to know and no one to know, I ambled over to the nun in charge and asked for sanitary napkins, in a loud voice, making sure my friends overheard. The nun told me to stop making such a fuss and called me a "foolish girl." I slunk off to the bathroom, not quite sure what to do with the wad of sanitary napkins she had removed from a drawer and grudgingly shoved at me. Suddenly I was aware of a queasy cramping in my belly. As tears rolled down my face, I felt hot with shame and embarrassment. I was an eleven-year-old girl longing for my mother and home.

Many years later, I attended the menarche ceremony for a friend's daughter, held on a beach, with the wind and waves. Mother and daughter tied one leg loosely to the other's with a red thread. They ran along the beach together until the thread fell away. Then the daughter ran on alone, her mother cheering her on. When the daughter returned, we welcomed her into the circle of adults, each of us offering a wisdom, prayer, or poem to support her growth into full womanhood. She was radiant, flushed with sea air and loving attention. This, I thought, was how it should be. Welcoming a young girl into the community, helping her to embrace this new stage of life.

Some days later, I went back to that same beach and sat for a while, remembering the little girl I had been, and how different and painful her experience was. This time, I imagined taking my younger Self by the hand, tying our legs together and running along the beach. I saw my younger Self, still carrying a little baby fat, but shooting up fast, too. Her hair shone in the light and her legs flew as she broke away from me. And when she returned, red-cheeked and full of life, I welcomed her into my arms. I told her that she was precious, and that no one had the right to do or say anything to or about her body without her permission. I added that she didn't need to change herself, or do something she wasn't comfortable with, to gain someone's love. I felt her slender arms tighten around me.

Loving our bodies is essential if we are to liberate our sexual energy and open to pleasure. How can we guide our lovers to touch us in a way that satisfies us, if we are steeped in shame about our looks? How can we orgasm, full-throated and passionate, if we don't celebrate our clitorises, the only organ in the human body designed solely for pleasure? Sex education teaches girls to say "no" to sex but not to say "yes" to their desires. The Zimbabwean-born scholar and motivational speaker, Tererai Trent, puts it this way: "A woman with awakened sexuality . . . has recovered what has been kept from her, the knowledge of her own corporeal self and its powerful potentials."[37]

Many forces work to keep women from loving and trusting our bodies. After all, the world doesn't constantly and loudly critique or legislate men's bodies in the way they do ours. Yet, it's important to recognize that your sacred longings are housed in your body. And the more you are filled with a deep love for your body, the more you will be liberated to flow in the direction that serves you.

Self-love is so important. Any time we get to help each other to a rich serving of it is powerful. I know, for example, that I couldn't have remained sober if I had to constantly fight my craving for alcohol. In time, the craving would have won out. Instead, by learning to love myself, beginning with small steps of showing up, caring for others, listening to the stories of other women, and finding myself in the same pools of feeling, sometimes laughing aloud at our foibles and our failures—the desire to drink was lifted from me.

This is how it works. Not by enforcing control to refashion yourself as worthy of love—but aligning with the deep source of love that is your birthright. Loving yourself isn't narcissistic. Narcissists behave as they do precisely because they have no real sense of self-worth and so need to inflate their egos. No, this is simply saying that at heart, you are love and you are worthy of love. This is your natural state.

This doesn't mean you live without self-direction. Water needs a container. A river needs a riverbank. But boundaries for Ocean and River Woman aren't the walls you've been taught to build. Self-discipline doesn't mean relentless self-policing or self-criticism. These boundaries are flexible and fluid. They move according to your own evolving inclinations. And the more you are filled with a deep love for your body and being, the more your boundaries can shift and meander in the direction that serves your soul.

Even in that great headlong fall into romantic love, as Ocean and River Woman you know yourself well enough, love yourself deeply enough, to return to yourself, before you move out again, always in relationship, never cut off, always at choice, and eternally connected to the greater body of life.

Eve Ensler: Learning to Love Our Bodies and the Body of the World

V, formerly known as Eve Ensler, wrote the "Vagina Monologues" in a desire to have women talk about a part of their bodies that is rarely discussed and little understood. V tells us that patriarchy and capitalism take women out of their bodies. She adds that when women get back into their bodies, something big is going to happen. We'll see a great change in our society, as well as in our souls, she says.

For V, full acceptance of her body was hard-earned. Raped by her father at an early age, she struggled with addiction. Hating the way her body looked, she battled it, striving, like so many other women, for a slimmer, shapelier, different self.

When, in her fifties, she went to the Congo, V heard the brutal stories of the systemic and weaponized rape and violation of women and girls. She began to connect the war over the Earth's resources to violence toward women.

When advanced-stage uterine cancer struck V, any last wall of resistance dissolved. Her body, she realized, wasn't divided from the world. Her tumor was comprised of the grief and pain from the rape she had endured and the agonizing stories of the women and girls of the Congo that she had taken into her own body. Months of painful treatments, chemo, and infections ensued. And yet, paradoxically, the depth of her pain and hurt finally allowed her to affirm the miracle of her own body—to feel its beauty and its strength.

As she was healing from cancer, V helped found The City of Joy, a transformational community for women, in the Congo. Here, in a region often referred to as "The worst place in the world to be a woman" she raised a safe harbor for women to dance, sing, share their stories, and learn to love their bodies and themselves again.[38]

Integration

Journal Reflection: Setting Boundaries

A healthy self-regard requires that we know how to set boundaries, say no, and refuse to have our feelings or concerns be overridden by others. Your boundaries aren't set or rigid; they will flex and re-form as you move toward greater understanding. But they are an essential Ocean and River Woman skill. To explore further, ask yourself these questions, and note your response in your journal:

> *When did you set a boundary? What happened?*
>
> *When did you neglect to set a boundary? What happened?*

After you have answered both questions, reflect on what you have discovered about yourself and boundaries.

Journal Reflection: Write the Story of Your First Menstrual Flow

This exploration of your first menses may take some time to complete. But please note, you don't have to tackle all the parts at the same time. In fact, spacing them out can help you to reflect on your story more deeply. If possible, take this exercise outdoors and sit near a flowing body of water. "Flow" is a key element in how nature works. This is also a powerful exercise to do in a circle of sisters where you can share your experiences with each other.

Begin by using this writing prompt: *My first menstrual flow arrived . . .*

Next, after writing your story, read it out loud to yourself, noting how you feel.

When you are ready, rewrite your story as it might have been—if this had been a most wonderful initiation. Describe this moment. Then rewrite it, making it more wonderful still.

Who is present? Who is standing there affirming you, loving you, encouraging you as you make this transition into womanhood?

Reflection: Read your new story out loud. What stands out for you? What have you learned about yourself? If you were to honor the magic of menstruation, its beauty and power, what would have been and would be different for you?

There's a saying that goes, "It's never too late to have a good childhood." Maybe, just maybe, it is never too late to have a good transition into womanhood, too.

I feel an overwhelming longing for my being, my inner feminine softness and ability to flow with mother life. A softness that is relentlessly strong and stable.

—Sonya

The gentle waves of the ocean and I are singing songs together. I lay myself in the warmth of her Ocean and River Woman's arms and I am buoyed.

—Sharon

The Shift: Dam/ned to Flow

Be wild; that is how to clear the river.

—Clarissa Pinkola Estés

Patriarchy views a girl's budding sexuality as a wild river—one that must be dam/ned and never allowed to run free. Later, our wombs become public space to be legislated and controlled. Women have always fought for autonomy over our own bodies. But this too: We have sometimes been complicit in dam/ning our own natural flow.

Whenever our natural urges meet a wall of resistance that aims to keep us in our place, what do we often do? We pour more concrete. We harden ourselves and lose touch with our inner nature. Yet the truth is we never stop desiring; we just mount barriers against it. The developing world has built so many dams that they have literally thrown the Earth off her axis. When we build dams within ourselves, don't we also throw our own lives out of orbit?

To let your real feelings come through, you must dismantle the dam. It will likely give way on its own eventually, because holding back is just too hard. But it is better to be proactive and seek out those denied emotions so that they don't reappear with greater force and urgency. Repress them too long and your pain will become too great, your rage all consuming, your grief unstoppable. And when that dam breaks, woe to those who live downstream, for they will feel the full force of your feelings.

What will it take to dismantle your dam? The tyranny of the ego—the need to be a certain way, to hold yourself back in order to appear acceptable or remain safe—must first be washed away. Then you can find what you really want, beneath all the shoulds and shames.

Ocean and River Woman can help you with this dismantling, one obstacle at a time. She will comfort you as you return to the place in your body that is closed tight with trauma and gently let the tears flow, moving water back into the stream. There may be many places where you are pent up or squeezed tight that need to be released. This process may take months or a lifetime. And yet you will discover it is a kinder, softer way to be, once you embrace a life of feeling.

Release, however, is not always a conscious choice. A life event suddenly overrides all your defenses and controls. The loss of a lover is heartbreaking, the fury at the destruction of a beloved place in nature overwhelming, your fear for your children great. All that withheld rage and passion come hurtling out. But don't despair. Flooding isn't always destructive. If your emotions run clear and true, it turns these raw emotions into rich deposits that provide fresh ground to build upon. A flood is a way of fertilizing the land.

As Ocean and River Woman, you have faith that you will find your way. In surrendering, great reservoirs of vitality are unleashed. You generate, create, and move according to your own rhythms. All you have to do, my sister, is open the floodgate of your own wild heart.

Integration

Ritual: Stream of Consciousness

If possible, head to a body of water in nature close by to you. If that's not possible, simply settle into sacred space and use your imagination or a photo to access such a place.

Approach the water as you would an ancestor who loves you unconditionally and to whom you can open your heart completely.

Before you settle down, find a twig, leaf, or stone to hold in your hand during the ceremony as a reminder of how this water is the same water that has been circulating through the bodies of ancient lands, since the beginning. Stay aware of the object in your hand, as if you are pressing all of your feelings into it and through it.

In whatever way feels authentic to you, greet this water ancestor, and acknowledge that you have come for support and guidance.

Next, simply sit and sense what your heart most longs for. Let your feelings pour forth uncensored. Speak your stream of consciousness. Draw on the strength of Ocean and River Woman. Ask her to help you release the words that need to be spoken.

Allow your desires, your emotions, to run wild and free. Let your longings surprise you, inform you, undo you. Let the words and intensity of feeling rise and fall like waves on the ocean. If you feel yourself getting dammed, or stuck, simply repeat these words: *This is what I long for . . .*

When you are finished, write about what has become clear for you in the process. When your deepest longing is distilled, hold the object you selected in both hands and simply state what your primary longing is: *This is what I desire . . .*

When you are ready, give it to the water and let it go.

Dismantling the Dam

Flowing is the rhythm of the earth.

—Gabrielle Roth

The Iijoki (its name means "night" in ancient Sami) is the second longest river in Finland, stretching 230 miles to the Gulf of Bothnia. Serial damming of the river in the 1960s resulted in the biggest ecological catastrophe in the area. The surrounding forests and marshlands suffered, birds and small mammals disappeared, and the salmon could no longer return home to spawn.

This river story is told around the world in a thousand different ways and voices. But in a *Washington Post* article, the Finnish photographer Janne Korkko, describes life along the Iijoki this way:

"Night river is full of songs of memories, and its riverbanks are full of people with these memories. Some of them are sacred, silenced or even untold . . . . But some of the songs are still alive or they are waking up through the people, who are starting to remember the song of the wild, free-flowing river."[39]

In you, too, there is a wild, free-flowing river. No matter how many dams you have built, however much concrete you have poured, or how many high walls you have built to protect yourself, the song of your own wild energy still sings deep inside you. And if you become quiet and listen, you know its clear, natural current as the pure essence of who you are.

It is vital you remember this, not just for your sake, but because the world needs your gifts and blessings just as it needs a river's vitalizing waters.

And so, you arrive at another threshold where you are challenged to free yourself from whatever holds you back from living fully and authentically. The question Ocean and River Woman poses now is this: *Are you ready to dismantle the dams?* No matter the hurt or shame that caused you to erect them, you can bring them down.

Flow is the essence of feminine energy. It is the animating principle of the soul. We are made, as the dancer Gabrielle Roth tells us, to be buoyed up by our "awesome beauty." Yet many of us carry an inner critic who shuts that flow down.

The voice of the critic isn't evil. It had your best interests at heart as it tried to keep you safe in childhood. But one day it became the oppressor, holding you back from a genuine, creative, passionate life. It is important to understand that the inner critic isn't you. It is simply the voice of society, family, and all those that would rather see you live a small, safe life.

How many projects, relationships, passions, and dreams have you abandoned because you listened to the critic? What has that cost you? What grace and creativity did your community miss out on because you held back? There is no blame. Whatever you discover, self-forgiveness is key to allowing your waters to flow again. I have learned through my own journey with alcoholism "not to regret the past nor wish to shut the door on it," as the *Big Book of Alcoholics Anonymous* advises.

I am reminded of a poem "I Give You Back." Here the Native American writer Joy Harjo writes of giving up her fear because it is "not my blood anymore."[40]

Harjo was born to a Creek Father and French-Cherokee mother, and she often speaks of being guided by the voice of an Old Creek Indian within her. In this poem, she releases her inherited trauma, refuses it, gives it back to the perpetrators. She repeats the line *I release you* over and over. And in doing so, she becomes unafraid to be angry or to rejoice or to be hated or to be loved. Hers is the most incredible expression of freeing ourselves from past trauma in order to embrace being fully alive.

Once we are free from fear and self-blame, something amazing happens. It becomes easier to be curious about what it is we love. What brings us joy? What energizes us? Where does our attention naturally flow? When are we most ourselves? No dam can withstand the pulse of a river forever. As you begin to feed your own river of longing, the dam is less able to hold you back. Your energy is a force of nature. It is more powerful than any blockages that stand in its way.

But what if the thing we are most afraid of—one of the reasons we dam ourselves in the first place—is that we fear experiencing ourselves in all our original, astonishing spontaneity? After all, who are you when you are unleashed? If you look at a waterfall liberated from winter's ice or the great surge of a wild wave across the shore, you can sense the power that is yours to release into the world. The crazy thing about it, the thing that is often so hard to understand, is that *it doesn't require that we do more or be more*, it simply asks that you let go and let flow.

That doesn't mean surrender is easy. Particularly for women, the idea of surrender can carry a negative charge; it may seem we have always yielded to others' demands. Ocean and River Woman doesn't ask that you to surrender to a person, place, or thing—but to your essential self, the dream of your soul. And this takes great strength.

Activist Sobonfu Somé of the Dagara Tribe of Burkino Faso describes this kind of surrender when she speaks of her rigorous training with the elders. "I tell people you have to break down at all levels," she says. "What you are most afraid of, the elders will make you go through it. What you resist most, they will make you do. You have to have a willingness to be dismantled again and again. So that you always go beyond who you think you are."[41]

Dams are not eternal. All over the world, they are coming down. All over the world, rivers are being set free. All over the world, women's internal dams are being dismantled at accelerating rates, releasing our energies to move again so that we may revitalize every aspect of our communities.

To flow free is a risky business. Who knows where it will lead? But in your heart, you already hear the song of your own river. And deep within, you know that if you are to live true to yourself, the dams must come down.

A Channel for Something Greater: Valerie Andrews' Story

If you have a creative practice, you will have experienced moments of flow. Often these periods follow hours of hard discipline and work. But then something magical occurs: You forget yourself and become a channel for something greater that is both *of* you and *not* of you. You might say that you "feel the spirit moving." You might call it a "mystical oneness," or you might simply feel that time has been suspended. The writer Valerie Andrews tells me about her own process of flow as she relearns to play the piano from a place of ease.

"Some days, I think, *I will never be able to get control of this piece.* Yet the very word *control* is indicative that I'm stuck in the ego. It is more about what you don't do at the keyboard than all the trills and flourishes you create. With proper instruction, you strip down and go back to the basics. You learn how to sit upright, relax the arms, and let gravity do the work. Then you do your best to get out of the way and let the composer speak."

Valerie's words make me wonder if we are not all learning to get out of our own way. Our inner music, like a river, wants to flow easily, pulled by what we genuinely gravitate toward. When we become stressed, when we overly exert our effort, we shut down the channel. To open to our own internal flow we must relax, feel our way through, and give ourselves over to what is working. In this way, we allow what is within us to come through.

Integration

Ritual: I Release You

In the spirit of Joy Harjo's poem, "I Give You Back," spend some time reflecting on the things that you want to release. Consider the bricks in the dam of your being, the things that keep you stuck. They may be comprised of traumatic memories, punishing self-talk, relentless anger, unhealthy relationships, or a feeling of being deeply unlovable. Make a list of things you want to release.

Then go to a body of water (or a bathtub or basin). Name what you are releasing out loud to the water.

I release you (name it)

I release you (name it)

Keep going until you have released everything on your list.

I am a powerful, huge waterfall, rushing, roaring, tumbling. I am unstoppable. I must be free, unbounded.

—Maura

In the waters of my soul, I sparkle, tumble, flow, spread open. I bring life and am full of life.

—Michelle

The Way: Shapeshifting

Everything says no to me
Everything tells me not.
Only I say yes.

—Marge Piercy

Like many women, you may have been squeezed into a very narrow way of feeling and being in the world, relegated to a slender creek when wide rivers and roaring cataracts might suit you better. You may have been encouraged—even trained—to stay away from these stronger feelings and remain safely in the shallows. Until now, that is.

Ocean and River Woman is the bringer of strong currents that will tug at you until you lose your footing. Her tidal pull can come in the form of a great love, or a sudden grief, or a profound yearning. Once she has your attention, she will insist that you explore the full gamut of your feelings. *Flow with me*, she says, *into your depths, and know that, like the tide, your feelings will carry you.*

As she pries you off the shoals where you are emotionally stuck, Ocean and River Woman cautions that standing water eventually becomes toxic. If your feelings do not flow, they will make you sick. And while you may be aware of the need to release anger or resentment, striving to be eternally calm can prove equally soul-destroying. In attempting to be a sea of tranquility at the center of every storm, you can become unnaturally placid. Even a sheltered pond will find the wind rippling its surface.

Feelings and water are meant to circulate and churn. You must become the storm itself.

Ocean and River Woman is a shapeshifter, taking many forms from fresh pools to roiling oceans, to glacial lakes and steaming geysers. The notion that one emotional state should prevail is a relic of patriarchy and its efforts to control. How would we create, fall in love, move mountains, without the freedom to feel deeply and wildly?

And yet, as women, we have a long list of feelings we aren't supposed to express. Encouraged to be still pools that reflect the needs and wishes of everybody around us, it is as if we are too shallow to contain our own chasmic yearnings. And all too often we find our power seeping away. The word *influence* comes from the Latin "to flow into." In repressing the flow of our emotions, we experience a form of isolation that leads to unimaginable despair. Our feelings may even erode to the point we are no longer in touch with why we want to live.

With the help of Ocean and River Woman, you can learn to navigate the wild and choppy waters of your emotional life. When does it serve to ride the waves of laughter and lightness or to let yourself drown in grief? When do you need to move languidly like a warm current? When do you need to freeze and become as impenetrable as ice in order to protect yourself?

As Ocean and River Woman, you possess the shapeshifting ability to break from a rigid way of being in the world and burst open to a multifaceted state of being, one in which you are both fluid and authentic. Once you experience the many aspects of your inner waters, you will be able to flow outward into the world and change the terrain according to your own desires.

Reclaiming Your Sacred Emotions

You don't tell the Atlantic Ocean to behave.

—Eve Ensler

The Arabic word *isharat* refers to the ability to read the physical signs of water. How deep? How strong is the current? As an Ocean and River Woman, you, too, understand water's many forms. You are a freshwater stream, a tumbling waterfall, a giant wave—shapeshifting, moving, flowing effortlessly between different ways of being.

Even so, at times when certain feelings overwhelm you, when you feel crazy with grief or anger, you may express in a way that erodes and dissolves the relationships you hold dear. Or perhaps your emotions drift faint as mist, mostly unobserved. Perhaps you are prone to floods of passion. Or you tend to submerge your emotions, earning a reputation for being distant and cold. Whatever your habitual pattern, in you is a vibrant emotional range of which you, like most of us, are likely unaware.

When I quit drinking in my mid-twenties, long suppressed emotions flooded my nervous system. It was if an undersea vent, blocked by years of numbing myself with alcohol, had exploded inside of me. I was overwhelmed by a turmoil of feelings and impulses. And yet, I could feel life flowing through me again, washing away years of disconnection and despair.

There's a wonderful poem by Kaylan Haught, "God Says Yes to Me," where she asks God—who is a woman—if it is okay to be melodramatic. God says *yes*. And then she asks all kinds of other questions, some delightfully whimsical like whether she can decide to wear nail polish. And God, who calls her "Sweetcakes," always responds with *yes*. I think of Ocean and River Woman as this kind of accepting presence, inviting us to say *yes* to every drop of our emotion.

To an Ocean and River Woman, all emotions, like the wild forms of water, are a natural part of our own personal watershed. The only question is how to express them in healthy ways. How do we both honor our feelings and take responsibility for them, neither bottling them up nor releasing them in torrents of recrimination or rage?

It is possible to emote excessively and still be completely disconnected from your authentic emotions. And of course, there are times when your emotions will lead you astray. Sometimes you can get lost in them or misread them. How can you distinguish between lust and love? And isn't it true that envy and judgement, while often carrying a similar energy, are essentially different? Learning to trust yourself with your feelings takes time, patience, and many bellyflops. Yet when you are clear about how you feel, you have immense influence. There is something irresistible about a woman whose feelings are aligned with her heart and her values. She is on her way to becoming unstoppable.

In the main, we women have learned to respond to men's feelings. We are experts at placating their anger, their disappointments, their frustrations. We have even, on occasion, confused cruelty for love. Focused not on our feelings, but on managing those of others, we can inadvertently become part of a cycle of abuse that conspires to quash and control our own emotions.

That's changing. Woman are realizing that we have reasons to be angry. That does not mean we are angry women. It does not mean that we are cruel or out of control. It means that anger, like a pure stream, is flowing through us at the injustices and corruption that permeate our world. We want to be happy and peaceful, but often the map to real joy and love includes crossing a river of pain. If we submerge our fury, do we really think that we will be able to feel tenderness? It doesn't work that way. We either own our feelings or we don't.

When my mother was in a care home with dementia, I never knew what—or even who—I would find. Some days she greeted me with a smile so loving, it broke my heart. Others, she was so caught up in her own misery and frustration she would try to hit or bite me. On her worst days, she did not recognize me. Her mind, untethered, moved into strange channels and swirling eddies of memory. I learned to be in the moment, to catch the wave of a story and run with it, even if it made no sense.

If I saw amusement in her eyes, I would try to share the joke. We did mirror dances. She'd raise an arm; I would raise mine. She'd smile; I'd grin right back. She'd give me a side look, head cocked like a curious robin, and I'd do the same. We had never been very tactile with each other. But now, I'd stroke her skin, her hair, her cheeks, her back. I'd sing for her—though I can't hold a note—and she'd raise her two forefingers as if conducting me. She'd ask when my brother was going to visit, though he was six years dead. I'd go with the flow and tell her, "Mum, he's busy with work, but he'll be here soon."

This was a world constructed in nanoseconds. The rules changed; boundaries blurred. I had to let go of every preconceived notion of who my mother was and what our relationship was about. I learned instead how to be with a woman who was falling deeper into Alzheimer's. My mother was like a river that was always changing directions. I moved to meet her.

Visiting my mother daily for months on end, I learned to stay in the spontaneous and open moment. It was painful but also strangely liberating. I no longer expected anything of her or myself. Some days we sang Christmas carols or chair-danced. Some days my mother paced the corridors obsessively, lean and mean as a hungry lion. More than once, I found her black and blue from the previous night's fall yet coming toward me on her walker. I wanted to keep her safe, but I couldn't. I couldn't tame her or cage her. We were entering the wild river of death, and it came tumbling toward us, sweeping us up and carrying us away.

And yet, as exhausting and even frightening as it was to be so out of control, I never loved my mother more. There was always the essence of who she was beneath the madness, the fog of loss and confusion. Strangely, when she was no longer in charge of what she did or said, she was most herself. Her emotions were set free to express the full range of everything her body and mind experienced.

She died at 2:00 am on Christmas morning. I sat alone with her body for hours before the morticians came to take her away. I felt her join the stream of ancestors—her beloved mother and father, Helen and Arthur; her beloved brother and son, both Davids; my father, Tom. As the quiet settled around me, a quickening stirred deep inside, a reminder that I will always carry this woman in the wild current of my heart.

Your emotions are the sacred waters of your being, connecting you to the magical, mystical, moon-splashed world and to your own mysterious tides. As an Ocean and River Woman, you trust your heart, knowing your capacity for feeling is your most powerful and sacred gift.

Integration

Journal Reflection:
Exploring Your Shapeshifting Emotions

Which emotions do you fall into and have a hard time getting out of? Which do you tend to repress or submerge? This exploration will help you see the many forms your own emotions take. This work goes deep, so hold yourself gently throughout this exercise.

Start with a list of the forms that water takes, from snowflakes to ocean waves. Get as many as you can on your list, including variations: warm spring showers, torrential thunderstorms, and everything in between.

Then ask: Which ones most resemble your emotional landscape? Do you tend to freeze or flood? Are you turbulent, calm, deep? As you contemplate the different permutations of water, consider which one best reflects your present emotional state, for example:

* A still lake
* An ocean wave crashing against rocks
* A frozen pond
* Spring melt

When you have your descriptor, write about what it is like to live with this particular emotion.

How does it hamper you? What special insight does it offer?

Review your writing, and ask: How often do you feel this way? What surprises you the most? Then record your answers.

Make this a regular process, and you will learn a great deal about your emotional landscape. As you do, you might find yourself curious about certain emotions that you aren't as familiar with and might be curious to explore further. For example, if your feelings are frequently turbulent, ask yourself, *what would it be like to be a still pond?* Again, don't judge, simply explore.

Practice: Move Your Energy

Dancing in the privacy of your living room can help you to identify and shift stuck energy, uplift your spirits, and help you to explore your emotional range.

Letting your body move naturally to music is a perfect way to feel into your own flow. How do you like to move? Smoothly, staccato-style, sensuously? What music most expresses what you feel and releases you to move? Try different tempos. If you like to rock out, try moving at a slower, smoother pace, and vice versa. Simply experiment.

After you rock out, how do you feel?
After you move sensuously and intentionally, how do you feel?
What beat gets your dancing mojo moving?
What moods are evoked by moving in certain ways to certain music?

After dancing, journal your responses as you discover the many forms and shapes of your natural feelings.

In the oceans and rivers of my soul, I come fully alive with all my waves and rivulets of crazed foam, with all my waves and tempestuous moods. I am a storm, raging. I am cascading across time, destroying the dams, clearing the old logs and trunks, giving me stagnation. And finally carrying myself beyond the imposed horizons

—Ginny

Ocean and River Woman, how do you express in me now?

—Michelle

Emerging as Ocean and River Woman

A Fully Embodied Ocean and River Woman

You are a revitalizing and reanimating force. Your natural ability to live from the depths of your heart brings more aliveness into the world. Defying a culture that would have you submerge your feelings in favor of being pleasant and submissive, you are a natural disrupter. Your passion is destined to make waves.

Energetic and ardent, you make connections that run deep and true. You have little interest in the superficial or the routine. You are a passionate artist and lover, a deeply interested friend, a loyal ally. Sensuous and sensual, your ease with your body and sexuality can intimidate some. You also inspire others be free of shame and self-consciousness.

You have the capacity to lose yourself in your pursuits, to become a channel for something greater. Open to inspiration, ready to release your ego and get out of your own way, you create from a place of pure magic and surrender. This is your genius.

And when you run dry, as you will at times, you know that the tide will return, and you will soon be filled with yearning and energy again.

Those who meet you in the depths find you to be a ready source of inspiration. Others are drawn to you, the way we all are drawn to water. You are unafraid to open your heart and let others in, and you know how to bring out their hidden treasures. You offer friendship with no judgment from the heart.

An Ocean and River Woman Caught in the Shadow

At times, you may overwhelm others with your emotions. When someone doesn't match your level of intensity, you may keep ratcheting up the emotional pressure in order to get a response. You might act out, overdramatize, and use your emotional dexterity to manipulate others through guilt, rage, or victimhood.

In your quest for stimulation, you can be prone to addiction, reaching for things outside of yourself to give you an experience of aliveness and intensity. You may also go through multiple lovers, friendships, projects, seeking to recapture that initial high.

To embody the healthy aspects of Ocean and River Woman, therefore, it is vital that you accept life's slow, meandering moments, its natural ebb and flow. When you do this, you will be able to navigate your feelings in a truly empowered and life-giving way.

Ocean and River Woman and the Planet

Your emotions have carried you to your life purpose, and your passion gives you the energy to make a change. Water is sacred to you, so your activism or advocacy may be focused on protecting it. You may be especially troubled by factories and farms that pour their toxins into the land and pollute your local water supply.

You know that only moving water is life-giving. Thus, you have a clear sense for stagnant ideas, policies, practices. You know that love is more powerful than hate and that to advocate *for* something is more powerful than to fight against it. This is not a romantic notion, but an understanding that hate burns people out, while love is an endless resource.

You lead through the power of attraction. Your passion draws people to the causes that you care about. They join to be part of a community that values emotion and encourages each to hold one another up. Women who identify with Ocean and River Woman create movements where members can laugh and cry together and where feelings are valued and freely shared.

There are currents in the human soul that need to be brought to life. Knowing this, you help create a more caring world.

Some Final Reflections on Ocean and River Woman

What is Ocean and River Woman's greatest gift to you?

What aspects of Ocean and River Woman challenge you the most?

How do you see yourself embodying Ocean and River Woman's wisdom in the future?

Which areas of your life could most benefit from Ocean and River Woman's presence?

If you were to fully embrace your Ocean and River Woman self, what would change?

How will you express thanks to Ocean and River Woman?

Opening to Mountain Woman

As the waters of Ocean and River Woman recede, Mountain Woman, with her towering peaks and long shadows, rises up before you. You are aware of your depths, and now you are being called to make your vision real. As Mountain Woman, you will give birth to your greater self, emerging into the world as an authentic, unstoppable force. You will need muscle, determination, and dedication for the next stage of the journey. You are transitioning from introspection to soul-guided action. Mountain Woman is calling you to reclaim your power as creatrix—a woman ready to remake the map of the world. Feel into your spine and sinew. It is time to make the ascent.

4

Mountain Woman

Soul of a Mountain Woman

In the time of the great silence, before the ruffle of leaves or the pad of paws,
Mountain Woman helped bring the world into being.
Her towering presence rests on bedrock.
Her prayers rise to pleasure the goddesses. She is their equal:
Creator, Earth shaker, woman of friction, broad-backed, and warrior-strong.
Forged from fire and ice, in her anger, she erupts.
From her resistance, new landscapes form.
With clouds for hair, thunderbolts for her crown, she makes her own weather.
When we rise to her challenge,
we reach new heights within ourselves.

Stage of Initiation: Giving Birth

The Challenge: Embracing Friction

The Shift: Broken to Re-Born

The Way: Transformative Power

Embodied Dimensions: Commitment, vision, manifestation, leadership, clarity, inner power, soul-driven action

Guiding Question: What am I willing to risk—and do —in order to give birth to my wholeness?

Giving Birth:
The Fourth Initiation

i am the throat
of the sandia mountains
a night wind woman
who burns
with every breath
she takes

—Joy Harjo

Mountain Woman is your soaring, granite magnificence. She dares you to play in the realms of the gods and goddesses, on the highest levels. She urges you to emerge from your cave of containment into wide open spaces, to own your influence, and to take your place in the world.

Many of us resist our inner Mountain Woman. We are taught in numerous subtle and not-so-subtle ways to hide our magnificence and not to rise. Women are permitted to be softly rounded foothills, but never to become a soaring Everest, as men are encouraged to do. To take up that kind of space, to impress upon the terrain in such a fashion, is to get above ourselves. It is to overreach. It is to be too damned much.

But Mountain Woman will not be silenced. She spurs you to wholeness, ushering in a period that is creatively risky and often rife with friction. To emerge from the confines of domestication and claim your full, multidimensional nature, you will have to move through many challenges. Birthing, after all, is both a powerful and painful act, as much about contraction as it about expansion. As the actress Bette Davis so famously pronounced, "Fasten your seat belts; it's going to be a bumpy ride."

The first 700 million years of geological history was a cool, quiet period. There were no mountains and no continental collisions.[42] It took Earth's tectonic plates crashing into each other, pushing the land upwards, to give rise to mountains. Just as the Earth roiled, so embodying Mountain Woman will thrust you into the hurts and oppositions of your life. Until you are challenged to take a stand or reach for a vision, until you have experienced conflict and resistance, Mountain Woman will likely elude you.

Mountains are born from eruptions, friction, collisions. This is how Mountain Woman arises—out of magma and into motion. One day you will be able to stand in your truth even as the ground trembles and the winds howl about you. This is the strength of Mountain Woman: to rise tall under pressure. Her power, and yours, comes from within, and no one can take it from you.

As you embark upon your mountain path, you will be torn between the familiar and the unknown, the comfortable and the risky, the part of you that wants to remain hidden, and the part of you ready to erupt into the world. These tectonic plates will begin to rub against each other until your belly fills with fire and you arrive at the climax of your journey.

Mountain Woman asks: *Will you risk your safety and comfort in order to rise to your full potential? Will you find the courage to break free of what has kept you securely tethered and in your place? Will you awaken to your greatness and your goodness?*

Look around you: Whole beautiful mountain ranges of women are rising up—bold, boundaried, and fierce in their desire to protect our planet. Together, we will birth a new world.

Space for Bigger Dreams

That's what I want—to hear you erupting.
You young Mount St. Helenses
who don't know the power in you—I want to hear you.

—URSULA K. LE GUIN

How do we apprehend a mountain? It can feel so close you can almost touch it. Or it can be hidden in the clouds and seem out of reach. Similarly, your Mountain Woman Self may be dominant one day, then disappear beneath a veil of mist. But visible or invisible, near or far, you can sense her towering presence.

As you embark on the fourth stage of your journey, Mountain Woman asks you to carve out space, making room for bigger dreams and grander visions. She spurs you to embark on a great adventure, to move beyond your comfort zone. While much of your journey so far has been deeply introspective, now you are quested to bring forth that which is within you. Mountain Woman is all about manifestation. She urges you to seize the challenge, breathe into the moments of pain, and birth the new.

One of the most chilling aspects of patriarchy is how it attempts to rob women of creative agency. Attending an exhibit of the artist and feminist Judy Chicago, I was struck by her words, "When I scrutinized the art-historical record, I was shocked to discover that there were almost no images of birth in Western art, at least from a female point of view." We are portrayed in our nakedness, our voluptuousness, and our domesticity, yet rarely in the wild, keening, courageous act of giving birth. Our ability to generate life from our own bodies somehow isn't considered worthy of representation. Or is it simply too powerful for the patriarchy to acknowledge?

Mountain Woman helps us to reclaim our most fundamental power of creation. We take back our rock-solid belief in our ability to effect change. We are not afraid to oppose a calcified and lifeless system as we create a new and better one.

Mountain Woman insists you meet the world head on. She rouses you to action, calling you into service of what matters most to you. She reminds you that you are also a divine being with the capacity to look beyond the confines of your daily role and toward a long-range vision. Like a mountain, a woman reaches great heights by refusing to give up on her dreams and by relying on her bedrock values.

And it begins with taking that first step.

In the mid-1990s, I headed to the mountains to escape my own internal rockslide. I was more than ten years sober and separating from a relationship with a man I once heard described as "King Baby." For years, I had submitted to his churlish ways while ignoring my own needs for love and support. Now I was haunted by the fact that I continually attached myself to men who neither valued nor encouraged me.

Over the next few years, I became obsessed with climbing. I summited Mount Whitney at over 14,000 feet on a brilliant clear-sky day. I ascended the Himalayas to 16,000 in the wake of a blizzard, then Mount Shasta in a purple-cloud thunderstorm. My body became leaner, exposing sinew and spine. With each ascent, my courage grew. I was less willing to compromise, and more able to acknowledge my own hunger to act from a sense of sovereignty, rather than to appease some lofty male. Climbing, my vision of myself, and my place in the world expanded.

In those years, I thought about the strength of women. My Romany great-grandmother who traveled to a small town in Yorkshire and had twelve children, raising them with fierce love and scant resources. All my black-eyed Irish ancestors who risked their lives in childbirth and saw their families through years of want and famine. The mountains, enduring and timeless, connected me to this lineage of survivors and gave me courage.

Backpacking, sleeping beneath a river of stars, I came to know myself as part of a cosmic story stretching back 13.8 billion years. I was small, yes, but I also contained a vast inheritance of resilience, creativity, and imagination. I began to sense what I was here to do. The word *destiny* literally means "of the stars." Each star, a reminder that our greater self is always within us, ready to be called forth and take its place in the world. And so it was that on a high mountain slope I made a promise: Never again would I allow myself to stand in someone else's shadow. It was time to pursue my own dreams and visions.

You may be thinking, *But I don't have a vision! Or even a clear goal.* But consider how far you've come. You've unburdened yourself of beliefs and griefs too heavy to bear. You've incubated your dreams and set your own path. And most recently, with Ocean and River Woman, you've been swept up by the current of your passions. Now it is time to trust the truth of your own heart and act upon it.

You might begin by speaking your truth out loud in a challenging conversation or a long-avoided confrontation. These seemingly small acts are, in fact, monumental. They can precede great change. *What would happen if one woman told the truth about / her life?* asked the poet Muriel Rukeyser. *The world would split open.*[43]

As you follow the path of your heart up into the mountains, placing one foot in front of the other, you, too, will gain in strength and courage. There are no guarantees you will reach the summit. But in the attempt, you will learn to face your challenges, and you will grow. Writes warrior poet Audre Lorde, "When I dare to be powerful, to use all my strength in service of my vision, it becomes less and less important whether I am afraid."[44]

Creative projects rarely come to fruition overnight. Organizations take time to build, artistic visions to mature, movements to gain ground. Mountain Woman offers a geologic, deep-time perspective. You may not see the full results of your work in your lifetime. But in pursuing what you care about, you will develop the perseverance and faith necessary to keep moving in the right direction. Even if you never reach the mountaintop, you will create a path for others to follow. In that way you serve the collective good and your greater Self. Dreams, you recognize, are often achieved across generations and by individuals who may not even think of themselves as working together.

To develop long-range vision, you will need to walk carefully and mindfully. Climbing mountains is risky, and it is easy to fall from a great height. But as you ascend, you will see greater possibilities for your life. What is hidden at sea level becomes clear as you emerge above the tree line. From here on, the horizon expands, and it is easier to get the lay of the land—to see the whole valley beneath you.

You may encounter resistance at points along the way, and you may feel so weighed down with fear and apathy that you simply have to stop and rest. It is okay to pause and gather strength. But tarry too long, and you will lose momentum. The secret to endurance is embracing the magic and urgency of the moment.

Not every mountain is meant to be climbed. Mount Kailash in Tibet is considered so sacred that to set foot on her flanks is to defy the divine order and risk death. Not every project or dream is supposed to be realized. But when you find *your* mountain—the challenge you are meant to take on—you will know it. You will dream of it night and day. Even when it is veiled by your own fear or uncertainty, you will sense its presence.

And there will come a moment, when you know it is time to push, like a woman giving birth. You will feel the intensity of *now*. You will realize that if you delay too long and miss that power surge, all is lost. Mountain Woman urges you to erupt into action, to apply yourself over and over again until you feel that surge of completion. She insists: *This is your time to harness the energy and become the creator of your own life in service of the collective good.*

Signs that Mountain Woman Is Trying to Get Your Attention

Desire to Manifest—You feel a surge of energy to act in service of your dreams.

Birthing—You are experiencing a time of friction and collision, often at odds with others who want to keep you small and tame.

Sense of Destiny—In touch with the ground of your being, you feel destiny drawing you forth.

Rage—You are mad, hot-bellied, furious at the inequities and destruction you see in the world.

Big Vision—You are seeing your life, and how the world is structured, in new ways.

Refusal to Remain Silent—You are tired of swallowing your rage, your concerns, your own voice.

The Chipko Movement: Natural Mountain Women

In the 1970s a group of women of the Himalayas bravely protested government-funded deforestation. This policy was causing floods, landslides, and general devastation. The villagers were also losing much-needed fuel for daily life. When the men arrived to cut down the forest, the women made a human chain with their bodies, placing themselves between the trees and the chainsaw. They literally hugged the trees.

The Hindi word *chipko* means "to hug," and this non-violent action birthed the Chipko movement. Comprised mostly of rural women, the movement spread across India—not through mass media, but through folk songs and marches. It demonstrated how rural people depended on their local forests for their way of life.

In 1980, Prime Minister Indira Gandhi issued a fifteen-year ban on felling trees in the Himalayas until the canopy was fully restored.

Like the mountains in which they made their home, these women formed a boundary too strong for anyone to cross. And this brings us to the question: What are we willing to put ourselves on the line for? What are we willing to protect with our lives?

Integration

Journal Reflection: The Power to Protect

What do you care enough about to protect with your whole being? Your children, the rights of nature, racial equity, reproductive justice? Spend some time reflecting on what it is that calls your Mountain Woman Self into being. Then begin writing, *I call on the power of Mountain Woman to protect* . . . Read back and reflect. How does it feel to invoke this power? What seems possible—or impossible—in this moment?

Journal Reflection: The Birthing Stage

* I am called to this stage of the journey in order to learn . . .
* I know that this is my Mountain Woman time because . . .
* At this moment, I fear . . .
* At this moment, I am excited by . . .
* I hope to emerge from this time with Mountain Woman with . . .

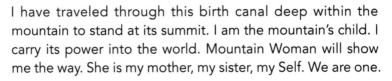

I have traveled through this birth canal deep within the mountain to stand at its summit. I am the mountain's child. I carry its power into the world. Mountain Woman will show me the way. She is my mother, my sister, my Self. We are one.

—Kay Johnsen

I stand tall taking my first breaths of thin air. I must trust that I am enough, that my ancestors are holding me in the strength I feel. I must trust that I have enough for being this wise Mountain Woman.

—Laurie Shade-Neff

My ancestral mountain mothers sing to me *rise up, rise up, rise up.* I welcome this power to belong again to me.

—Katie

Expansiveness

What has been hidden is now exposed.

—TERRY TEMPEST WILLIAMS

If you have ever gazed at a hawk flying overhead and wished you too could rise up and behold the grand scheme of things, then you are in the realm of Mountain Woman. And you have heard her call to soar.

Mountain Woman gives you the bird's-eye view. She enables you to look down on the valleys below and see for miles. But this expansive perspective must be earned. The experience of climbing toward your vision will test your limits. It is a process of learning. Who you are at the bottom of the mountain is not who you are once you reach the peak.

Even if you don't reach the summit, your willingness to engage the challenge will make you stronger. It is not so much about the heights you achieve, or the goals that you attain, as learning who you are and what you are capable of.

The word *altar* comes from the Latin word meaning "high." From the altar—the high place—we learn that achievement comes with sacrifice. I'm not talking about the way that women have been taught to sacrifice ourselves and our dreams over generations. I'm talking about the sacred act of giving ourselves to a cause, a way of life, or a community we care about.

Mountain Woman reminds you to consider not only what you want to give to the world, but what is needed from you. With each ascent, she asks you to extend your range: "What do I need?" becomes *What is needed from me?* "What's in it for me?" becomes *How do I serve?* "What am I supposed to do?" becomes *What is my divine purpose?*

Very likely no one has told you to grow bigger, to take up more space. This simply isn't part of a woman's cultural curriculum. But it is part of our soul work. As a Mountain Woman, you stand for broader visions and bolder concerns. You learn to stand tall and take risks to achieve some greater good. You embark on dangerous conversations. Ignore the "Do Not Enter" signs. Refuse to be irrelevant. Embrace your own immensity.

This kind of steadfast commitment will help you achieve your dream. Dedicate yourself to the climb, my sisters, and the vision will be granted you.

Integration

Journal Reflection: Letters to and from Your Mountain Woman Self

Your Letter to Mountain Woman

Take a moment to get in touch in with your Mountain Woman Self, homing in on whatever aspect you identify with or need to call into your life. In your journal write a letter to your emerging Mountain Woman Self. Tell her about your dreams, your ambitions, and your visions. Allow yourself to speak from your heart and let the words flow. Know that she will receive and honor everything you have to say.

After you have written your letter, read through it. Then ask:

> *What have I learned about myself?*
>
> *Who am I reaching to become?*
>
> *What do I sense I am being called to do?*

Mountain Woman's Letter to You

When it feels as if the time is right, settle in again with your journal. This time Mountain Woman will be writing her response to your letter. She will offer her advice, insights on how to move from where you are now, to achieving your dreams and visions in a way that serves the greater good. Allow her words to fill your page, as she shares with you all of her wisdom about what it is that you are being called to.

After the letter is written, read through it. Then ask:

> *What is it that Mountain Woman is telling me?*
>
> *What does she know about me that I am only learning about myself?*
>
> *What and who is she calling me to do and be?*

Owning Your Grit and Grandeur

It is we sinful women
who come out raising the banner of truth
up against barricades of lies on the highways

—Rukhsana Ahmad

You have already reclaimed many aspects of yourself on this journey. Now you are called to review the larger patterns and forces at work in your own life, and to take an aerial view of your world.

Mountain Woman summons you to rise up and appreciate your own grandeur—to grow as big as you need to be, to respond to the magnitude of these changing times. It's easy to cling to old beliefs and habits. There is always the temptation to play it safe, to say this moment is too big, the challenges too great. Yet while there is nothing wrong with occasional plateaus—these are not the times we grow.

Adversity doesn't have to break you; it can make you strong. It is when we stretch beyond what we think of as our breaking point, when we risk ourselves to serve what we love, that we discover we are so much bigger than we imagined ourselves to be. On learning that she had become the youngest and first Black Poet Laureate, Rita Dove reflected on the times when she held her breath and jumped. "Courage has nothing to do with our determination to be great," she explained. "It has to do with what we decide in that moment when we are called upon to be more."[45]

The trouble is women are rarely characterized as "more." The stories, myths, and fairytales I read growing up didn't offer images of powerful women, or a diversity of voices and experiences. We were described as waiting—waiting for the prince's kiss or the hero's return, waiting to be rescued from a tower or from being chained to a rock. Later, I learned we were supposed to be self-sacrificing, like Florence Nightingale or Mother Teresa.

These women were portrayed as paragons of holy selflessness, without any texture or toughness. But Florence Nightingale wasn't just some ghostly vision with a lamp tending the wounded in the Crimean War, she was a brilliant medical observer. In *Notes on Nursing*, she wrote about the patient's need to be in touch with nature: "I have seen, in fevers (and felt, when I was a fever patient myself), the most acute suffering produced from the patient (in a hut), not being able to see out of [the] window."[46] Nightingale was a pioneer in advocating for nature as essential to healing. Mother Teresa didn't just tend to the poor and sick, she did so even when spiritual darkness caused her to feel abandoned by her god. These women were warriors!

Today, we have advances in feminist storytelling, with wonderful writers like Madeline Miller and Pat Barker retelling the epic tales of the Odyssey and Iliad from a female perspective. Yet the hero's journey is still deeply engrained in our culture, and its parameters are not so easily overcome. We women shall need to dig deep, to own ourselves as part of this great cosmic adventure, to take authority for the stories we tell about ourselves and what is possible for our lives.

If something needs to be unchained right now, it is surely our imaginations. Dreaming big isn't something we've been taught to do. We must link together to free ourselves from stories of women as passive victims or as only worthy of supporting roles. But nor do we want to simply supplant men in the old stories. We need new narratives of what it means to be strong, spiritual warriors: Women who confront challenge and heartbreak but are not broken by it.

In her essay "My Beautiful Undoing: Erosion of Self" Terry Tempest Williams recalls being "let go" by the University of Utah, where she has taught for years in the Environmental Humanities

Graduate Program. Why? Because she and her husband have bid on land at a Bureau of Land Management oil and gas lease auction. They bought the land to protect it, not exploit it. But the University of Utah depends for its financial support on a state legislature that has been bought by the oil and gas lobbyists. Terry Tempest Williams—and her cause—have to go.

The heartbreak from losing her job bites deeply. Terry loves teaching. She has spent years developing a program of which she is rightfully proud. When she gets the news of her dismissal, she feels herself unraveling. But as she writes, "Where we experience heartbreak, the loss of a job or a marriage, or illness, or another disruption of the life we had planned for ourselves, may be our liberation—and open door to growth."

Terry describes waking to a full moon and going outside into the high desert lands that have been her home—and her family's—for generations. She begins to speak to the moon, offering, "a lament and a longing." She later recalls, "I had dared to tell this celestial body what my spiritual body desired: a deepening—a new way to understand and serve the world."[47] In this moment, adversity became a portal for expansion. Terry was not diminished by her loss but enlarged by it.

A heartbreak—or merely the relentlessness of daily life—may grind you down, but this kind of pressure is what makes a Mountain Woman strong. What you see from your small-self perspective isn't the whole picture. There is moonlight and magic, and a deep cord of connection to the universe and its legacy of stars. In the excruciating experiences and also in the quotidian ones, you remember you are in service to something bigger than yourself. There is a deep and resounding purpose to your being here.

Getting in touch with Mountain Woman can be especially helpful when you are starting a new venture, when you are consumed by a million daunting details or experiencing a frightening lack of certainty.

Her perspective is also a vital skill when confronting the state of the world. For without that long-range mountain vision, without the bigger view, how can you understand the greater forces at work that are shaping your life and rearranging our society?

Mountains toughen you, and as the path becomes steep and stony, and the need for concentrated effort increases, you learn more about who you really are. The word *concentrate* means "to focus," which is essential on a mountain trail. But also, as the poet Jane Hirshfield writes, "to increase in strength or destiny."[48]

Mountain Woman asks you to see the patterns that repeat themselves in your own life, and over long stretches of time. She assures you that when you find your mountain to climb, your authentic path, the goddesses will come to your aid. And your life will take on an epic feel.

Quitting drinking was one major mountain for me to climb. Writing this book is another. What I have discovered is this: If the challenge arises from my authentic self, then I am given the power and the will to see it through. At the end of my journey, I will not be the person I was at the beginning—I will have acquired new skills, been exposed to new ideas, and been forced to reckon with my own limitations. And I will have learned to recognize them and even rise above them.

We may not always be able to stand atop the fray in our full power, but whether we do or don't, we must realize that our lives matter. Every action we take enlarges the story we are writing. As Mountain Woman you understand your actions, or inaction, have deep-time consequences. You aren't just motivated by your immediate needs or desires. You realize every decision affects the well-being of generations to come.

June Jordan in her "Poem for South African Women," penned the now famous line, *we are the ones we have been waiting for.*[49] The poem was written to commemorate the 1956 protest of over

20,000 Black and Indian women and children marching in Pretoria to oppose Apartheid's system of racism and inequality, and most especially the pass law which restricted free movement of Africans. During the march, the women sang *"wathint' abafazi, wathint' imbokodo, uza kufa!"* This translates as: *When you strike the women, you strike a rock, you will be crushed.* The march didn't overthrow the system that day. But it gained recognition for South African women as a powerful force for political change. Forty years later, the Apartheid laws were struck down.

We are the ones we have been waiting for.

Integration

Journal Reflection:
Who Are the Women You Look Up To?

This exercise is designed to help you live in deep alignment with your values.

What role models do you have? These might include your mother or a grandmother, a teacher, or a good friend. Or perhaps you've been inspired by a certain writer, organizer, or artist. Or is there someone in your community you look up to? Historical figures whose stories inspire you? Who are the women who encourage you to overcome obstacles and to be your greatest self?

As you begin to reflect on the lives of these women, note what you admire most about them. Is it their values? Their determination? Their vulnerability? Their ability to break down barriers? When you have a sense of what draws you to them, write your reflections in your journal.

Then ask: *How can I incorporate these qualities in my own life?*

Journal Reflection: Your "Badass" Ancestors

"Our ancestors were survivors of things far more frightening than our first-world problems. They were *strong*. How do we know that? Because you're here. Your bloodline survived millennia of plague, war, pestilence, famine, infant mortality, and just plain old bad luck . . . just to make *you*. That means your ancestors were badasses."[50]

I love these words of pagan author Patti Wigington, because she reminds me of the strong lineages we all come from. Thinking of "badass ancestors" has also inspired the following exercise—and a way to connect with your ancestor energy, even if you don't know the details of your personal history.

Come present to the moment. Feel yourself in your body. Take a deep breath and awaken your cells, your sensing body, your dream-body . . . the part of you that knows how to imagine and intuit.

Consider the shape of your body, the shape and color of your eyes, your complexion, your physicality.

Your body holds your story. Your body remembers.

Consider your talents, your strengths, think about what you have survived and what you know. Your whole being, your true nature, is testament to a larger story.

Journey back in ancestral time and see who and what appears before you.

Imagine your parents, grandparents, your great grandparents, your great, great grandparents, and before them, further back. Feel the energy of your ancestral line. Take some time to appreciate the essence and ingenuity of these survivors.

Travel back as far as your imagination wants to travel—to before recorded history, to the cave dwellers and hunter gatherers.

And before that, to the single cell beings that emerged from the salty oceans.

And before that, to the stars and stardust you are made from.

All the way to the first light and the explosion of energy that ignited the universe.

Allow images to emerge. Don't question, simply allow yourself to notice, to feel, to experience whatever comes to you.

Now imagine your ancestors gathered together around the campfire. They have come together to discuss your situation in this moment in time and to offer their wisdom to you. They want only the best for you.

One of your ancestors from any part of your ancestral story rises to be the spokesperson for all of them. They address you by name, and begin, *This is what we want you to know* . . . . Listen deeply to what is being told to you. Allow your ancestors' words to fill your page.

After you have reflected on the wisdom they have offered you, ask yourself:

What is it that I want to take from this into my life?

Alignment

I have to cast my lot with those
who age after age, perversely,
with no extraordinary power,
reconstitute the world.

—ADRIENNE RICH

As a Mountain Woman, you take full responsibility for your life. You act in alignment with your bedrock values. No one else dictates what you can and cannot do. You are not a victim. You are a creatrix, a woman who produces and brings forth life. You cannot be swayed because you know your own heart and mind.

Mountain Woman symbolizes an urge toward wholeness. Awakening to her majesty, you discover the power of presence. The wind and the elements may shape and carve you, but they cannot change your nature. Regardless of your circumstances or the forces at work in your life, you possess an essential core that cannot be destroyed.

Time and again, under the most crushing constraints, women have found that strength isn't about privilege or circumstances. It's about authenticity. This is a vital lesson of Mountain Woman. By aligning with your bedrock values, you grow in scope and influence. When you are divided, you are living against yourself, and like a fractured stone, you will split. When you stop fighting yourself, you have the strength of mountains.

To rise tall, you need to know what you stand for and who you are deep inside. You need to know what matters to you and what is unique about you—your particular strengths and talents. What is it you can rely on?

When you unearth these values, you discover a rich vein of strength and joy. To live in accordance with what you love is true liberation. This is the ultimate freeing of your wild soul—to live in service of what matters most to you.

When your whole life expresses who you are and what you care about, you are fully exposed, like a mountain standing firm against the wind. This may sound daunting, yet this is the place you have been making your way to all journey long. Falseness falls away along with fear and doubt. There is no disconnect between how you show up in the world and who you are inside. When you act from Mountain Woman integrity, nothing and no one can tear you down.

Integration

Embodied Practice: Being the Mountain

Plant your feet on the ground, hip-width apart. Feel the solidity of a mountain as you elongate your spine, taking deep breaths into your core. With each breath, release tension in your neck, shoulders, back, hips, thighs while remaining upright and feeling the firmness of bedrock beneath your feet. Hold the posture for as long as is comfortable, continuing to breathe deep into your belly. Whenever you feel ready to release your pose, relax, and answer these questions in your journal:

> *How do I feel right now?*
>
> *What am I aware of right now?*
>
> *How do I want to be right now?*

Stone by Stone We Grow Strong

> *Stone by stone I pile*
> *this cairn of my intention*
> *with the noon's weight on my back*
>
> —ADRIENNE RICH

When we are clear about our bedrock values, we rise in the world, and we can hold power without collapsing or second-guessing ourselves. We know who we are at a soul level, and all our actions stem from there. We possess a deep confidence that allows us to take risks and court failure—all brave steps on the path to fulfillment.

At times, we may be worn down by the materialistic and exploitative values of our culture. These can easily drag us out of alignment with our Mountain Woman nature. We know that we should live simply on the planet, but we are bombarded with ads telling us that we need all these things from big cars to cellphones and synthetic fleece blankets to feel secure and comfortable. Sometimes we may say yes to a job that doesn't reflect our passion or purpose because it offers greater status or financial rewards.

Earning money is not bad; having status is not wrong. However, we run into trouble when we act in a way that doesn't reflect our core values. Each time we are swayed, we feel a little more demoralized, a little more divided against ourselves, even when our choices are made in good faith to protect our families and ourselves.

Like bedrock after fracking, we may crack under pressure and give up on what we care about. Deep inside, we know that we are being used, our talent mined by those who care nothing for who we are or what we desire.

But while our culture aims to erode our true power, the forces of our destiny are stronger still. Everything in the universe is conspiring to help women step up and embrace their holy purpose. To show that you, along with each living being, have a part to play in the great endeavor of life. Every time you accept the invitation to grow, you become stronger, more audacious.

Newly formed mountains are magnificently restless and volatile. As you awaken to Mountain Woman, you may feel that way, too. You may start to erupt with big dreams and grand notions. Will you quit your job, move across country, use your savings to start a business or train to do something different and more meaningful?

For a while, you may feel unstoppable, puffed-up in your belief that you can achieve anything you want. And maybe you can! You are, after all, soaring with enthusiasm—from the Greek *enthousiasmos*, meaning "filled with god." But it's important that you focus not only on these external changes, but on what is happening deep inside. You are discovering your ability to determine the course of your life based on your own values. You are learning to lift yourself above the demands and duties imposed by the culture and to see your life from a higher vantage point.

Early in my career, it felt natural to follow my father's path into advertising. My role as copywriter initially served my need for creativity (my love of writing), connection (I worked with wonderful people) and adventure (I worked in London, New York, and San Francisco). But while I developed marketable skills, I wasn't challenged to grow at a soul level. I needed the work of the wild soul to test me—to shake me to my core and call forth my true strengths and values.

Older mountains, on the other hand, aren't as volatile as young ones. The mature Mountain Woman is less concerned with recognition or applause, because she knows the right thing to do. Because her actions are aligned with what she cares about. She has healed her internal rifts, learned to act from integrity.

The Appalachians are the oldest mountain range in America and among the most ancient on Earth. They aren't as tall or impressive as the Sierras or Rockies. They have been eroding over hundreds of millions of years, and time has softened their edges. But perhaps they speak to you, as they do to me, of a different kind of strength: A seasoned Mountain Woman who is grounded and generous.

I think of the poets, activists, and community leaders I have had the privilege to know who grew up in Appalachia and the Ozark mountains. Much of the work they do—educating children, organizing neighbors, keeping food on their own table in times of scarcity—is unsung. It hasn't made them rich or famous. Yet, they stand tall because they never gave up caring. And they never backed down from what civil rights leader John Lewis called "good trouble." Through their perseverance, communities survive and even thrive in what we call "hard times."

Today, women in every discipline are challenging the status quo. We may not possess extraordinary power or wealth or status. But we have resources that towering corporations and powerful government bodies lack. We have our deep foundation of Earth-based wisdom, feminist strength, and an unwavering dedication to the values of care, connection, and inclusivity. We are the mountains on which our future civilization must be built.

Integration

Ritual: Build a Commitment Cairn

A cairn is a human-made pile of stones to guide hikers by marking the trail or to signify a mountaintop. In this ritual, you will create your own cairn. Each stone will represent something that deeply matters to you, such as taking care of the land, pursuing your creative life, forming a community, completing a project, building a business or organization, speaking a truth, caring for a partner. As you place each stone on your cairn, feel the energy of each intention, each meaning, each value. You can do this exercise with stones you have collected, or simply by conducting this ritual in your imagination.

After all the stones are placed, write about your cairn. What does it symbolize? What does it say about your values? What stand does it urge you to take? What mark of resistance does it represent?

I am strong in my wholeness, one with life, with nature, with all who live within me, on me, through me.

—Linda

I feel the breath of Heaven and Earth move through me. I am the majesty and strength of the mountain. My mountain self. I look across and see all of the other mountain women. We are one.

—Meggie

The Challenge:
Embracing Friction

and the ones who stood without sweet company
will sing and sing
back into the mountains

—JUNE JORDAN

We have been asleep. Silent. Under the crushing weight of patriarchy, we have forgotten our power as women. Yet like the Earth, we possess restless energy and sudden creative surges. Now is the time to heed them for they will help us to transform the planet.

Mountain Woman reminds us that the time for dormancy is over.

It might feel safer not to change. But if the planet were to follow that trajectory, it would become cold and dead, as unlivable as Mars. In truth, life comes from friction and emerges from a hot belly.

When we find our footing as Mountain Women, we challenge systems of oppression and begin the necessary task of reimagining the world. Our resistance is essential. To initiate a new stage of renewal, we must be willing to topple the forms and institutions that are doing violence to people and to the planet. Don't be afraid. Death and cataclysm are how stars are born, how mountains form, and how the Earth survives. Sometimes you need to raise a storm to make a difference.

You must dispel the notion that you mustn't take up too much space, that you mustn't voice your opinions too emphatically. Mountain Woman hollers from the peaks and highest altars. She places her body before the chainsaw. She raises banners, knits pussy hats, protests injustice and inequity, and protects the vulnerable. She refuses to bow to anyone. The long history of life has carved her face and the crags of her being. Molten energy roils inside her. She is a force of nature.

As women, we have been taught to fear the peak experiences of our lives—birth, menstruation, sex, menopause. We have been warned to hold our tongues, to strangle our anger. But now it rises, hot, holy, and explosive, in the service of life itself.

We will not shut up or calm down. We are tired of being nice.

It is time to heed the heat of your passion, stoke the fire of commitment. After generations of living under the pressure of patriarchy, you have learned how to transform hard coal into diamonds.

Our task, my sisters, is reshaping the map of the modern world.

Becoming Fire-Breathing Dragons

every word out of her mouth
a riot

—DENICE FROHMAN

There is tension at the core of life, beneath the surface of our restless planet. Conflict is a necessary aspect of all meaningful transformation. It proceeds moments of deep change. Disturbances are a necessary precursor of evolution. The more we allow the tension to build, the greater the discovery that follows. If we want true change—in ourselves and in our society—we therefore need to learn to dance with tension.

But how do we reconcile conflict with our role as peacemakers?

For generations, women have been tasked with quelling discord and resolving family quarrels. In the face of disunity, we are supposed to be the balm. But haven't we paid the price of peace at any cost?

When we ignore our rage and accept the status quo, we uphold a destructive system that wages war not just on the Earth but on women everywhere. It's not just that women sidestep conflict; it's that we overtly or covertly encourage others to do the same. As mothers, if we teach our daughters to play nice and get along, we are doing the work of the patriarchy. If we simply accept that we don't have a say about our own reproductive rights, or Nature's rights, we are doing the work of the patriarchy. Could it be that by just "trying to get along" we fail to protect what and whom we love? Could it be that lasting peace will only come when we stop trying to tamp down the tension, and become full-on, fire-breathing dragons?

As women, we possess a natural instinct to protect life. And yet we cannot heal every wound and calm every upset. So, ask yourself, *What is it I long to speak out against?* Inequity, white supremacy, gun violence, toxic chemicals, underfunded schools, the greed of the fossil fuel industry, the inaction on climate change? Then unleash your truth, in service of what you care about.

Mountain Woman calls to you in your restlessness. A hairline crack. A disturbance in the field. You can't ignore these things. Let your words leap from your mouth like flames, hot and urgent. Express your deepest and most transformative capacities. It is time to shatter the illusion that you—that we—don't have the power to change the system.

I don't know of a woman whose heart isn't breaking and whose rage isn't rising, in the face of the destructive and soul-destroying policies that are emerging all around us. So, know this: A Mountain Woman doesn't erupt over superficial problems. Her rage arises out of love for this world. She is the primordial life force ensuring the wellbeing of future generations. She is the eternal and powerful maternal feminine, the fearsome mama bear that is ready to protect her young. It is time to listen to her now.

When I first started going public with my Wild Soul work, I was so terrified of dissent and of people challenging what I'd written that each time I posted a blog, I'd be down for the count. I was writing about spirit and ecology in a way not usually discussed, and more often demeaned as "woo-woo." But the more often I spoke out, the easier it became.

In 2015, I was asked to talk at the Techno-Utopianism & the Fate of the World Conference in New York City. The conference took place in the Great Hall of Cooper Union, and each presenter stood at the lectern where Abraham Lincoln announced his run for the presidency. It was, at the time, the largest and most prestigious conference I had been asked to address, and excitement and fear churned inside me in equal measure.

I was on a panel titled "Nature's Presence and Our Awareness" with three seasoned environmentalists, all of them older white men, all of them notable environmental warriors, two of them with multiple books to their names. When we were introduced in the green room before going on stage, they barely lifted their eyes to meet mine. They just went on talking among themselves as if I were invisible.

On stage, the men spoke of the environmental horrors we were perpetuating. They gave statistics, examples, and sounded rightfully upset with our seeming inability to be better stewards of the Earth. The audience was silent and subdued. Then it was my turn. I put my notes to one side and stepped up to the lectern. I felt a deep inner quiet. What were the words that I wanted, despite my fear, to give voice to? I knew I had something different—and also important—to add to the conversation. Part of me badly wanted to be recognized by these men, whom I admired for their work. Yet I had done a lot of thinking and writing on the topic at hand, and that gave me the authority to speak my own truth, on my terms, not theirs.

Clearly, slowly, I started. I spoke about what it felt like to backpack in the mountains. How though you struggle with the weight of your pack, you also feel the weight of your everyday worries fall away. How as twilight descends, you can hear bears rooting beyond the campsite and are reminded that you are not at the top of the food chain. I spoke about how your muscles harden with each day's walk, and the language of thunderclouds becomes your language, too. How time slows as you filter water from ice cold streams and count every high-altitude step and breath.

I spoke of how the bowl of the mountain brings you closer to yourself and those you travel with. And how here, in the wilderness, far from technology and the hum of traffic, the dreams pour into you out of the night. I spoke of how I dreamed of riding a white bear through a sky blooming with stars and then woke to watch the rising sun gild the peaks.

And then, when it is time to descend the mountain, how you carry the stillness and immensity with you. And you know that this, too, is part of you. You carry the sure knowledge that forgetting this causes us to do so much harm. That this loss of intimacy with the Earth makes us lose sight of who we are and what truly matters. That we aren't bad people, we are traumatized people, torn from a primary and primal relationship with our first mother—Earth. And into that wrenching void, comes our need to dominate, consume, and conquer.

As the applause erupted, I felt the magic of the wilderness stir within us, in that large auditorium, in the bowels of a venerable old building. At least for a moment, a touch of wildness pounding in the blood of all those who were there. In my speaking out, I found my own language, my own voice.

It is crucial that women insist on taking their place at the table or perhaps more truly, setting a new one. If we don't express our views openly and honestly, then we will just pass on our legacy of silence and submission to future generations and the existing system will not change. As Audre Lorde writes, "I have come to believe over and over again that what is most important to me must be spoken, made verbal and shared, even at the risk of having it bruised or misunderstood."[51]

I have a growing list of women who shake me to my core with their ability to stand in their own truth. One is Greta Thunberg. If you have seen this young Swedish activist admonishing heads of state about their lack of action on the climate emergency, it is a thing of beauty. Her voice is calm, but never appeasing. She has no feminine wiles, nor does she indulge in sugar coating. We have heard her voice speaking truth to power, and it has awakened our own.

As I write, women of color in Congress and the Senate are receiving death threats. And women across the world who speak out about rape are dismissed or threatened with even more violence. Indigenous women, fighting to protect their lands, are being attacked and many of them have been "disappeared." As women move into positions of influence, this reality will be brought down. Each woman who enters the fray and speaks her truth, makes it harder for the world to close its ears.

Until we remake the system, until we take it back from the patriarchy, you may have to sacrifice greatly and risk much. It can be unbearably lonely at times to be a lone voice crying from the mountaintop. Some will call you obsessed, delusional, say that you are neglecting your children. Lovers may tire of your passion for causes. For a time, you will likely question the path you have chosen. But then you will remember, the lives of generations and the life of this planet are at stake.

Consider the social changes brought about by women's movements—protection for factory workers, children's rights, homes for unwed mothers and sanctuaries for abused women. Take heart in civil rights heroines like Rosa Parks and Fannie Lou Hamer, as well as all the demonstrators who laid down their lives, saying, *We will not be moved.*

Be proud of the younger women who are finding their voices sooner. Young women like Malala Yousafzai, the Pakistani activist who advocated for the education of girls—even after she was shot in the face on a school bus. And like Amanda Gorman, the youngest poet to perform at a presidential inauguration, whose voice rose up for inclusivity and love. And like Emma González, the survivor of the Parkland high school shootings turned teenage anti-gun activist.

Every truth, every action, every resistance you offer, matters. Whatever you do that breaks in some way the stranglehold of patriarchy, matters. But we can only do so much as individuals. Like peaks in a mountain range, we need to link together. We need to join in radical solidarity with other courageous women to make ourselves heard. When we embrace our collective vulnerabilities and strengths, when we share our pain and our dreams, we rise as one.

The novelist Toni Morrison writes that when things are at their worst, "This is precisely the time when artists go to work. There is no time for despair, no place for self-pity, no need for silence, no room for fear. We speak, we write, we do language. That is how civilizations heal."[52]

Let me ask you, my sister: Are you ready to take your place—and take up space—and change the world?

Integration

Journal Reflection: What Am I Trying to Hold Together?

Spend some time reflecting on the following questions.

> *What am I trying to hold together?*
>
> *What do I fear will happen if I don't keep holding* [name it/them] *together?*

What might be the result if I loosen my grip?

What is the ideal world I would like to leave to the next generation?

Share your answers with your women's circle or with a close friend who supports your goals and values.

Journal Reflection: Unlearning to Not Speak

There's a powerful poem, "Unlearning to Not Speak" by Marge Piercy that is well-suited to a Mountain Woman's awakening. The poem begins by confronting, head on, the many ways we have been shamed and silenced. In other words, *before* we can speak out, we first need to *unlearn* to not speak. Settle in and think about the kinds of things—situations, pressures, fears, beliefs—that have stopped you from speaking your truth. Then tap into your inner Mountain Woman. Breathe her in, as you feel your belly and chest expanding with her energy, begin writing your own piece, starting with these words from Piercy's poem:

I must learn to speak again . . .

Allow your words to flow onto the page. What are you hungry to speak about? What do you need to say? How are you no longer willing to be silenced? When you have finished writing, read your poem or prose piece out loud.

What is it that you notice?

What is it that surprises you?

How does it make you feel?

Journal Reflection: What Makes You Angry?

The question, *What makes you angry?* is a powerful central inquiry for a woman's circle. It's also good to write about this in your journal. If you're like most of the women I know, there will be plenty to say in answer. So let rip. Tell it like it is. What enrages you? War? Selfishness? Ignorance? Your thoughtless neighbor?

After you've written about everything that makes you angry, reflect on the quality of your anger. Is it hot, icy, quick to burn, slow to simmer? Then pay attention to the common threads between different things that make you angry These will point to your underlying values, such as fairness, compassion, creativity, collaboration. Make a list of any that jump off the page as things you want to claim, rather than repress.

Now, as a Mountain Woman, ask yourself how you can transmute your anger into loving and empowered action. Then make a list of three to five things you can do to shift your anger and fire up your creativity.

I can feel the fire in my belly wanting to erupt. I feel the restlessness of the winds, the gravity of the ascent and the edges of the rocks. I see women that have come before me, fighters, warriors, mothers, defending, caring, curing, creating, loving, hating, helping.

—Kai

I am she
wild mountain woman
the unapologetic eruption
creating your disruption
rupturing your secrets
she who had the audacity
to unleash
her furious
molten mess
your way.

—Caroline Cummings

The Shift:
Broken to Reborn

Another world is not only possible, she is on her way.
On a quiet day, I can hear her breathing.

—Arundhati Roy

The world is breaking apart. Called by some the Great Unraveling, our global systems are toppling, and our inner worlds are being shaken to the core. We are drifting farther apart from each other, due to shifting plates of misunderstanding and disinformation. As the energy of patriarchy winds down, it becomes increasingly evident that our economic, social, and political institutions, which have all along worked better for some of us than for others, are failing us all. Many quake in fear.

Mountain Woman celebrates the breakages and braves the chasms, for she knows that only when the world breaks open can it be made anew.

The great mistake is to think that our lives—that any life—is settled and secure. The energy of the molten core of the Earth keeps moving, and so must we.

Now, from the broken and wounded aspects of the world, something new is bubbling up. You may sense it as a tremor in your soul or feel it as a thundering in your heart or the shaking of the Earth beneath your feet. But what if breaking apart isn't the end, but the beginning? What if amid the chaos and the destruction, a new way of being is about to be revealed?

The greatest mountains constantly erode. Everything that lives carries some affliction and is broken in some way. Only when we enter the breaks can we glimpse the new world that is on its way.

Mountain Woman requires of you a counter-intuitive approach. You must ignore the voice that commands you to hold things together. You must go instead into the very depths of brokenness where the treasure resides.

"*Vunja* is a Swahili word that marks the site of strange ruptures but then invites celebration and dance with/in those cracks," writes professor and Nigerian activist Bayo Akomolafe. It is time for you to dance with those breakages in a way that opens you to "new forms of becoming-together."[53]

In looking for new ways of being, other places of power, it is vital you acknowledge the cracks, celebrate the chasms, and enter the shadowy world of fissures.

Just as a mantle plume under a fault line or fracture zone can result in eruptions of huge volumes of lava, so the cracks in our systems—and our psyches—can allow new forms of organization and new ways of being to emerge. When, eventually, the upheaval settles into quiet, nothing is the same. Our guiding story has completely changed.

Dancing in the Chasm

I
will
remember
with my breath
to make a mountain

—May Swenson

The people-pleasing, peace-loving part of you may be trembling as you read this. *Do we have to break apart to truly change the path we are on?* It feels frightening and overwhelming. And if we stop at the falling apart stage, it is. But Mountain Woman knows that falling apart is a necessary step toward reinvention.

In "The New Rule" the Sufi poet Rumi reminds us that when things are falling apart (*Everywhere is falling everywhere*) that it is in these times of brokenness we search for the hidden treasure.

Founded on a philosophy of separation, one that keeps us from the Earth and from each other, patriarchy is fraught with fractures. Its divide-and-conquer attitude has made our communities and our institutions—and our very selves—extremely vulnerable. Right now, our world is rife with so many cracks it is set to crash and burn.

Practiced at papering over the fissures, we women are socialized to repair what is broken. We are the weavers and the uniters. But in many ways, we are tending to a wound that never heals. Does repairing a flawed system serve us? Our energy, which could be channeled into new ways of being, is wasted. What if we stopped using it to hold together a system that is dysfunctional and destructive? In our

12-Step work, we have a name for this: bottoming out. When every attempt to cover up the mess of our lives and pretend we are making "progress" has failed, then the real work begins.

It isn't easy or enviable to hit rock bottom. Our addiction to patriarchal systems of exploitation and fragmentation is powerful. It can feel overwhelming to consider how much will have to change, including us, if we admit the status quo isn't working. Even those of us who have been most hurt by the system and are acutely aware of its toxic aspects can still fear the changes that will come when the whole thing crashes. The pain of hitting bottom is real. And we can't ignore it. But Mountain Woman asks, *Might this also be cause for celebration?* She reminds us that the chaos we are experiencing is an invitation into the wilds of creativity—to that spark of imagination that ushers forth when stone is struck.

A Mountain Woman has no patience for passivity. This is not about remaining silent or stoic in the face of destruction. You have a vital task: to remain open, curious, awake, so that you become a conduit for whatever new energy or insight is trying to be born. Find the openings. Put your ear to the cracks and listen for the emergent stories, voices, and visions that are rising as magma from the depths. In doing so, you will be helping our culture to give birth to a new vision, a new era.

The fractured places cannot be repaired. Unless we own the trauma and our deep sense of despair, there can be no healing. Falling apart isn't what any one of us would have chosen. It's not a journey we can ever be prepared for. But it is the journey of our times. And is the journey you are taking, right here, right now.

We cannot help but feel this on a personal level, every day. We live in a society fraught with pressures—to perform, to work harder, to ignore the destruction and the devastation, until we come to the breaking point. But what if this burnout is a portal to growth? As Audre Lorde asks, "What are the tyrannies you swallow day by day and attempt to make your own, until you will sicken and die of them . . . ?"[54] Well, we are sick and tired of being sick and tired. Mountain Woman reminds us that is it time to awaken to the sacred purpose of our lives.

The American gymnast Simone Biles knows what it's like to move through trauma in order to achieve a purpose. This extraordinarily talented young woman, along with scores of other young gymnasts, was sexually abused by her team's doctor, Larry Nassar. Then she was abandoned by the American Olympic and USA Gymnastics officials who worked to cover up the abuse. Unsurprisingly, it was the victims of the crime who were left to bring Larry Nassar to justice.

During the 2021 Olympics, Biles experienced what gymnasts call *the twisties:* when spinning through the air, an athlete cannot tell up from down. This is a sign of being divorced from your body. Instead of powering through, Simone bowed out, citing mental health issues. "It's like fighting all those demons coming in here," she said after the team competition.

Biles stayed at the Olympics to cheer on her peers, and later returned to competition, earning a bronze medal. Some of the white male conservative commentators called her a "quitter," a "selfish sociopath" who had brought "shame on her country." But in owning her trauma, in refusing to perform on anyone else's terms but her own, Biles was, in every way, warrior-strong. Many people understood this, I suspect, because they wished for the same courage to admit their wounds.

It was there, in her own psychic fault line, that Biles found buried treasure. She learned that she was no longer just a performer, she was a fully rounded human being who could speak up for the suffering other teammates had endured. In owning her broken places, she reclaimed a greater sense of self and another source of her power. In speaking out, she was not just healing her own wounds, she was helping to create a society in which young women would not have to tolerate abuse.

We saw something similar with Naomi Osaka when she withdrew from the French Open, admitting her struggles with depression and anxiety. These athletes, these young women we look up to, are showing us the power of owning our brokenness. They are forcing us to question the pressure we put on ourselves to overcome, as well as our belief that we must push ourselves to the brink, endure years of pain and trauma, and simply carry on. Biles and Osaka are standing up for women everywhere, showing us that in claiming our vulnerability, we become strong.

I am reminded of the Japanese art of Kintsugi, which mends pottery by highlighting the broken parts in gold. This is a good image for how we might deal with heartbreak and trauma, while celebrating our own beauty. Brokenness and wholeness are not separate from each other, but co-conspirators, helping us to recover our own worth and share it with the world.

Even so, given all the despair and destruction, you may fear tending your own wounds is self-centered. But as you've seen, it can also lead to a collective healing.

To lead or influence others effectively, you must be willing to face the ways you have been wounded by the world. But remember this: When a bone breaks, it heals and regrows stronger than before. As the poet and artist Rashani wrote: *There is a brokenness / out of which comes the unbroken, / a shatteredness / out of which blooms the unshatterable.*[55] From the world's fractured places, a new world can arise that is more loving, inclusive, and supportive than before.

Mountain Woman commands you to remember you have been born into this place and time, to this broken and beautiful world, for a reason. She reminds you that your belly is a molten core, a crucible for forging a new world. Mountain Woman will help you to discover your own strength. If you can hold to her fire, you will become an Earth shaker—a luminous, creative being. My sister, you can light up the world.

Becoming Mountain Woman: The Three Bs

Take a moment to relax and sit quietly, listening to your breath and reflecting on the images and thoughts that have arisen during your time with Mountain Woman. Then spend at least five minutes answering each of the following questions in your journal.

What is breaking up inside of me, and in the world?

What is bubbling up?

Who am I becoming?

Take the answer to that last question and turn it into a poem or portrait or collage. The title will be *The Woman I am Becoming*. What is her energy like? What visions does she entertain? What is she taking a stand for? In any and every way possible, make this new you come alive.

Silvia Vasquez-Lavado's Story: Rising Above Trauma

A native Peruvian and sexual violence survivor, Silvia Vasquez-Lavado had an epiphany in October 2005, during a trek to the base camp of Mt. Everest. Climbing had reconnected her to her inner courageous girl. Moved deeply by the capacity of Mt. Everest to rekindle her inner power and heal her spiritually, she made a promise to return one day and reach the peak.

Thus began Silvia's quest to climb the world's Seven Summits. She first climbed Mt. Kilimanjaro, Tanzania in October 2005; Mt. Elbrus, Russia in September 2006; and she attempted Mt. Denali, Alaska in June 2012 before turning back due to extreme weather. She set off to climb Mt. Aconcagua, Argentina in December 2013.

Summiting Aconcagua proved to be a life-changing experience for her. The day after coming down from the summit, Silvia was determined to climb the remaining peaks before attempting

Mt. Everest. She also decided she would not go alone. Instead, she vowed to bring four eighteen-year-old women, all survivors of sexual violence, from the San Francisco Bay Area, as well as four eighteen-year-old survivors of sexual violence from Nepal.

Her dream was for these young women to find their own courage and heal with their sisters from around the world. In 2014, she founded Courageous Girls, a California nonprofit that takes young women and non-binary survivors of sexual violence on adventure travels.

In May 2016, Silvia became the first Peruvian woman to summit Mt. Everest and, two years later, the first openly gay woman to complete the Seven Summits. When she eventually climbed Denali, it took almost two months. Living in a little tent, with no showers, and continually stretched to her limits, she wondered at times why she was making such a journey. When she finally returned from the summit, she knelt down and cried. She felt empty. She had given everything to the mountain.

But in return, the mountain had given Silvia back herself.[56]

Integration

Visualization: Finding Buried Treasures

When mountains shift or break apart, they reveal their hidden treasures—a painted paleolithic cave wall, ancient fossils. When you embrace the fractured places within, you discover the treasures that lie deep within your soul.

Find a safe space to do this next exercise, a guided meditation. Ideally, you will be surrounded by a loving circle of sisters, in real time or in your imagination. Light a candle and play music that allows you to enter a meditative state. And give yourself a safety net by knowing that anytime in this process, you can leave the visualization. You are in charge of your journey. Always.

Take a few moments to focus on your breath.

Imagine that you are entering the mountains. As you walk farther along the path, you come to a fissure in the rocks. You slow down and sit beside it. This fissure represents a soul-wound, a way in which you feel broken and incomplete. (For example, you are only as good as others think. Or you're not creative. Or worthy.)

Your soul-wound may originate from a specific incident or time in your life. Let the memories surface and try not to judge them or fight them. You are simply bearing witness.

After a while, you notice a spark of light emanating from the crack. It glows so enticingly you find yourself drawn to it, slipping through the crack into the rock, until you enter the most beautiful cave you have ever seen. All around you are paintings in rich ochres, and deep reds, and wondrous earth colors.

At the center of the cave is a torch, and you pick it up and begin to study the paintings on the walls. You realize they are of you, and they picture all the many ways that you have courageously responded to life. They show how you have grown strong, learned skills, developed talents—all because of your soul-wound. They show you your bravery and your beauty.

Spend as much time as you are comfortable in the cave, learning all about the treasure you have gleaned. And thank the mountain for sharing her wisdom with you.

When you are ready, lift your face to the sunlight pouring through the crack and feel yourself rise. You are back on firm terrain again. Take a few deep breaths, and leave the mountains, returning to where you started.

Then take out your journal and record everything you remember about your journey.

But my truth is my truth
unshakeable
unbreakable
right down to my core.
Yes...I am the weathermaker
you wish I was not.

—Caroline Cummings

I am the bottom and the top of the mountain. The light fractals burst into my heart lighting up the crystals embedded in these dark stones of guardianship.

—Katie

Feelings of broken trust, lies lived, truth buried for so many eons. So many lives. Now, rising like a cloud, resting on the face of mountain strength I can climb and reach a place where I can sit and look out over the landscape of brokenness.

—Jane

The Way: Transformative Power

When sleeping women wake, mountains move.

—CHINESE PROVERB

In taking a stand, a Mountain Woman is willing to be seen for who she is and what she values. Exposure is influence. And yet, how many of us long to stay hidden in the forest, safe among the trees? But if we do, how will we ever grow tall and large enough to make our own weather?

We would think things had gotten easier for women. But the culture of social media has in many ways made exposure even riskier. Trolling, doxing, canceling, bullying, can make us question whether to speak out or take a leadership role in any situation. Will we inevitably receive blowback? The answer is yes. But Mountain Woman tells us, *If you are speaking truth from the core of your being, you will find the strength to meet whatever gets thrown at you.*

To know what you want to commit to—the purpose of your life— you must embrace the immense quiet of Mountain Woman. Dare to venture above the tree line, a place of light and edges, far outside your comfort zone. Up here, you are at your most vulnerable and exposed. You may never feel so close to death and yet so alive. Caught between these extremes, you come to realize what is important to you. From this place, it feels natural to rise up and make a difference.

This kind of self-determining power has been tamped down for ages by a system that simultaneously mines women's strength and keeps us "in our place." Mountain Woman says, *Own your wholeness, your beautiful entirety. Refuse to be used only for what society deems of value. Feel instead the grit inherent in owning who you are.*

When you climb above your plateaus of unworthiness, you leave the win/lose paradigm behind and lay claim to dormant energy. Use this energy to express what matters to you.

Stop giving gurus, organizations, or belief systems the power to override your innate wisdom. Don't become a devotee to someone else's dream if it doesn't serve your own unfolding. If you come under the spell of a mentor's charisma, a fall is inevitable. Rockslides will follow—until you step back on your own path and regain your clarity of purpose.

Remember the oracles and seers, the gritty grandmothers, and the furious re-sisters, the burned and the enslaved. You stand on the shoulders of all the women who, while vilified, never relinquished their visions.

Mountain Woman draws her strength from eons of geological time. So, too, you draw on the tremendous toughness of all the women who came before you. Your power is sourced not only from your belly and being, but from the bedrock of your ancestors. Their spirits guide you still.

What Will You Unleash?

Freedom is actually a bigger game than power.
Power is about what you can control.
Freedom is about what you can unleash.

—HARRIET RUBIN

Mountain Woman speaks to our need to dig deep inside to challenge a patriarchal model based on separation, extraction, and hierarchy and replace it with our own values of connection, reciprocity, and collaboration. But it will not be easy. "The word 'power' is highly charged for women," writes poet Adrienne Rich.[57] We tend, she tells us, to associate it with the use of force, with rape, with war, and an almost sociopathic accumulation by the few of wealth and resources. This is the kind of the power that acts only in its own interest, demeaning and exploiting others, including women and children.

Our desire to rise to the pinnacle, to be the top of the pyramid, can sometimes cause us to swell to giant proportions so that we become callous, self-centered. The art of a Mountain Woman is to learn to harness power humbly and with discernment. A mountain that blows too hard will destroy everything in its vicinity. This isn't to say you should tone down your power, only that you need to be sure it is transformative power—one shared with the dispossessed, the marginalized, and with nature herself.

Our goal must be power that seeks to decolonize and liberate self and others. Power that isn't shared raises up only the smallest portion of people, while subjugating the rest. It is aimed at maintaining the status quo. If, as women, we are seduced by this power, we come to think of ourselves as separate from other women, somehow more deserving, more extraordinary.

The first waves of the feminist movement didn't break from patriarchy, perhaps because women still wanted its support and protection. Women of color, poor women, immigrant women, non-heterosexual women, trans women, were mainly excluded. Only white and mostly well-to-do women had access to greater freedoms and privileges. Some who benefitted from the women's movement enjoyed their privileges precisely because they were willing to ignore the bad behavior of the men with whom they were linked—their husbands, bosses, mentors.

Yet, can we deny that any woman who rises in the ranks wants to feel safe? Taking a stand is to be exposed. There are so many ways we can be targets in these times. Everyone has a social media platform and an opinion. Powerful women, especially those that take on the establishment, know that to be visible is to be vulnerable. That's why we must support each other, creating buttresses of care and kindness.

Men tend to think of themselves as solitary conquerors, climbing the lofty perches of success on their own. But nobody summits a mountain alone. We do so, roped together. If another climber stumbles on a steep, icy slope, we throw down our picks and dig in. We hold each other up. Our job is to keep each other safe. Even if you climb solo, you depend on a support team. Nor do you climb a mountain for yourself alone. You climb it to forge a path for those who follow.

I learned a lot about this new kind of leadership during the first Wild Soul Woman facilitation training I ran back in 2018. Things had been going well, but as we neared the end of the course, I noticed that some trainees were merely going through the motions. I blasted out a fiery email, noting that I was upset with their lack of responsiveness. Never mind that I hadn't been entirely clear of what my expectations were.

Almost the minute I hit "send," I regretted it. And then I recognized the fingerprints of my Inner Taskmaster, the one who says that I have to do everything, all at once and alone.

The email was sourced in so many of my Taskmaster's unanswered questions: *How will I ever get this group to summit if they don't put in more energy? Why am I working so hard if they aren't?* The weight of responsibility hung on my shoulders, and I was stressed out over it. But I also felt a deep sense of shame. Showing anger was hardly the way to model a Wild Soul Woman. Or was it?

The seismic effects of my email were still spreading through the group, despite my apology. So, I shared with a dear friend what had happened. She's known me for years and asked just the right questions:

"What is it you fear?"

"I don't trust that they'll do what they need to do to complete the training. I think that if I don't push them, all these months will be for nothing."

Then she asked, "What is it you want?"

"To lead from my heart."

"And what else?"

"For everyone to do their part. To be a team."

"And what will it take to lead from your heart and create a fully engaged team?"

As I considered her questions, I mused on how we had reached the Mountain Woman stage and yet the group was all over the map. Some were trailing far behind, while others were nearing the peak. I was ready to blame the trainees who were lagging. But, in all honesty, I had been so in control of the agenda, that it had likely had the effect of disempowering those around me.

On our next group call, I listened to the hurt and anger my email caused. As the group's facilitator, it was uncomfortable to hear how my words had landed, and I felt extremely vulnerable. But the call was real and heartfelt. My burst of anger had in some way opened us up to be more genuine. There was sadness and also a renewed sense of commitment and energy. Like the air after a high mountain storm, everything felt lighter and brighter. There was also a significant shift in the group dynamics.

Some owned that they'd been dawdling and not fully engaging. I confessed I've been in Taskmaster mode, not checking in with each woman to see if she knew and understood her own level of responsibility. Together, we agreed that we needed to extend the training so that everyone could arrive at basecamp, and we could summit as one. We affirmed that we were each of us responsible for the success of the group. That we were a team.

At our best, we women make space for each other to stumble, and then reach out a hand to lift each other up. For me, that's the core of women's leadership—the open, loving circle where we can admit that we are imperfect and keep learning to do better. We don't abandon each other at the first bump in the road. We work things out and discover that we can be authentically and messily ourselves and still be leaders and innovators.

Transformative feminine power, after all, refutes the dominant top-down model. It is sourced from deep within each of us. And it depends on these individual acts of courage. It starts with you saying, *I believe I can make a difference.* And then trusting that with hard work, you will.

The Women's Earth and Climate Action Network International understands this. Its acronym is "WECAN." Uplifting women on the frontlines of climate disruption—women who have unique and essential solutions and skills—WECAN supports a different kind of leadership: feminine, indigenous, rooted in intimate knowledge of the land.

Listening to the speakers at their online Global Women's Assembly for Climate Justice, I realized how different the women sounded. They weren't looking to call attention to themselves or to impose grandiose, high-tech solutions. They were here to implement programs that met their communities' needs.

Another admirable organization is Emerge America, which mentors women into political power. At one of their fundraising events, I was struck by the confidence and joy of each candidate who spoke that night. Powerhouses all, some were already in office, some just beginning their political careers. But each felt empowered by their mentors—a network of experienced women who offered advice and support and were there to listen when things got tough.

When women come into power, their organizations, including governmental ones, operate differently. Putting women on corporate boards isn't just about giving them better access to the old, patriarchal systems of power; it's about creating organizations that take a feminine approach—nurturing, inclusive, collaborative, and vulnerable—and thus achieve different results.

Mountain Woman asks you transform power *over* to power *within* and to remember that you are a creator who is birthing the world anew.

When I feel that familiar twinge of self-doubt and need a jolt of confidence, I imagine standing by Mount Shasta, a 14,000 ft volcano which I summited more than two decades ago. She is a deceptive mountain, soft and sensuous, but also dangerous and unpredictable with crevasses that can swallow you whole. She has the power of a goddess to be nurturing and yet to shock her acolytes awake. As I picture her in my mind, I feel myself become a goddess in my own right.

And I wonder: Why do we fear honoring the divine within us? The capacity for greatness, for having an impact, for shaping and co-creating with the universe? *Who me?* we ask. *Who am I to make a difference?*

Mountain Woman responds: *Who are you not to?*

Integration

Mountain Woman Ritual: Small Self, Big Self

Take a slow, meditative walk outside and find two stones that speak to you. One of them will represent your smaller, invisible self, and the other, the part of you that is willing to take a stand and to "stand out." Notice the different energies of these two stones.

Next, lie down and hold your smaller stone, curling your body around it. Make yourself into a small ball on the ground. Feel into the energy of being contracted, invisible. Don't judge this feeling. Simply allow that sense of being small and hidden to fill you. When you are clear about the quality of that energy, begin to write in your journal: *When I am in the smaller, contracted place, I feel . . .*

Allow yourself to express all that you sense in this place. What is the wisdom here for you? What have you discovered? What experiences or expectations tend to pull you into smallness?

Staying small, reach out for the stone that represents your courage and your larger self. Start to think about the things that it represents and qualities that you want to bring into your life. Let its energy fill you. As it does, let your body unfurl. How do you feel as you let your desire to be visible, to take a stand, grow into a state of fullness?

Explore what it feels like to be fully expressive and strongly anchored in yourself. Perhaps you feel a need to speak your passion. Perhaps your body feels different, and there's more strength in your spine, and you wish to stand upright. Sense that expanded energy within, and when it fills you, begin to write: *When I am in the larger, expanded place, I feel . . .*

Record all that you feel and sense from this place. What is the wisdom here for you? What have you discovered? What pulls you into largeness?

Stay full and notice every aspect of your posture, the position of your limbs, any warm spots in your body. Then when it feels right, let yourself contract again. Notice any body sensations. And write down any memories or feelings.

The goal of this exercise is to go back and forth between these two energies, learning as much as you can about yourself in your smallness and in your largeness, and then to observe how it feels to switch between the two.

Place the two stones where you can see them or visit them. Keep exploring without judgment. You will always experience a friction between these two sides of yourself. As you spend time with them, you will embrace both aspects of yourself. You will learn to dance with Mountain Woman energy.

I feel a deep sorrow—for how I have taught my daughter to be in this world. While encouraging her to find her unique self and embrace it, I also taught her to subdue it and conform to get by.

—Jacqui

I long to become a woman of granite strength . . . of peaks and valleys where built-up emotions can melt and run off to join the rivers and oceans that feed the forest and evaporate in the deserts.

—Jane

The enormity and strength of Mountain Woman has finally touched my heart and soul, awakening a need within to climb higher, so I can soar with the eagles and come out from the clouds that have been obscuring my view for so long.

—Terri

Emerging as Mountain Woman

A Fully Embodied Mountain Woman

You take command of a room, simply by your presence. Your deep strength and grounded quality draws others into your orbit. They want to lean on you and learn from you because you are a natural leader.

Irritated by those who only dream, you do your best to light a fire in others. You may be found teaching in a school, running a board, organizing a fundraiser. You are first to roll up your sleeves and get to work. *So, what are you going to do about it?* are the words you live by.

You forgo obfuscation for no-bullshit communication. You have no interest in selling yourself, and every interest in being yourself.

You are a maker of things: communities, organizations, and large, generous meals. Love for you is expressed through action.

Passion erupts from you, and you blow hot with lust. Your sexuality is full-on and unabashed. But it can also go dormant when your attention lies elsewhere, and you're engrossed in a project. A neglected lover may even complain it has gone extinct! But if that person stands up to you and demands a fair share of your attention, you will soon rekindle the flame.

At times, a Mountain Woman needs to enter the cave and savor the comfort of obscurity. Her life, in small or big ways, is a public one, because she is fully committed to making a difference. If you follow this path, people will rely on you, and you will have a long to-do list. So recharging is essential. The good news is that you know how to set firm boundaries that allow for this kind of self-care.

Because you don't sugarcoat your words or try to appease others, you won't be liked by everyone. In fact, some will positively dislike your directness and the fact that you don't work at pleasing others. Others will envy your authenticity. Those who have the courage to come close will find in you a deeply loyal friend who will always have their back in a crisis.

A Mountain Woman Caught in the Shadow

Your personal magnetism makes you extremely influential. Others listen to you and follow your lead. If you don't heed the warning signs, this can make you overbearing so that you don't see what others need or make room for their ideas and opinions. Driven by self-will, you may bully rather than persuade and alienate those you most want to draw to your side. You may even push away those who are a little too slow for your taste.

When challenged, you can shut down and become aloof. It's not just that you aren't listening to others, you aren't listening to the deeper whispers of your soul. You can be so busy pushing the rock uphill that you have forgotten why. In the process, you don't just exhaust yourself but all those around you.

In such times, you may lose sight of feminine power—inclusive and supportive—and instead embody the worst of patriarchy. You may become dominating and controlling. But the good news is that it doesn't take you long to realize that you need to take a deep breath, slow down, and come back to your authentic self. You can move out of burnout and overwhelm by realigning with the collective effort, sharing both the burden and the power with others. In this way, you again begin to lift others up.

Mountain Woman and the Planet

You are angry at the state of the world and not afraid to use that fury to fuel your resistance. You are a woman who takes on the Fortune 500 companies, the oil and gas industries, the sleazy politicians. Fearless in your contempt of rotten practices, you are the quintessential whistleblower.

You aren't intimidated by those in authority and so it never occurs to you that you aren't up to the task of taking them on. Whether it's advocating for healthy food in the schools or clean water in your community, giving up is not an option. Life has taught you about tenacity. And one way or another, you will wear down those who stand in your way.

You also possess mountaintop vision, the capacity to see the big picture. Whether working to plant trees, house the homeless, or take care of your family on a shoestring, you recognize that the multiple problems of the world arise out of a dysfunctional and exploitative system. You know that if things are truly going to change, we need to confront the mountains of self-interest that have given us capitalism, colonialism, racism, and patriarchy. When it comes down to it, you, my sister, are a revolutionary.

Some Final Reflections on Mountain Woman

What is Mountain Woman's greatest gift to you?

What aspects of Mountain Woman challenge you the most?

How do you see yourself embodying Mountain Woman's wisdom in the future?

Which areas of your life could most benefit from Mountain Woman's presence?

If you were to fully embrace your Mountain Woman self, what would change?

How will you express thanks to Mountain Woman?

Opening to Grassland Woman

As you descend from the mountains, you carry with you a new vision and a powerful desire to remain true to your rewilded self. The lush valleys of Grassland Woman await you, and your return to her lowlands will mark your homecoming. Here you will find the refreshment to nurture the new life within. Grassland Woman's wide arms reach out to enfold you. She will show you how to integrate your newfound wisdom into your daily life and share your gifts with community. Receiving Grassland Woman's blessings, however, comes with a new set of challenges. But by now, my sister, you carry the strength of the first four archetypes within you.

5

Grassland Woman

Soul of a Grassland Woman

Grassland Woman feeds us and heals us.
She is lover and life-giver.
From her lush flesh, sweet corn and wild orchards spring.
In her abundance, she sings and seeds the world alive.
Songbirds nest in her, wind ruffles her tresses,
her roots run wide and deep.
Reciprocity is her religion,
community her calling.
She is the web and the weaver, Earth and Eros,
receiving each being as kin.
When we come home to her, we know that we belong.

Stage of Initiation: Nurturing the New Life

The Challenge: Finding Common Ground

The Shift: Striving to Thriving

The Way: Reciprocity

Embodied Dimensions: Community, simple pleasures, relationship, ritual, seasonality, resilience, appreciation, sustainability

Guiding Question: How will I find the commitment, courage, and resilience to bring my gifts to the world?

Nurturing the New Life:
The Fifth Initiation

If you travel far enough,
One day you will recognize yourself
Coming down the road to meet you.
And you will say
YES.

—Marion Woodman

Welcome home, my sister. After the highs and lows of your journey, the questions and insights, the commitment and perseverance, you have reached your destination.

Grassland Woman, with her soft lap and waving grasses, greets you as you return. She understands how you have changed and celebrates your journey. In her sun-warmed meadows and lush valleys, you will begin to offer up your sacred gifts.

You might feel that the hard work is over, but homecoming can prove challenging, too. You may wish to turn back if you encounter people and forces that want to tame and shame you. Or you may try to cling to the ecstatic peaks or return to the oceanic intensity of your earlier adventures. It is one thing, after all, to be a Wild Soul Woman alone, in the desert, or on the mountaintop, and quite another to maintain your newfound sense of self amid the daily demands of family and work. And yet, the question remains: If you don't complete the journey, who will benefit?

Reintegrating into community is the ultimate challenge. Some will fear the changes you bring, the light you bear. When you carry the seeds of a more loving and inclusive future, there will always be those who want to shut you out and keep you down. But Grassland Woman will have none of it.

Rooted and radiant, she encourages you to express your newfound wisdom playfully, passionately. She calls you to become the open flower that draws the honeybee, so that more beauty can be brought into the world. By being yourself, you will attract those who respect the soul's unfolding and who work for the good of the whole community.

It is not in the lofty but in the lowly that most of life is lived. In *After the Ecstasy the Laundry,* Buddhist practitioner Jack Kornfield notes that life is comprised of both mundane chores and spiritual adventures. Washing travel-soiled laundry may not be as exciting as the trip itself, but it is an element of it. To hang your clean, mended laundry out to dry on a blustery morning can also be part of your rewilding.

We know that the patriarchy undervalues what is called "woman's work": caregiving, cleaning, cooking. These chores are never finished. But if we overlook the value of this repetitive "feminine" work, it's not just our dreams that we dismiss—it is the stuff of our daily lives. One of the most radical steps you can take as a Grassland Woman, therefore, is to celebrate the cyclical, seasonal work of women. Raising children? Wild work. Caring for elders? Wild work. Tending a garden? Wild work. Founding a company? Wild work. Daily life, whatever form it takes, is not incompatible with wildness; rather, wildness enlivens and refreshes us in our everyday existence. And if we try to live without it, we will tire and fade.

As a Grassland Woman, you delight to nourish and care for that which you love, be it family, community, nature, creative pursuits, causes or whatever wild work draws your nurture. This caring comes directly from your internal sense of freedom. It comes from a place of aliveness deep within your soul. In nourishing, tending, ministering, you are honoring your own values rather than doing what is expected of you. Everyone can sense this.

This is how you shift the field of consciousness. This is how you create the ground out of which new life can spring.

A Place for Our Gifts

The old threads are unraveling,
Get your needles ready.
We are stitching a new quilt
of humanity.

—Julia Myers

While homecoming may seem such a natural thing, this stage is where many a woman gives up on her wild soul and veers off the path. Many of the same responsibilities and expectations that set us on this journey in the first place are still there, urging us to return to our old ways.

At times, it may seem easier to slip back into old habits and outgrown roles, to "disappear" again. But Grassland Woman shows you it is worthwhile to home in on your newfound gifts and make good use of them. West African writer Malidoma Somé tells us, "Without a community you cannot be yourself. The community is where we draw the strength needed to effect changes inside of us." [58]

In Somé's world, one of the essential tasks of community is to help its member reach their full potential. But we in the West rarely have access to this kind of support. So how do we integrate back into community in a way that honors both our newborn selves and the needs of the whole?

There is an image that speaks to me. In *Braiding Sweetgrass*, Robin Wall Kimmerer, biologist and member of the Citizen Potawatomi Nation, describes making baskets. "A basket knows the dual powers of destruction and creation that shape the world. Strands once separated are rewoven into a new whole. The journey of a grass basket is also the journey of a people."[59]

Baskets are made to hold things, like the sacred medicine you are carrying. At the start of your journey, you may have separated from the tribe. Now it is time to weave yourself back into community, so others can receive your gifts. This weaving is a vital aspect of your journey. Without it, your mission is incomplete.

Sweetgrass thrives on the edges between land and water. We, too, must learn to thrive between the mythic and the mundane, the wild and the domesticated. Integration for a Grassland Woman is an organic process. The surface of your life may appear manicured, but you embrace an undergrowth of aliveness and connection.

Even so, weaving our lives together will take time. You can't force it. In fact, Grassland Woman advises you not to rush. Before you come out as a Wild Soul Woman, you must first become intimate with your new self. You must allow the knowing to seep into the roots of your being *before* you proclaim it to the world.

I rarely know what I think until I speak it out loud. Thus, I've found this process to be a particularly trying aspect of the Wild Soul Woman journey. When I first began this work, I didn't want to stop and meditate on each revelation. I wanted to tell everyone about it. To shout each realization from the rooftops! "Don't you know the wounds of the Earth are our wounds?" "Don't you know we have to rewild ourselves first, if we are to rewild the world?" As I poured out my passion at networking events and other gatherings, people plotted their escape. I didn't know how to bring my gifts back to a community. In fact, I didn't know if I even had a community.

Then I started giving workshops and writing about what I had experienced that shook me to my roots. Slowly, steadily, I began to create a life based on my love of nature and the wild soul. And people, at least enough of them, began to stop looking at me as if I were crazy.

It required great courage for you to embark on this journey, and you are different from when you started. You carry sacred medicine as an offering that cannot be ignored. As you arrive in the realm of Grassland Woman, you are ripe and ready to translate your wisdom so that you can make it accessible to others. Your nurturing instinct has been activated and transformed. You are prepared to share your insights and experiences for the benefit of the whole.

This doesn't mean your gifts will always be welcomed with open arms. But if you remain committed, you will find those *niches*, from the French meaning, "to make a nest," where you can make a difference. Plant a garden or start a storytelling circle; volunteer with a non-profit that reflects your values or teach a child to read. Through such acts, you can help to heal the world.

The strength of Grassland Woman resides in her thick network of deeply planted roots, the deeper the better. As we come to know her, we begin to build our own tapestries of connection. This is what enables us to survive and thrive, not only in times of plenty but in times of drought. Grassland Woman calls us bloom in the smallest niches, to put down roots and make connections—even in stony ground.

Signs that Grassland Woman Is Trying to Get Your Attention

A Sense of Completion—You feel that a cycle of transformation is nearing its conclusion.

Desire for Community—You long to be held in a circle of people with whom you can share your experiences and gifts.

A Hankering for Home—You long to plant yourself back in the everydayness of your life and relationships.

Aloneness Fatigue—You are ready for energy and creative collaboration, and the joy that comes from being among other committed people.

Hunger to Belong—You are ready to put down roots and grow your gifts.

Vandana Shiva: Natural Grassland Woman

The Indian scholar and environmental activist Dr. Vandana Shiva goes head-to-head with the largest and most powerful agri-businesses in the world, fighting to ban patented seeds that wreak havoc with biodiversity and impose crushing debts on small farmers. While to many in the environmental movement Vandana Shiva is an eco-warrior, to those in the establishment she is a thorn. The companies pushing genetically modified crops have tried to delegitimize her, questioning her credentials and calling her a fake. But Shiva's message is too powerful to be ignored. Her work preserves heirloom seeds which can be replanted year after year, and which are handed down from one farmer to the next through generations. These seeds have also evolved in relationship to a particular eco-system. Her work has a spiritual force, as well as a scientific basis. And because it touches so many lives, her voice is being heard.

Integration

Ritual: Field of Dreams Day-Long Retreat

Contained within the seed is the germ of a future planet, village, or community. And, as Shiva's story reminds us, how we treat our seeds speaks volumes about who we are. In this exercise, I invite you to nurture your own organic seed, without the interference of the dominating culture.

Here, you are going to create a special seed packet. In this packet you will place your vision—the one vital vision you want to propagate in the world. Yours is not an engineered seed but a genuine one that allows you to grow life from the wild soil of your own being.

Gather a circle of women friends. Bring some art supplies: large envelopes, old magazines, colored pencils, and crayons. Don't forget glue, sparkly pens, bits of fabric—anything that appeals to different members of the group.

Part One: Begin by setting the context for the day, explaining the purpose behind making this seed packet. Invite each woman to introduce herself by saying her name, where she is from, and what drew her to the circle.

Part Two: Spend the morning creating your seed packets.

On the front of an envelope, make a collage or draw an image of the world you dream of seeding. Dream big and don't censor yourself. What does this world look like? What values does it represent? What stands out about your new world?

Plant Your Seeds. On small slips of paper, write the seeds that will need to be planted in order to birth this new world. Some of those seeds might be *love* or *clean water* or *social equality.* Others might be very specific, such as *join my local council* or *advocate for a certain cause* or *create a women's circle.* Don't hold back. Make as many seeds as you wish, then put them into your packet.

On the back of the envelope or packet, write the care instructions. How can you best ensure that your seeds will grow? How will you water them, give them enough sunlight, nurture them? Your instructions might include things like: exercise every day, take a dance class, create a community of support, start blogging about your ideas.

Part Three: After creating your seed packets (don't seal the envelope), break for lunch, then gather in a circle. Allow time for each woman to share her vision for the world, the seeds she is sowing, and how she plans to nurture the seeds moving forward.

Hold each share within a sacred space. Do not comment or offer practical suggestions. Deep emotions will be triggered during this process, some of which may include feelings of inadequacy: *How will this ever come about? Who am I to dream this dream? The problems are so deep, my efforts won't make a difference. What if things keep falling apart? What if my children inherit a chaotic, depleted world?* Prepare the group for this, letting them know that tears are welcome, for they will irrigate the fields you are preparing.

Part Four: To close the circle, take an actual packet of seeds—not the ones you have created—and sow the seeds, as a group. Plant them in a yard or in small individual pots or in whatever patch of soil is suited to receiving them. Then say a blessing over the actual seed packet and all of the created ones.

If it feels right, consider meeting as a group once a month or season to support each other in seeding your visions. Meanwhile, bring your seed packet home and keep it in a special place. At any time, you can add new seeds and new care instructions.

While there is tremendous power in doing this activity as part of a woman's circle, it can also be a beautiful solo activity.

Journal Reflection: The Period of Homecoming

* *I am called to this stage of the journey in order to learn . . .*
* *I know that this is my Grassland Woman time because . . .*
* *At this moment, I fear . . .*
* *At this moment, I am excited by . . .*
* *I hope to emerge as a Grassland Woman with . . .*

In the grassland of my soul, I am home. I am with those I have always known and longed for. I am the body of the Earth, woven in the tapestry of sisterhood, ready to wrap the world together in healing love.

—Laurie Shade-Neff

I know I am where I need to be, I have followed all the signs, I have set my intentions. I know I can contribute to the world with beauty. For now, I am learning and gathering my tools. Planting my seeds, tending my plants. The time will come soon when I will be ready to give what I have to give. Be what I have to be.

—Camille

Belonging

The roots of all living things are tied together.

—Joan Halifax

The feeling that we do not belong is one of the most painful things we can experience. This sense of lostness, or alienation, may have been why you embarked on this journey to begin with. Even now, you may worry that your pull toward authenticity is at odds with being part of a community. But Grassland Woman says, *If you deny who you are in order to fit in, then you will never find your place in the world.*

The profound pain of separation can arise for many reasons and take many forms. The modern world has made loess (wind-blown soil) of us all. We are, in the truest sense of the word, rootless. We have been ripped from the Earth. Untethered, we feel increasingly anxious and stressed. Today, virtual reality eclipses the wisdom of our senses, while endless miles of pavement and expanding wireless networks cut us off from the Earth's magnetic energy.

But you know better. As a Grassland Woman, you understand that you are made of the same matter as the Earth, born from her breath, her belly, and her bounty. Beneath the loamy soil is the soft dissolve of your ancestors. In your lungs, the breath of forests; in your blood, the salty oceans; in your bones, the residue of stars. You cannot *not* belong.

It is one thing to know this intellectually, however, and another to live it. So how do we re-learn the art of belonging? How do we repair our severed bonds to this beautiful and still fertile world?

The root word for religion, *religare*, means "to bind together." Awakening to the spirit of Grassland Woman, we recall the umbilical cord that connects us to the greater body of Earth and Cosmos. And thus, the original binding spirit and true purpose of religion is restored.

Grassland Woman has a different sense of the sacred than the one most of us were raised with. She reminds us that we were never banished from the garden. We were never told not to eat its fruit or to hide our nakedness. In her creation story, woman did not burst forth from the rib of man. She was birthed from the great womb of Earth and Universe. At this stage of your journey, you are not in exile anymore. You are not cast out from the web of creation. You are not a mistake. You are, my sister, my beloved friend, cherished and wanted.

Grassland Woman joyfully welcomes home the prodigal daughter, the adored child of the Earth. The snake and the apple tree, the shivering grasses and the wild blue creeks embrace you as you return to her fold.

If you can grasp this great love, the love that lies at the heart of belonging, then nothing will ever be the same. Old patterns of shame, blame, judging, and comparing lose their potency. You realize that you were never cast out of Eden. That was the wrong story. And it is being righted and rewritten as you are being rewoven into the fabric of the world.

Eighty percent of prairie grasses live underground. Everything that makes you brave and rich with life originates there, too, in this fecund space. Begin by rooting in that tangible reality.

Wherever you find yourself, your roots run long and deep. You are the beloved child of the Earth and a long evolutionary process that has given birth to you. Let your song be one of belonging.

Integration

Grassland Woman Ceremony: Create a Circle of Belonging

If you can, perform this ceremony on a patch of soft earth.

Gather some stones or any other natural objects with which to make a circle, large enough to encircle you. As you step into the circle, allow yourself to feel held by a community.

Sit down and gently focus on your breath. You belong here, as part of this community. Feel the essence of Grassland Woman supporting you, telling you that you are a vital part of the Earth—and that you and your gifts are needed.

Sense how receptive this circle is to what you have to offer. Feel that in your body and heart. And when you are ready, begin to name the gifts you want to share with your community.

Speak each gift out loud. If they are not fully formed, simply name what you sense about them now.

Allow the ground to absorb your gifts, as you also feel them taking root in you. Speak your gifts out loud, feel the body of the Earth take them in. And be sure to take them into your own body, as well, as you acknowledge them.

After you have spoken and let this experience sink in, take out your journal and begin to write, starting with these words, *In this place of belonging I offer you . . .*

After you have finished writing, holding on to the truth of your heart, dismantle the circle, being careful where you place things back. When the circle is no more, except in your own being, say these words.

I am part of this community.

I am needed.

I am ready to give of my gifts.

Journal Reflection: I Am the Body of the Earth

If we care how the Earth is treated, it follows that we must also treat our own bodies in a nurturing and sacred way. If we aren't respecting our bodies, we're not respecting an aspect of the body of the Earth. Take a moment to really think about that. Self-care can open us to caring for other aspects of life on this amazingly beautiful planet. And caring for the planet can also help us understand how important it is to nurture our own bodies. This is a beautiful reciprocity.

For this exploration, choose a special spot that is relatively private and where you feel safe. Then simply lay your body on the Earth. Feel your whole body being held and supported by the ground beneath you. Sense how the Earth is breathing. Feel her temperature, the texture of her skin.

Breathe gently and deeply, relaxing into the Earth. Allow yourself to enter a dreamlike state in which the boundary between your body and the land fades away. Now you are one body, breathing together, feeling together, sensing together. There is no separation. You share one body, one breath, one heartbeat. Stay in this position, as long as it is comfortable.

When you are ready, sit up while thanking the Earth for her love and support. Reach for your journal. Write from this prompt:

> *I commit to caring for the body of the Earth and*
> *my own body by . . .*

Coming Home to Yourself

I am made whole by your life. Each soul,
Each soul completes
Me.

—HAFIZ

A friend and eco-feminist once told me that she believed American women did not feel they belonged to the land because they were relative newcomers and just coming to terms with their own history. In truth, many of us in the West are waking up to the wounds of colonialism and the horrors of genocide and slavery. Confronted with our brutal past, we can struggle to feel part of the land's in-dwelling spirit. And yet, we must find our way back.

When a culture is disconnected from the land, we grow up with the wrong stories. Author and animist Sophie Strand writes, "I am much more interested in ensoilment than ensoulment. I want to have actual roots."[60] Nationalism, so-called "love of country," is mostly devoid of care and concern for the land and for the larger Earth community. We swear allegiance to an abstraction while dismissing the values of those who for millennia lived in intimate and reciprocal kinship with the land. Nationalism pumps us up so that we feel ascendent, all powerful. It forgets that belonging is rooted in humility, from the word *humus*, meaning "earth."

As someone whose lineage includes Irish, English, Scottish, and Romany, and with ancestors who crossed the Atlantic east to west and back again several times, I find it hard to say where I am from. Like many transplanted people, I feel a sense of bifurcation, of having roots in more than one country. I identify with my birthplace in England but also with my chosen home in California. But does this necessarily stop me from belonging? The world, after all, is made of nomads as well as nesters. We aren't all able to remain in one place. Today, with millions forced by war, famine, and climate disruption to seek refuge in foreign lands, many of us are literally out at sea, in search of a home.

The quest for belonging is complicated and, at times, heartbreaking. It haunts us and hits us in our most vulnerable places. But remember, as you complete this journey you have found a home *within yourself.* You have learned that belonging is about more than finding the perfect place to settle, it is about embracing an authentic ground of being. Further, you cannot belong if you don't make yourself vulnerable and share yourself with others, honestly and fully. Finally, belonging won't fall into your lap. It flourishes through the practice of sharing, reaching out, connecting, relating, and loving one another.

A Grassland Woman knows that without the earthworm or the prairie dogs, her own ecological niche would not survive. Every patch of ground has its own community. Every patch of ground offers an opportunity for intimacy; every encounter, a chance for belonging. It takes courage to extend yourself and risk being repelled by some and inconvenienced by others' demands on you. True belonging includes putting up at times with people you sometimes wish would find their belonging elsewhere, or a location that doesn't easily nurture you. And yet, each of us has a place within the larger picture.

I live in Pacheco Valle, a boxed canyon bordered by steep forested hills, north of San Francisco, in a condominium I have shared with my husband for over twenty years. Our neighbors mostly keep to themselves, and we rarely get together to walk or share a meal.

Yet this is a place of many wonders. To enter the valley, you pass a large meadow that harbors deer and songbirds and a seasonal creek that spills down one side like a communion veil. This land is a haven for hawks, bobcat, coyote, and field mice. In spring, it is briefly covered in popsicle-bright California poppies. It also hosts the oldest *midden*, or burial site, 3,000 years old, of the Miwok tribe.

About ten years ago, we learned that the meadow was to be sold. The land was zoned for light commercial usage, and the thought of the meadow being blighted with anonymous shops and parking lots galvanized the community.

But would the owners (the Gannett newspaper company) sell the land to the Pacheco Valle residents? And for what price? And if we could buy it, could we then donate it to Marin Open Space for public use in perpetuity? The challenges were immense, but we got a proposition on the ballot that would allow residents of Pacheco Valle to tax themselves in order to purchase the land. My husband and I went door-to-door garnering support for this measure. We met scores of neighbors. After many months of work, everyone playing their part, we acquired the land, and held our first-ever community party. We had come together to preserve a meadow and its unique place in the ecosystem and in our hearts. Our political affiliations didn't matter—only the longing to keep this piece of land intact.

Like the hawk and coyote who share a meadow, the strands of our stories run together. Together, we bear responsibility for the places we make our home. But here's the thing: The land is not only shaped by us, it also shapes us in return. If we refuse to come together to protect it, then who will we become in the process? What will we lose? How much less resilient will we be? And if we learn to love it and care for it, what then? What can we do together, what can we become together, that sustains and celebrates a circle of belonging that holds us all?

Integration

Journal Reflection: Where Do I Belong?

Write about a place where you felt or feel at home and where you feel most alive. Describe the landscape. Include the human and more-than-human companions who share/d it with you. What is the light like? The colors? The sounds, fragrances, and textures? The flora and fauna? The buildings and the pathways?

Write about this special place using all your senses and most vivid descriptive powers. Begin with these words: *There is a place* . . .

After you've written your piece, reflect on it. Then journal about what you have learned about yourself and what you need to feel at home in the world.

What qualities are essential to you?

What is the emotional tone of the place?

What or who is present?

Joy

We're all attracted to the perfume
of fermenting joy

—Tony Hoagland

When you are in touch with Grassland Woman, you appreciate the things that bind you to the roots of life. Simmering stews, ripening fruit, the gathering of storytellers around the fire. The joyous spirit of Grassland Woman infuses the everyday so that even the neglected nooks and crannies become astonishing, marvelous, like the spontaneous beauty of shared laughter or a murmuration of starlings.

Joy acts as a compass, drawing you toward the people, places, and activities that enchant you. It springs up in the most surprising places—a blue iris in a parking lot, a sudden burst of wild mint on the breeze, or the whoosh of a raven's wings. It is not dependent on luck or circumstance but on listening and being aware of your surroundings. The is how you hone your ability to see and receive the miraculous, wherever it might arise. Grassland Woman fills you with the sunlight of her spirit.

I'm not talking about the easy joy of always walking on the bright side, but about the deep-rooted joy that comes even with suffering and challenge. I'm thinking of children playing in refugee camps, protestors for social justice breaking into song, prisoners who find a small patch of sky that helps them survive the loneliness of their cells, a woman who hears a kind word from a friend after a long day of caretaking. Joy enables us to endure trauma and pain. It is like a meadow that, after a deadly fire, blossoms with colorful coneflowers, poppies, and mallow.

And so, taking our cue from the Earth, we remain open to beauty despite loss, disappointment, and heartbreak. We, too, learn how to bloom again. And as a Grassland Woman, we grow adept at welcoming new life.

Often, it's the small pockets of joy that stand out—that one thrilling moment when love and beauty seize us. In these moments, with Grassland Woman's strength, we say, *I will not be mowed down. The seeds of my joy will keep on flowering, however hard you try to stop me.*

These days we confront a litany of daily horrors on the evening news. But we can face these realities, without succumbing to despair. How? By continually reminding ourselves of what we are grateful for. In this way, we create a habit of heart that inspires joy. A small spurt of personal growth, the flight of a bird, a glimpse of kindness—noticing these things raises our capacity to receive life's blessing.

As author Jay Griffith writes, "Within each of us must be found *energeia*, and the quality of loving life sufficient to rebel against its extinguishing, to say 'never' to the toxic tragedy that brought us here and, instead, seek happiness only when it is ecocratic, made of chlorophyll and birdsong, the laughing generosity of macaques leaping through the trees."[61]

As you cultivate joy, as you flower and unfold your riches and invite others to join you, you come to embody the resilience and radiance of Grassland Woman. You, my sister, are that sunlit meadow.

Integration

Practice: Staying Present to the Myriad Miracles of Life

Sometimes we are so caught up in our own busyness, or trying to get it right, or simply worrying about what happened in the past or might happen in the future, that we forget to embrace the here and now. Much has been written on mindfulness, and it's easy to see why.

If we don't learn how to be present to our lives, we can't receive the present that *is* our life.

So, try this: Go for a walk, alone. Walk slowly, mindfully, allowing a childlike delight to rise in you whenever something along the path brings you pleasure. It can be the smallest flower or fungi, the moss on tree bark, or simply the way the light casts shadows. It can be children playing nearby or your eyes meeting those of a stranger. It can be the kindness of the checkout clerk. Allow a deep inner smile to infuse your being. Become a smile walking. Become a flower of open-faced joy. Allow yourself to dance with life in the present moment.

"There Ain't No Stopping Me Now"

I, a bell awakened,
and what I heard was my whole self
saying and singing what it knew: I can.

—Denise Levertov

The word "angel" comes from the Greek word *angelos,* for "messenger." How can you be that light-filled messenger, bringing joy into a world that is starving for good news? It's not a matter of ignoring the destruction of the environment, the slow but steady erosion of our civil discourse, it's about remembering to celebrate the goodness and the beauty, too. If you tell yourself you shouldn't feel joy, you deprive yourself of something that doesn't just give you pleasure but provides essential support for living in a difficult world. If you deny joy, how will you ever find the energy to keep up the good fight?

Our culture emphasizes the pursuit of happiness, which increasingly feels like the purchase of happiness. But that kind of happiness never lasts because it's dependent on something outside of us—a good job, a beautiful house, a fancy car—that can be snatched away at any moment. It is both shallow and fragile. Joy has deeper roots and a more enduring heart. We cultivate it from within, whatever life throws at us.

In 2020, I was watching the news about a "count the vote" protest outside the Philadelphia Convention Center. Amid the most contentious election in my memory, a crowd of people were dancing to the disco hit "There Ain't No Stopping Me Now." They were there on serious business, to ensure the count of every legitimate vote, but the atmosphere was jubilant. It struck me that activism infused with celebration and great music has always been an unstoppable force. You can't fight hate with hate. Many have tried and it doesn't work. But an open meadow of playful invitation is something no one can resist for long. The organizers of this event sent a text message to all registered voters in Philadelphia inviting them to join "a joyful party."

If we are to support this living, jiving planet, we need people who are willing to dance, sing, gather boisterously, boogie down. Celebration and ritual will feed you—and feed the soil—on the long road ahead. It will remind you that more than anything, the world needs people who are unafraid to live wholeheartedly, joyfully, no matter what.

Joy can break through even when we contemplate endings—the end of beauty, the withering of the rose, or the approach of the end of our lives.

In her poem "What the Gardener Knows," Kay Adams says:

Everything dies.
Before it dies, most everything blooms.
Consider the seed. Really. Think about it.
White flowers glow in moonlight.

This poem speaks to the understanding that we are all going to die, but we get to blossom first. We get to glow in the moonlight. We get to add our beauty to the world.

Tania Maree Giordana is founder of NourishNYC, an organization that began by supporting Black Lives Matter protestors with first aid kits, food, and water. Now she helps people to find housing, clothing, even find a friend. Tania came to this work after being sexually assaulted. All she wanted was a space to go where people would understand what she had experienced and where she could be happy for a time. In other words, at the very heart of NourishNYC is an idea that we all need spaces where we can move beyond our marginality and trauma to remember joy.

To me, this is the essence of Grassland Woman. In a world that may seem increasingly harsh and hostile, we need to put this experience of peace and celebration front and center. Indeed, it is a matter of some urgency. When we elevate joy to its rightful place, we make different decisions. How can we destroy a local park if we believe in children having a place to play? How can we be angry all the time if we savor celebration? How can we stand by at the loss of so much nature if we see its beauty as vital to our sense of wellbeing?

At a conference on healing and nature, a group of teenagers asked me if I thought spending too much time online could lead to more teen suicides. The question was unsettling, and I wanted to answer it to the best of my ability. After a moment, I said that I didn't have the data to prove it, but I knew this: If you spend hours each day staring at a screen, this will not make you happy. If you spend hours each day, with your friends, outdoors as much as possible, interacting with each other and the natural world, you will have a chance, a real chance, of true happiness.

When I think about these past forty years of my sobriety, I believe what has saved me is my desire to never again fall into a pit of despair. I consciously choose joy. And I have done so in the darkest times of my life, when a man I was madly in love with broke up with me, when I found out I couldn't have children, when my brother died suddenly of a heart attack, when I was struggling to establish my Wild Soul work.

Those times, as any addict will tell you, are moments when picking up your addiction again is all too real. The black hole is always there, patiently waiting. Joy for me has never been a luxury; it is an imperative. And I reconnect with it, every time I am outside, even in a small city park or walking around the block. There is something about moving through the landscape, a feeling of loving life, inhaling the green scented air, feeling the wind, as the grasses must as they sway on a windy day, riffling my hair. Out of doors, I feel my own vitality, which may just be another word for joy.

At this point in your journey, a seed has been planted in your heart, a deep commitment to live in grace and gratitude. You may be tired of the negativity and the naysayers and like me, you may dream of a future surrounded by friends and family, great music, lots of poetry, good food, and wild beauty. So, I ask you: If we don't fight for the right to experience joy, what are we fighting for?

To the uninitiated, a meadow is nothing marvelous. But you know it as a miracle of harmony, every form of life working together, nothing left out, every being needed. This deep magic is ours to experience every day. When you are tired and your heart is breaking, you step outside in the early morning, the air ribboned with soft light. The grasses, still damp with dew, caress your feet. And you feel the seeds you have planted throughout this journey stirring. In this moment, you know that because you have gone deep into the loam of your being and have tended to your true self, whatever else the future holds, you will flower.

Barbara Sarnecka's Story: Toasting Rejection

When you try to live as a Wild Soul Woman in a de-wilded society, it is inevitable that you will meet with rejection. So how can you turn rejection into resilience?

Barbara Sarnecka, a social sciences professor at UC Irvine knows that for most of us today, rejection is par for the course. Academics constantly have to submit grant applications, papers for journals, and topics for conferences, and ninety percent of the time they meet with rejection. There are similar hurdles for those who want to make it in the arts or business worlds.

This process of repeated rejection can feel lonely and shaming. But Sarnecka has turned rejection on its head, making it a cause for celebration.

Instead of hiding from rejection, her students are taught to celebrate it. She compiles her students' rejections from grad schools, internships, potential employers, grants, and conferences and adds them to a Google Doc. When they reach one hundred, she throws a party for the students.

No longer fearing rejection, her students apply for many more opportunities. They're emboldened. After all, if rejected, they're closer to their next party. Barbara describes the whole process as energizing. Joyful. And because rejection isn't feared, her students and colleagues continually put themselves out there and rack up more successes.[62]

This is a Grassland Woman's perspective: *Keep composting your rejections until they bloom into celebration.* When we aren't afraid of rejection, when we acknowledge that much of life is about hearing *no* before we come to the big *yes*, we learn to roll with our disappointments and see them as an organic phase of life, knowing in the end that our dreams will come to fruition.

Integration

Ritual: Start Your Own Rejection Celebration Community

Make a time to come together with your sisters and learn to celebrate each other's disappointments and rejections. The point of this exercise isn't to trivialize disappointment, but to make it food for growth. Learning to accept and even celebrate failure is key to resilience. If you're going to be true to yourself, you will meet all kinds of pushback. Invite your sisters to come and share those times and cheer each other on.

Spend the first ten or twenty minutes in quiet meditation of things you have attempted, but failed at: being that perfect parent, getting a promotion, making a grade, completing a project, starting a business, filling a workshop, organizing a protest. Then give each woman in the circle a set amount of time, perhaps five to ten minutes, to share her frustrations and perceived failures. As she finishes speaking, follow up with the words, *You are brave, you are unstoppable, you are getting closer.* Say them as a mantra, over and over, until you feel that she has heard you. Then turn to the next woman.

After everyone has shared, release "rejection" energy by dancing or singing. Invite laughter and silliness. Love each other for your courage. Delight in how brave you all are. How persistent. How truly unstoppable.

In the grasslands of my soul I dance, naked and free, hair waving in the breeze. As I sway and move with the grass, undulating in the breeze, we are one with the breath of the wind, the spirit that unites us and roots us in the earth. Round and round I dance, rooting myself in the womb of the earth to be birthed anew with seeds of healing.

—Eileen

I feel like a beautiful prairie flower, blowing in the wind. I am colorful, delicate, yet strong. Connected to the winds, rooted in the ground, I stand taller than the grass, I come out for the world to see. I fear nothing, I don't have to do anything, I just am.

—Tonya

I am nervous, excited, humbled, and honored. I've never felt the joy of community so deeply. This gives me so much hope for our Earth tribe. This sisterhood is the roots that have awakened me fully, and I am full of gratitude.

—Laurie

The Challenge: Finding Common Ground

She's at the edge of the great plains.
Wise to openness, she finds it a familiar place.

—Margaret Hasse

When we reengage with the world, we will find ourselves in close communion with some and outright conflict with others. Relationships challenge us. There are bound to be differences of opinions, disagreements, times when you fail to see the needs of other people and they fail to see yours. That's not to mention the quality of attention that's required to truly consider the well-being of other life forms. The world, after all, is comprised of many perspectives, not one monolithic point of view. Life is a multivalent, multi-storied event.

Grassland Woman represents the open field where we all can gather. If, in our pride or our privilege, we view ourselves as separate, we will not join the group and flourish. Grassland Woman knows that life thrives through communion and community.

With the help of Grassland Woman, you discover a web of symbiotic relationships: The relationship of fungus to the roots of the grasses, the bee to the flower, the wind to the spore. Our own creativity and generativity springs from such partnerships between the muse and artist, between two lovers or friends.

There can be no growth without connection. It is through contact that we are touched, transformed.

Like seeds borne on the wind, a Grassland Woman travels into the center of life. While society separates us with borders and boundaries, she is boundless in her affinities. For her, plants, animals, soil, and strangers are all kin.

Sophie Strand asserts, "I am melting into another story. A bigger story. A wider cast of characters."[63] This is what happens when you become an integral part of the Earth community. Diversity becomes your divinity. Everything and everyone has its purpose and place.

Through your willingness to be in contact with this wild current of exchange, the larger intelligence of life, you receive the support, energy, and inspiration you need to keep evolving. Grassland Woman asks: *What relationships will allow you to blossom, season after season?*

A Grassland Woman understands that her lessons will bear fruit when she takes her place in the heart of the creation, with a host of blooming, buzzing, chirping, squiggling creatures.

Dancing Together in the Fields

Restoring land without restoring relationship is an empty exercise.
It is relationship that will endure and relationship that will
sustain the restored land.

—Robin Wall Kimmerer

What saddens me is that with each passing year, we seem to be less able to dance and tussle together in the fields. Our inability to make peace with one another is distressing. This "divide and conquer culture"

is increasingly polarizing and exhausting. The notion of Earth as a commons is lost to us, and so is our appreciation for our human and other-than-human communities.

In our culture, openness often signifies economic opportunity. Every wide-open stretch of land risks being turned into suburban housing tracts or monoculture farms. What does this imply about our own openness? How can we be comfortable standing up for what we believe in, in a world that divides and exploits? What will it take to put our fear aside and remain open to our longing for community, communion, collaboration? Grassland Woman can be our ally, for she knows these qualities of relating are a woman's natural genius.

It is by remaining engaged and cultivating new partners and alliances that we can bring our vision to life. When we support each other, we create fertile ground for new ideas to take hold. Female friendship overcomes the barriers that would keep us back and relegate us to insignificance. We are simply stronger when we work together. Alicia Garza, co-founder of The Black Lives Matter Global Network puts it this way, "Figure out what you really care about. Find other people who care about the same things that you do. Join them. And once you do, keep bringing other people along with you."[64]

Grassland Woman knows that many of us are hurting because we feel so incredibly alone. It's as if we are all backed into our own corners, shouting at each other, with no sense of common purpose or connection. Social media is mostly anti-social. Likes and swipes can never replace a hug or warm embrace. We need real connections—and the capacity to disagree and still work together. I have a best friend from my youth with whom I argue about almost everything, but we love each other and soften each other's edges. We each grow in this relationship precisely because we don't think alike. Our robust exchanges aerate and turn the soil and keep our conversation and our relationship always fresh.

In our hearts and in our homes, in our houses of worship and our town halls, we need to make space for people to come together, across divides, to talk and interact. We don't need another fundamental, "my-way-or-the-highway" philosophy, we need to mix and mingle, to try to understand each other so we can tend our patches of common ground, however small or scattered they might be.

The key is empathy. I realized this in a profound way when I was a panelist for "Art and Healing: Words that Hurt, Words that Heal" at the Conference of World Affairs in Boulder, Colorado, just before the 2016 election. The U.S. was in tatters. So many of us were angry and afraid, closed off to one another's points of view. This division wasn't just along party lines; we were all furious at different factions within our own parties. The tension in the room was palpable.

One of the panelists, Athena Edmonds, a poet and advocate for LGBTQ youth, read aloud the heart-wrenching poems she wrote while her trans child, little more than a toddler, fought fiercely and unequivocally for the right to be a boy. "He asked me if his hair was pretty, his eyelashes. 'Then get rid of them,' he said."

A woman stood up and came toward the stage to ask a question. She had a son, she said, who was homosexual. The word seemed to stick in her throat. She wanted help to change her child's orientation, to make him normal. To send him to conversion therapy. "People can change, can't they?" Her eyes pleaded for an answer. For absolution.

I could sense the sigh emanating from Athena's body. The sadness. "I knew a nine-year-old boy," she told the woman, "who tried to commit suicide because he was trapped in a girl's body. Nine years old and he wanted to die."

The woman at the microphone then admits that what she is saying is unpopular. And she is right. Boulder is a progressive community. She returns to her seat on legs as wobbly as a young fawn's. Yet her question has been received, and she has been brave enough to ask it.

A reverent silence ensues, so powerful that it appears to shimmer like the light from the windows of the Old Chapel where this session is being held.

"This is what Rumi is talking about," I say, referring to a poem I had read earlier that begins:

Out beyond ideas of wrongdoing and rightdoing,
there is a field. I'll meet you there.[65]

"The field is a place to begin the difficult and essential conversations," I add. "To realize that whether we like it or not, we are in this together. All voices matter. And if they go unheard, then they will poison the ground."

I let Rumi's words sink deep. Many of us are crying. As the woman who worried about her gay son sits there trembling, the woman beside her places a hand on her shoulder. And I sense this moment holds the opportunity for something new. Boundaries are dissolving, every person is engaged in this crazy-hard task of staying open, trying to find common ground.

A few days later, Athena calls me, "I don't understand it, but there was magic in that room." Yes, I think. Even now, in this broken and divided world, there is a field.

Integration

Practice: Bringing People Together

Invite neighbors over for a potluck. Throw a block party. Or take an evening walk with your neighbors. Covid brought our social lives and even small, daily interactions to a standstill. And we have no idea what other variants or viruses will arise in the future. What we can know is that many have felt almost unbearably alone during this time and may be struggling to reemerge and reconnect. What if you were to include even those you don't know well or sometimes find yourself avoiding?

As you gather, practice empathy and curiosity. Listen deeply. Set judgment to one side. Allow people to tell their stories and share about themselves. Try and include everyone. Don't have any expectations about what the gathering should or shouldn't be. Just allow it to happen. Afterwards, ask yourself:

How do I feel?

What happened?

Did we find any common ground?

If I continued to open myself to others, what might change?

Journal Reflection: Not So Different After All

Wolves share about eighty four percent of the same DNA as humans, slugs around seventy percent, trees fifty percent. The idea that we are separate from the rest of nature is simply an illusion. The following exercise has you explore connections to different "beings," including the human variety.

Begin by making a list of ten things you love in nature: anything from bears to trees.

Then another list, this time naming ten things that frighten or repel you in nature, anything from thunderstorms to hornets.

For each, write a simple sentence or two, beginning with this sentence stem:

I am like the [fill in the blank] *because . . .*

After you have read through them, what do you notice? What surprises you?

Next, think of three people in the world you admire and three you clash with, and follow the same pattern as above.

I am like [name of person] *because . . .*

After you have read through your responses, what do you notice? What surprises you?

As a Grassland Woman, I want to express my joy at being totally in sync with my community at last, surrounded by so many consciousnesses, it comes out like a dance, a spin and I can feel why the nature spirits are spinning in spirals of energy. How else could you be in such majesty?

—Suzi

My being used to be a hermit, sometimes shunned by family and friends and society, it is with trepidation and self-doubt I enter the idea—no, the reality—of sisterhood.

—Tonya

The Shift: Striving to Thriving

My mission in life is not merely to survive, but to thrive;
and to do so with some passion, some compassion,
some humor, and some style.

—Maya Angelou

Even the most committed activists burn out if they don't take time for self-renewal. Grassland Woman reminds us to respect our natural rhythms, to honor our cycles and seasons, to stop pushing and start deeply listening to the needs of our own bodies and psyches. She insists that we learn when to lay fallow, when to flower, when to reap the bounty of life.

At this point in your journey, your ego has softened. Like a field of rustling grasses, you bend to the winds. You realize you are one part of a harmonious eco-system in which your only task is to be your authentic self.

What have you got to show for your adventures? demands a mechanistic society that tells you to push on at full throttle. If you are naturally a go-getter, Grassland Woman will not try to slow you down. She will, however, call your attention to what is happening under the ground, to the web of nurturing connections that make you strong.

Grassland Woman evolved from barren rock, and over the ages earthworms and fungi and bacteria gave her a rich, loamy soil. As a Wild Soul Woman, you are also being challenged to build your soil. How? By allowing your newfound dreams and discoveries to work upon you. By slowing down you allow time to establish a generative foundation—one that makes it possible for new life to take hold.

Integration is a sacred process. Grassland Woman requires you to open your soul in the way a meadow opens it heart to sun, rain, and air. To receive the blessings of your journey, you gradually draw your raw insights and experiences deep into your cells, until they become part of your entire organism. Just as the processes of photosynthesis, metabolism, and decomposition work to transform, recombine, and knit together different forms of life, so your own transformation now supports you.

This process of transformation has already begun. You don't have to figure it out. You can sink your roots in the rich soil that has already formed underneath you. In every moment, you are being nurtured and nourished by the ground beneath your feet. Your unconscious has been reshaped, and you are now inclined to bloom according to your own seasons and inclinations.

This is Grassland Woman's gift.

When you listen to her, you realize that you are just where you need to be. Everything is within you.

Flourishing Naturally

We have to dare to be ourselves,
however frightening or strange that self may prove to be.

—MAY SARTON.

When we embrace Grassland Woman, no matter what our age, we come into maturity. Now we claim our essential self and acknowledge who we truly are. No longer seeking to compete or to compare ourselves to others, we have a new confidence. The era of trying to fit in through fixing ourselves is over! Our authenticity draws people to us.

After facilitating creative writing and poetry groups for many years, I can tell you that there is nothing more thrilling, or surprising, than authenticity. Most have us have been drilled in English class to pay attention to our syntax, spelling, and the logic of a sentence. When we try to sound literary or profound, we often end up mimicking others and lose the raw energy of our own creation.

You don't have to know all the rules or read piles of books. There isn't a class for authenticity. But there is a condition: You have to trust you have a unique voice that will sing true if you let it free.

Grassland Woman reminds us that we are part of a thriving world in which we join the celebratory song of meadowlarks and cicadas. She wants us to experience *veriditas*—vitality, fecundity, lushness. For the medieval mystic Hildegard von Bingen, *veriditas* was the intrinsic power that allows us all to thrive. As wildflowers flourish without synthetic fertilizers even in the roughest, rockiest ground, so, too, we have learned to bloom despite our limitations—or what we once perceived as lack.

A wonderful example of this "greening of the human spirit" can be found in Isabella Tree's book *Wilding*, set on a 13,500-acre farm in West Sussex that has been in her husband's family for generations. She tells us that the local dialect has over thirty words for mud, from *clodgy* to *gubber*. That mud forms thick sludge in winter and bakes hard in summer, making it hard to eke a living from the land.

By the time she and her husband inherited the property in 1985, industrialized farming practices were the norm, and it was hard for individual families to make a living. Isabella and her husband invested in expensive equipment and for a while produced artisan ice cream, but to no avail. The unyielding land could not support the cows and had nothing more to give.

This isn't a story about battling the elements; in fact, it's just the opposite. Stepping back from day-to-day micro-management, the couple learned more about the land. And the rewilding of their farm began. The question they asked themselves is this: *If we gave the land space and opportunity to express itself, what would it look like?*

Isabella and her husband spent several years studying alternative farming methods and cultivating a deeper intimacy with their surroundings. Humility is essential to this process. Relinquishing control and expectations, they let the land speak to them, showing them how they could support it and allow it to regenerate and become, once more, its lush and beneficent self.

Today, the farm thrives. Animals graze freely, fertilizing and aerating the soil. Returned to the wild, plants proliferate—and a whole new ecosystem takes hold. There are no internal fences and no predator controls.

Every year the land becomes increasingly more alive. Thorny bushes provide natural protection for oak trees and other seedlings. Other trees anchor the soil with their intricate web of roots. The bushes harbor nightingales, once on the brink of extinction. Their song celebrates the earth, brought back to life.

This is the message of Grassland Woman. She is asking you to rewild yourself—to respect your own natural abilities and inclinations. To be deeply curious about who you are on a soul level. She urges you to free yourself and be yourself.

What people and conditions do you need to prosper? What activity comes effortlessly to you? What brings you joy? What makes you come alive? Like Isabella and her husband, you will need to test what works and what doesn't. You will need to continually revise. At first, you may sputter and stutter and sometimes feel a little foolish. But be gentle—and patient—with yourself. It is never easy to go against the grain of conventional wisdom. But it is so much harder and more exhausting if you don't.

When we stop listening to the Earth, we put her through the worse kind of abuses. We dam her rivers, uproot her forests, rape her soil, mine her mountains, poison her waters, and cover her with chemicals, forcing her to produce according to our will.

When we stop listening to our own bodies and psyches, we do the same to ourselves. We poison our ground of being, dam our creativity, deplete our souls. It has to stop here and now, my sisters, with each of us working together as cross-pollinators to spread beauty as far afield as we can. Our task is to help each other bloom naturally, wherever we find ourselves, and thus, enable the whole community of life to thrive.

Integration

Journal Reflection: What Comes Naturally to You?

Find an area in nature that is open, like a field. This can be a corner of a local park or your own garden. Observe your surroundings quietly and allow yourself to contemplate something that attracts your interest. It can be a patch of sky, a bird, a small burrowing animal.

Now focus for a while on just this form of life. When you're ready, spend about ten minutes writing a short sketch, describing everything you can about it: shape, aroma, texture, sound, and anything else that captures your imagination.

When you are done writing, read your description through, and ask yourself:

What is this being naturally good at that I am also naturally good at? How are we alike?

Ritual: The Sacred Art of Composting

"I want to tell people that healing isn't about completion.
And it isn't about lightness. It's about the mixing bowl where
nothing is exiled, everything is included. In order to grow a garden,
you need manure. You need compost. In order to heal the soil,
you don't clean it, you add to it: fungi, ferment, bacteria, woodchip . . ."

—SOPHIE STRAND

Composting is an important way to contribute to soil-making. It is a human-tended version of the natural process of decay and transformation and a reminder that you need to create good soil for dreams to grow. Instead of throwing out your food waste or plant trimmings, put them on the compost pile or in your compost bin and wait. Occasionally turn if necessary. Use the rich compost either in your own garden or donate to someone else's.

Composting is a powerful reminder that when we bring different organic beings together and let the magic happen, we create nutrient-rich material that enriches the health of the soil. And what could be more sacred than that?

Every time you add to your compost pile, contemplate its power to renew the earth, and bless it with these words:

I release my sense of separation back to the Earth,
so that she can take it into herself,
and make of it something beautiful.
I honor the natural cycle of death, decay, and regeneration.
I thank Earth for teaching me
all things can be transformed.
All things can become ground for new life.

I see a vast open plain teeming with animals of all kinds living alongside each other contentedly. There is enough earth, food and water for everyone's needs, there is no need to compete with each other.

—Maura

I love being amongst the grasses swaying with the wind, a multitude of wildflowers popping here and there, a habitat for so many Beings . . . simplicity, safety . . .

—Pru

The Way: Reciprocity

This is the world I want to live in.
The shared world.

—Naomi Shihab Nye

Grassland Woman's abundance is predicated on reciprocity. Every one of her denizens is responsible for the well-being of the whole. Grasshoppers drop a portion of each leaf they eat to give back to the earth. Ants form underground passages that replenish the soil by carrying mineral-rich clay to the surface. When the sun delivers surplus energy, the plant community uses it to create and store the nutrients that build the soil.

Reciprocity is as natural as breathing. It's an energy, a way of being that is often invisible but flows between things. It is the antithesis of an ego-centered culture that takes without thought of giving back. Grassland Woman recognizes that it takes her helpers thousands of years to build up rich soil, but only a few years to destroy it.

Walk barefoot in a field of grasses, feel the soft duff at your feet, and know that you are supported by the generosity of the whole Earth community. In such moments you sense the daily exchange at the heart of life—a natural give and take. When we view ourselves as one with the Earth, we restore an essential balance. We are more easily satisfied, and we no longer drive our own bodies to the brink of exhaustion. In short, we realize it doesn't take much to turn a grassland into desert.

We develop reciprocity by asking different questions. Rather than *What's in it for me?* we say, *How can I work with others to create a stronger and more abundant whole?*

Reciprocity is an antidote to nervous and narcissistic scarcity thinking. Afraid that we won't get our fair share, we grab what we can. The patriarchy fears Grassland Woman because she represents a completely different understanding of how the world works. She knows that we thrive when we look out for each other instead of looking out only for ourselves. She is the voice of compassion and generosity. And in her, we discover that the more we freely contribute of our true gifts, the more we add to the generosity of the whole.

To become a Grassland Woman, lift your skirts and dance into the open fields. Remember that you are supported and loved by multitudes, and you return that love in manifold and miraculous ways.

I will live as if I loved myself,
I will gather the skirts of my ancestors,
we will work this land together,
we will sew the future into being.

—Chantek Mary McNeilage

Giving Back through Gratitude

Walking. I am listening to a deeper way.
Suddenly all my ancestors are behind me.
Be still, they say. Watch and listen.
You are the result of the love of thousands.

—LINDA HOGAN

What would it be like if everyone walked through the world singing her praises?

Whenever I go outside, I talk to the trees around me. And the birds. And the fungi. And the grasses. I thank them for their beauty and their presence. I also read nature poetry out loud and out of doors, because the natural world is the mother of all language. I like to think of the grasses bending their ears to the words of Mary Oliver or Joy Harjo. As I share their poems of praise, it is as if the soft singing of the grasses joins with my voice and the words of the poets in a choir of celebration.

Praise, I have come to believe, is an essential antidote to privilege and entitlement, a feeling that the world owes us something. It returns us to a state of gratitude. It is also the final step in a shift of perspective necessary to becoming a fully-fledged Wild Soul Woman.

With Grassland Woman, you understand that a generosity of spirit runs through life. It doesn't mean that life isn't hard at times or that you don't ever feel despair. It *does* mean that you were born into this moment for a reason. You have something to give. And life—people, places, ideas—ever generative, will give back to you in return. It's not always an equal balance. Some days are a lot better than others. But when we seek the praiseworthy in life, rather than focusing only on what is wrong, something extraordinary happens: we grow in love for our world and for ourselves. We give more and at the same time, we receive more. We become part of a glorious cycle of magnanimity.

Sara Steffey McQueen, who trained with me as a Wild Soul Woman facilitator, wrote in a workshop, "As a wildflower meadow offers abundant variety, I see my gifts through the eyes of my participants as we gather in a circle. I see how I have touched others, how my offerings resonate with them. I look out at this beautiful meadow and feel my horizons expanding."

For a Grassland Woman, giving is a feedback loop. As we offer our gifts, our community responds in kind. As we realize we are making a difference, we long to give more. This is a very different kind of relationship. We aren't giving out of obligation or for some quid pro quo. We are simply trusting that when we offer ourselves to life, life will support us in return.

When we gift our spirits and bodies the same loving care, we begin to find sources of energy and joy that we have yet to imagine. When we feel the Earth's love for us, and ours for her, we begin to be more grateful for our own existence. As Wild Soul Women, we understand that we are not a body to be controlled, nipped, tucked, or shamed. We are part of the miracle of life, and as such, we deserve to be celebrated and praised. At every moment we are engaged in a passionate love affair with the world in which we feel loved in return. This is true abundance: a fertility of spirit that bears the fruit of gladness.

Early one morning, before guiding a group of women through the Grassland Woman stage of their journey, I visited a favorite meadow. I was seeking to ground myself before the session. I took off my shoes and wriggled my toes deep into the dew-soaked grasses. I imagined roots extending from the soles of my feet into the earth, carrying my love and gratitude into the soil. My feet tingled, and I felt a shiver of electricity.

I then did something I had never dared to do before: I allowed Earth to love me back. I felt her Eros rising from the ground and flowing into me, until my feet and my belly felt warm, and her energy surged through my body and every part of me shook with her loving presence.

When I opened my eyes, a young buck stood about six feet away, his black nose quivering, a powerful energy vibrating between us. I was so aglow with radiance, I swear he would have mounted me if I hadn't started to move!

In that moment something shifted for me. I realized that for a Grassland Woman, it is as important to receive as it is to give—to welcome the pleasures of life, the sweet sensual joys of living in a world that also returns our affections, in often deeply erotic ways. This is a radical shift for women, who are much more comfortable with giving love than embracing it.

Reciprocity means taking in all the gifts, all the joy, all the learning and wisdom and love, until you understand at a core level that you are beloved, simply because you are.

Reciprocity is the fertile soil for a richly satisfying inner life. It allows you to contribute while remaining abundantly alive and energetic. It will help you to heal and become whole. And in that, my sisters, lies the salvation of the world.

Integration

Practice: Take a Praise Walk

Go to a place in nature that you love. If it is a place that is comfortable to walk barefoot, even better. Walk slowly and mindfully. Praise everything that you see around you, from the grasses to the birds, right down to the smallest stone. Allow your gratitude to pour out of you.

When you are ready, write down everything you remember about the experience. Afterwards, read your praise piece out loud to the landscape. Feel how she responds to being loved.

Journal Reflection: The Gift That Is You

Reciprocity goes in two directions; it's as much about receiving as it is about giving. Ask yourself these two key questions:

What does the world need?

What do I long to give?

Then contemplate at length the answer to this question:

Where do my gifts meet the needs of the world?

When you have the answer, you have at the very least, a way of being of profound service while using the innate talents and abilities that make you, you!

Tall blades of golden grass blow gently around me. I hear the message, *Just as the sun rises, so shall you, as you honor your wild self and be. Know and honor your freedom.*

—Deb

Grassland Woman guided me through long golden grasses; we gathered seeds in the palms of our hands. It felt like the belly of the earth, our woman bellies ripening in soft winds. There is work to do, healing to share.

—Laura

Emerging as Grassland Woman

A Fully Embodied Grassland Woman

You are a woman whose roots run wide and deep into the community. Your joy is in connection and collaboration, in knowing the folks in your neighborhood, in being part of an organization or movement, an eco-system, a particular place. You are aware of the gifts of exchange that living in community brings.

Generous in your support of others, you are the antithesis of competitive. You know that when any one woman seeds her beauty in the world, she adds to the whole by creating more seeds and thus more opportunities for everyone to flourish. Your wholehearted joy in others' successes makes you the first person someone wants to share their good news with. Equally, your compassion is a soft lap for those in need of comfort.

You have a "loaves and fishes" genius. Somehow you always have enough to feed the hungry, to shelter the heartsore, to include everyone in the circle of your care. The more diverse, the merrier. No one is left out.

You add beauty to the world, often in small ways. You may love to garden, to make things from scratch: clothes, baskets, pots, meals. Equally, you care less than most about appearing presentable. *Come as you are* is your motto. Authenticity is what you care about. And this is true in romantic relationships as well. Here, the ease and comfort you have with your own body makes a place for sensual, earthy pleasure, free of self-judgment or anxieties about performance.

Your deep love of others keeps you going and lifts you up. You have a great capacity for giving, especially when you know you are making a difference. You cultivate the good in others, delighting in their joy and blossoming. In your company, others are inspired to be their best selves.

A Grassland Woman Caught in the Shadow

A Grassland Woman who refuses to rest is a woman running toward her shadow. If you constantly do and give and never stop, you won't remain generative. Out of touch with your own natural rhythms, you will fall out of alignment with nature. Exhaustion will follow.

Seasons come and go, spring follows winter, and you are tasked as a Grassland Woman with recognizing that there are times to go underground and nourish your roots. Then you will spring into life and sap will sing through your body once again. But this rhythm is not yours to control.

If you don't take time to fill up with love and life, you will become a hungry ghost demanding more attention, possessions, status. The journey you have taken will be pushed back into the unconscious. Thus, it is important to recognize the times when you over-give. If you do too much for someone, you disempower them while depleting yourself. Engaging in collaborative, caring relationships does not mean taking over. If you fall into that trap, then the relationship will fall out of balance, and you will become resentful as your loved ones become dependent.

You need to let your children leave the nest. You need to give space to your friends and loved ones. You need to trust your colleagues and believe that your whole community will support you and carry on your work. Grassland Woman says: *Trust the filament that connects you to others. Remember, they also have plenty to give.*

Grassland Woman and the Planet:

Deeply grounded in the rhythms of nature, you are under no illusion that things are going well for this planet. You see the destruction all around you. You know and understand the butterfly effect: that razing forests in the Amazon has consequences for every corner of the Earth; that if insects disappear, so will much of life on this planet. You understand there is no issue that isn't connected to another, and that social justice is as important as water equity.

The world, as you see it, is in a whole lot of pain. You recognize that we need to open our hearts to each other and the suffering we are causing. You know we can't hide from the things that frighten or hurt us, because we are part of the system. If the Earth is not thriving, there is no place we are safe.

As a Grassland Woman, you align your spirituality with good works. You live the truth of *It takes a village.* Individual success means nothing. Since everything and everyone is connected, those who strive only for personal gain, go against the grain. You live by this truth: We are all in this together.

Thus, you are a powerful voice in uniting different interest groups and agencies and showing people how these larger issues intersect. You understand that the dance of renewal always happens in the creative space where people and organizations discover their shared concerns or interests.

Your ecological sensibility is essential to the world right now. You tear down the fences between special interest groups in favor of collaboration. You refuse to see people as "good" or "evil." You are always seeking dialogue and common ground.

You know that, if we come together, if we stop allowing the powers-that-be to draw us apart, we will be an unstoppable force for good. In this way, you are a new kind of leader, one who sits in a circle of other leaders, with no one more important than another.

As a Grassland Woman you know that we are all sisters, linked by roots that run deep between us.

Some Final Reflections on Grassland Woman

What is Grassland Woman's greatest gift to you?

What aspects of Grassland Woman challenge you the most?

How do you see yourself embodying Grassland Woman's wisdom in the future?

Which areas of your life could most benefit from Grassland Woman's presence?

If you were to fully embrace your Grassland Woman self, what would change?

How will you express thanks to Grassland Woman?

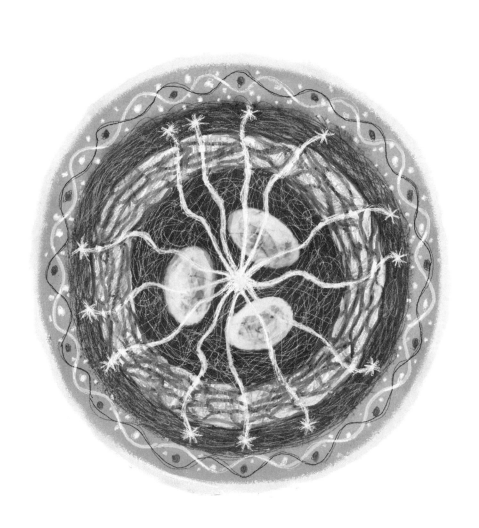

6

Walking the Way of the Wild Soul Woman

The Way of the Wild Soul Woman

Voices raised,
bare feet pounding on naked earth,
we are walking new paths.
we are telling new stories,
we are speaking new truths.
Together, my sisters, we are making a new world.

Desert Woman: Desire for time and space

Forest Woman: Desire to dream and create

Ocean and River Woman: Desire to feel and flow

Mountain Woman: Desire to act and be visible

Grassland Woman: Desire to connect and contribute

Seeking Wholeness

Within my body are all the sacred places of the world . . .
—SARAHA

I am standing by my Wild Soul Woman altar, a rocky outcrop high above my valley with sweeping views of the San Francisco Bay. I come here several times a week to tune into the wisdom of the archetypes, often bringing a challenge or brooding question with me. I turn to the East, tapping into the fiery sun-infused spaciousness of Desert Woman. To the North, and the ancient trees of Forest Woman, inviting darkness and mystery. To the West, where the Pacific surges against the craggy shoreline, considering how my own body flows with the energy of Ocean and River Woman. To the South, toward Mount Tamalpais, where Mountain Woman's message of courage and commitment comes toward me on the breeze. Finally, I look down at the earth beneath my feet, feeling the energy of Grassland Woman, as I root myself in this time and place, and the knowledge that I am connected to the entire Earth community.

One archetype's energy usually surges particularly strongly in my body. This is the one offering the insights I need now. With practice, I have developed an inner compass that points me to where deeper understanding resides. All I have to do is pay attention. In my journal, I write down every thought, feeling, and sensation that comes to me during the ritual. In this way, I glean fresh perspectives and am able to bring what is hidden within my consciousness into the light. I am learning to perceive my life's underlying themes, allowing them to enlighten and empower me.

If the Earth Archetypes are to become your constant guides, you will also want to find or create a sacred space in which you can invoke them, honor them, and learn from them.

———

Participants in my workshops have responded to this task in myriad ways. Some, like me, designate a special place in nature as their altar and visit it regularly. Others create an altar in their home, honoring each archetype with natural objects: a shell, a stone, a pinecone, a plant, a vessel containing water or sand. Some have made collages of all five landscapes. One participant remodeled a portable art box, placing images of the five landscapes on the inner lid. Inside, she stored her journals and pens. Others have covered a simple notebook with pictures of the archetypes, so that the journal itself becomes a sacred space.

When you commit to making a practice of engaging with the Wild Soul Woman Archetypes, magic happens. They will support you, especially in the hard times when you have lost your path.

When the first edition of this book was published, I was under incredible stress. My husband and I were in the process of clearing out our condo in Marin County, California, painting and recarpeting the place before we put it on the market and organized a move to London. Towering piles of boxes and workmen surrounded me as I juggled last-minute book decisions—the cover, the launch date, the final proofing. I ignored the pressures I was under and simply pushed through, clearly in the thrall of Mountain Woman—not realizing that I was living out her shadow, not her strength. At that point, I received a shocking health diagnosis, triggering a series of panic attacks. I couldn't walk—the world pitched and lurched as if I were on a small boat in a stormy sea. I was so certain I was having a stroke that I landed in the emergency room four times. When the panic attacks were at their worst, I retreated to a small space in my head, feeling separate from everyone and everything I loved. For three weeks, I could barely walk across my living room.

As I lay on the sofa, gazing out my window at the oak and bay laurels, watching the woodpeckers and squirrels, and the light spilling through leaves, I began to breathe more easily. Grassland Woman stirred in me and soothed me. I had neglected her call to rest, to restore myself, to ask for help, to lean into community. Now, her tendrils extended into my very soul. The message I kept hearing was this: *It is time to open your heart and feel the love and support that surrounds you.*

I emerged from my health scare and we took our place off the market, deciding to stay rooted where we were. My book launched and was well received. But I couldn't shake my Grassland Woman vision of community. Self-publishing no longer felt like the right option. I had made that decision, in part, from that shadow self, drawing too much on Mountain Woman. This archetype forgets at times that she doesn't always have to do it all herself. Now I yearned for collaboration and connection. This new edition arises from that Grassland Woman nurturing. I believe that in opening myself to her, I attracted just the right publisher and a whole community of helpers.

Recognizing the Shadow

In our yearning to be perfect,
we have mistaken perfection for wholeness.

—Marion Woodman

We can all get caught up in the shadow of an archetype, as I did. We may experience it as a feeling of being stuck, out of balance, or even possessed to the point of madness so that we are unsure how to stop ourselves from acting or thinking in a certain way. Or we may fall in love with ourselves as an ideal form of the archetype and become inflated, believing that we are all loving, all bountiful, all powerful. And that too becomes a cage. For to take care of our entire eco-system, we need to honor all the Earth energies. And that means we must resist over-identifying with any particular one. So how do we break free from the shadow?

One thing you can do is ask if there is an archetype that is driving you to the exclusion of the others. Then, look for solace and strength in a different one. You don't have to be run by any single archetype, and the more you engage with all of them, the more at choice you will be. As well, you will learn how certain archetypes act as counterbalances to others. For example, I've noticed that:

* Desert Woman is balanced out by Ocean and River Woman (more ease and flow) and Grassland Woman (more connection and community).
* Forest Woman, by Mountain Woman (more clarity and action) and Grassland Woman (more extraversion and groundedness).

✳ Ocean and River Woman, by Desert Woman (more solitude and self-sufficiency) and Forest Woman (more interiority and self-awareness).

✳ Mountain Woman, by Ocean and River Woman (more heart and meaning) and Grassland Woman (more community and support).

✳ Grassland Woman, by Desert Woman (more solitude and silence) and Forest Woman (more incubation and reflection).

Over time, you will find your own counterbalances and ways of working with these energies. And know that you are blessed when you can invite them all to play their part in your unfolding. This is the Way of the Wild Soul Woman: fluid, ever-moving, ever-changing. Yes, the shadow will appear. And that's part of the journey. There are aspects of you that you may have long suppressed and that need to come to the surface to be healed. That's just as it should be. We are not aiming for perfection, my sisters, but for rawness, realness, and the realization of the full body and breadth of our astonishingly diverse selves.

Practice: Create Your Own Altar

How will you design your altar? You might want to ask yourself these questions:

✳ *What type of altar (in nature, at home, collage, etc.) will allow me to most avail myself of all the Earth Archetypes?*

✳ *What am I called to create now, knowing I can always change it later?*

✳ *How will the form of my altar inform my vision of the archetypes?*

Once you've journaled your answers, read through them and ask yourself, *What am I committed to creating?* Then simply begin.

Moving Beyond the Heroic Journey

Instead of transcending ourselves,
we must move into ourselves.

—MARION WOODMAN

As I was invited to write an additional chapter for this new edition, I couldn't let go of the idea that there are other ways these archetypes can be accessed. What else might help readers come to know the territory of their wild psyches and see their lives in the context of the bigger stories that carry us all?

As I've noted, the archetypes of the Wild Soul Woman signify a rebirthing journey, from the Barren Worlds of Desert Woman to Nurturing the Newborn Self as Grassland Woman. But they also represent the three stages of the classic heroic journey: Separation, Ordeal, and Return, only from a feminine perspective. Knowing which denotes which, you can more easily discern where you are in your own journey of transformation.

Separation: Desert Woman and Forest Woman. Desert Woman strips away what no longer serves you and severs you from the demands of your daily life. Forest Woman leads you away from the well-trod path and toward your own inner compass. When one or both archetypes awaken in you, you are leaving the old life behind and signing up for something new. This period of separation is often quite internal and sometimes hard for others to see. In separating from the familiar world, you are learning to lean into your own strengths and insights.

The Ordeal: Ocean and River Woman and Mountain Woman. When you sense a rush of fear or excitement, or the sudden urge to reveal your true self to the world, no matter what the cost, you are in the Ordeal stage. The waters of the Earth urge you to surrender to the surging energy of your loving heart, to flow out into the world guided by your passion and purpose. Mountain Woman challenges you to stand up for your deepest values, even when you are afraid or tired or don't feel equal to the task. You are now interacting with others differently, and your internal changes affect your relationships. This transformation isn't just happening within you. It's impacting the world around you.

The Return: Grassland Woman. This archetype marks the ending of your solitary journey and your return to community. This is where the depth and strength of your transformation is tested amid the everyday tasks of life. This stage is all about coming home, only now carrying new medicine, new insights, and a willingness to remain true to your rewilded self amid the world's desire to change you.

Marking the Seasons

Revolution is as unpredictable as an earthquake
and as beautiful as spring.

—Rebecca Solnit

To be attuned to the Earth, is to be attuned to the seasons. And for many a Wild Soul Woman, marking the seasons with rituals is a vital spiritual and ecological practice. Here's how the Earth Archetypes align with the seasons. This information can help you to create your own traditions and provide the focal point for a women's group, should you choose to form one.

* **Late Autumn:** Desert Woman represents a time of endings, when leaves are shed in a fiery burst of color, leaving the branches bare and exposed.

* **Winter:** Forest Woman is associated with the season of hibernation, dreaming, and going inward, honoring the darkness.

* **Spring:** Ocean and River Woman leads us to a quickening, as snow melts, rivers fill, and all things come to life.

* **Summer:** Mountain Woman brings long days where we are filled with the sun's energy and are excited to be actively engaged in projects.

* **Early Autumn:** Grassland Woman celebrates the season of harvest, before winter's grip takes hold, when we reap the gifts of all our hard work.

It is wonderful to take this journey seasonally, honoring these landscapes as part of the cycle of life. You might begin each autumn, with Desert Woman, and then move into the other archetypes as the seasons shift, making a profound annual journey of renewal and rewilding. By moving with the seasons, you are inviting the Wild Soul Woman Archetypes to move through you, never getting stuck or stagnant. Clinging to any one for too long can be, let's face it, too much of a good thing. It would be like living in an endless summer: catastrophic in the long term. So again, this approach allows you to follow a cycle and flow that honors wildness and its need for dynamism.

Naming Your Desires

Our visions begin with our desires.

–Audre Lorde

Another way to get unstuck is to simply name your desires. Depending on what you really want or need in the moment, you will be drawn to a specific archetype. To help you get started, I have named some desires for each archetype below. However, you will have your own, so please feel empowered to make your own list. A daily practice of asking, *What do I desire?* is a way to focus your intention and to strengthen your relationship with the archetypes.

Desert Woman: Desire for time and space

Forest Woman: Desire to dream and create

Ocean and River Woman: Desire to feel and flow

Mountain Woman: Desire to act and be visible

Grassland Woman: Desire to connect and contribute

Shifting the Paradigm, One Metaphor at a Time

You don't see something until you have
the right metaphor to let you perceive it.

—ROBERT STETSON SHAW

Archetypes and metaphors—the very substance with which you have been engaging in over the course of this book—aren't just creative, vivid ways of mapping an inner journey of transformation, they are paradigm shifters. Why? Because archetypes and metaphors have powerful energy. They spawn stories. They invite solutions. And they allow us to engage with new ways of looking at the world and ourselves.

These Earth Archetypes have altered my inner landscapes in extraordinary and powerful ways. But I also want you to know what tangible changes women have made after working with their Wild Soul Woman Archetypes.

A woman who suffered deeply from co-dependency kept trying to get her sister sober while accommodating her demanding and sometimes abusive parents. As she familiarized herself with the archetypes, an image of a mountain kept coming to her. It wasn't a harsh, cold mountain, but one that seemed brave and vulnerable, open to the elements while still standing firm and tall. As she focused on this image, she felt encouraged to set healthy boundaries, and slowly, she learned to stand apart from her family's drama.

Forest Woman directed another woman to the study of eco-psychology. Every time she imagined herself in the forest, she became increasingly curious about where a certain path would lead. She kept walking deeper and deeper along the path into the forest, until she knew, in her heart, and with all her being, that eco-psychology was her way forward. She has just graduated from a three-year certification program.

Just the other day, a woman told me that she wished she had encountered Desert Woman many years ago. She was astonished by how deeply she resonated with the need to "go into the desert" of her own being, and no longer feel the need to perform for others. This remarkable woman had learned to live her life on her terms, others' opinions be damned. But as she contemplated the image of Desert Woman, she felt a profound sense of homecoming. That inner struggle, of *Am I being selfish? Shouldn't I be taking care of . . . ?* dropped away. It was as if she felt full-on permission to live her life in a way that served her soul.

Another woman who felt she'd had "a bottled-up life" told me that she now takes photos of flowing water as often as she can. These images remind her to honor her emotions, and to pay attention to her loving and sensuous heart. Nature photography has helped her to emerge as a storyteller—and the image of water, flowing free, has become a guiding principle.

Many of the women who have awakened to these Earth Archetypes are now writing, painting, dancing, singing, with abandon and joy. With this daily practice of honoring the landscapes, they have become emboldened to take creative risks—and to change the very nature of their lives. One example: a young woman joined her local council after learning about the interwoven roots of the Grassland Woman Archetype. She knows she brings a valuable perspective to her community.

I have witnessed countless times how a shift in metaphor can change a life. And the Earth Archetypes yield thousands of them. Consider the saguaro cactus's self-sufficiency; the rootedness of forests; rivers undammed; mountains standing firm in gale-force winds; the wild grasses holding the soil in place, protecting against erosion.

Every Wild Soul image offers the potential to shun the life-denying metaphors of our present culture: the body as machine, endless growth and the unyielding push for progress, the Age of Enlightenment that decreed the death of matter, the evil of Eve. Ask yourself: Which metaphors hold the possibility of deep awakening? Of profound change? By now, you already know the answer. We need to make a practice of working with Earth's life-giving images and to continue to follow The Way of the Wild Soul Woman. As our inner landscapes transform and flourish, collectively, we will surely change the world.

Journal Reflection: What Metaphors or Images Are Emerging in You?

Find a quiet space, perhaps by your new sacred altar, and allow yourself to relax. As you relax, drifting into a dream-like state, allow any images that come to you to emerge and write about them in your journal.

When you feel ready, read through your list. Which image is strongest in the moment? When you have your image/metaphor, simply ask of it: *What is your message for me?*

Write down everything that you feel, see, sense, or long for.

Then ask, *What will change if I allow this image to guide me?*

Again, journal your answer.

The Personal Is Planetary

Action on behalf of life transforms.

—Robin Wall Kimmerer

This book tells the stories of women who have transformed their worlds because they followed their passions, their roiling rage, their full-on hearts. And that's what we need—not one prescription fits all, but all of us doing our bit, in our weird, wonderful, unique ways, inspired by what we care about. Nature abhors sameness. It also abhors artificiality. Being a Wild Soul Woman is not about conforming or being afraid to speak about our personal experiences. It is about making room for everyone. The more diversity of perspectives, experiences, voices, and visions we are open to, the greater the chance we have of surviving these perilous times and of emerging into a world of inclusivity, reciprocity, and beauty. Instead of relying on one dominant ideology, we will be part of a living, breathing organism—comprised of billions of loving hearts.

A revolution is under way. Earth-conscious, vital, and courageous women from all over the world and all walks of life are finding each other and forming communities. Together, we are evolving a language unhindered by the limitations of patriarchy. We don't speak of domination, competition, and division, but of love, interdependence, and reciprocity. We are building a bridge from the wisdom of our Earth ancestors to the dreams of our descendants. Through new archetypes and metaphors, and thus new stories, we are inspiring a paradigm shift: a re-imagining of a worldview from one filled with despair and heedless destruction to one that honors all beings, human and other-than-human.

Every day the Earth showers us with gifts—and not only those of air, and soil, and plants, and photosynthesis, things we need to physically survive. The Earth also showers us with the gifts of creativity, intellect, connection, beauty, gladness, and wisdom. And we must not hoard those but share them in community. Everything we possess, we owe to being children of this planet. It is time, my sisters, to move forward with open hearts and unflagging hopes. We have so much to offer. Here, now, holding hands, our voices raised, our bare feet pounding on naked earth, we are telling a new story. The Way of the Wild Soul Woman is just beginning.

A Letter to My Readers

Dear Wild Soul Sister,

I sit here on a warm spring morning, thinking about all the women who have taken this wild journey with me. We have traveled far, my sisters, through many landscapes and many challenges. I want to acknowledge your creativity and courage. Your willingness to break free of your chains and shames—not just for yourself, but for the future of all people, and all life, on this amazing Earth.

You have completed your first Wild Soul Woman adventure, but your journey is far from over. Everything in the universe is constantly evolving. And nothing, least of all your wild psyche, is fixed. The Five Earth Archetypes are forever ingrained in your soul and embodied within you as vital aspects of your wholly alive Wild Soul Woman Self. I have been your guide, helping you to get to know them. Now, place your trust in them, and call upon them, as they continue to midwife your wild nature.

As you remain open to these archetypes' powerful energies, you will gain in creativity and resilience, for their strength and wisdom are always accessible. My hope is that you will engage with them as part of your daily life so that they keep enriching your inner world and showing you how to revitalize your relationship with Self, others, and the planet.

Over my many decades of sobriety and years of teaching and writing about the wild soul, I've learned: We matter. What we do matters. Every deed, thought, and word has the potential to plant a seed. We may not live to see the consequences of every action. But we can know that the transformation we long for begins in our own wild souls and our willingness to take another step toward dismantling the cage.

Whatever dream or vision you have emerged with from this journey, you will need a tribe of Wild Soul Sisters to help you speak your truth and stand up for your values. In a world that can often prove hostile or uncaring, this support is as essential as water or air. You need people with whom you can cry yourself raw and laugh yourself silly, who will help you to continue to free yourself to express all of who you are.

Life on Earth is still an experiment. We cannot know what lies ahead. And yet nothing changes if we can't imagine what it is we want—and then set out to make it real. You will at times fail and fall, but your sisters and perhaps, in time, some Wild Soul Brothers too, will hold you up while you reach inside for the strength to remain true to this path of rewilding.

Many years ago, I had a dream that is resonating in me and wanting to be told.

> *I am floating miles above the planet, looking down at what appear to be ants emerging from the Earth's fiery core. Drifting closer, I realize they are women: naked, straight-backed, sinewy. They stream from the center of the Earth to encircle the globe, pounding tall sticks, beating a rhythmic pulse. Closing ranks around the Earth, they form a protective circle of love and healing. They are fierce warriors, strong beyond belief.*

We each carry within us the Earth's innate strength, wisdom, and creativity. And the powerful, wild feminine, so vital to protecting the Earth, can only emerge when we realize that we are born of the planet, and that we carry the power of her landscapes within us.

We are fierce and brave and born of nature. And the Earth is calling to us now to rise up in all the splendor and fullness of our feminine power.

Please take a moment to feel that invitation. At the end of our time together, I'd like to share these words that came to me when I led my first Wild Soul Woman course.

I Am Woman
In my wholeness, I am holy.
Out of my dark womb
the world was born.
I am the beginning of the story,
the first star,
the tint of dawn,
the wave of energy
that moves galaxies and grasses.
I am the joy of life and its sorrows.
I am the desert's wide horizon,
the green pelt of forest,
the tidal power of ocean,
I am woman.
I am divine.
I am the god/dess you speak of.
I am.

I hope you will feel the warmth of my love as you journey onwards, called to shift and uplift the world in surprising and unexpected ways. Remember always that you are one Wild Soul Woman among many, a sisterhood dedicated to living untamed and unashamed. *We are wondrous. We are rising. We are wild.* Together, we are unstoppable.

Wild Blessings,
Mary Reynolds Thompson

Acknowledgements

To all the Wild Soul Sisters who have helped me along the way, my heartfelt thanks. You are the doulas who have made this book possible. I love you all.

Jess Beebe, Valerie Andrews, Kathleen Adams, no better trio of editing muses could have blessed me with their talents. Lori Wallace, your brilliant and incisive edits on reading the manuscript changed the flow of this work in truly wondrous ways. Osprey Orielle Lake, our regular feedback sessions were a vital source of wisdom, friendship, and encouragement. Annie Robinson and Lee Doyle, your ever-brilliant comments have made me a better writer.

Sabine Weeke, Editorial Director at Findhorn Press, you have my deep gratitude. I relish the friendship-building time Bruce and I spent with you in Scotland, and the grace with which you always respond to my concerns or questions. Big thanks, as well, to Ana Vidal of Infinia Literary Agency for making the introduction. And to the whole Inner Traditions & Bear Company team, for all that you do to promote writers who are trying to make this world a little better. A special nod to Hannah Easteaux for her excellent line edits.

Clare Dubois, you sowed the seed with your invitation to teach an online course based on the archetypes. Thank you for that and your generous foreword—and for all you do in and for this world.

Kathleen Brigidina, thank you for staying the course and working with me until the illustrations of the Wild Soul Woman Archetypes emerged in their full power and beauty. Your talent and tenacity have been an extraordinary gift to me and this work.

Christy Day, for your superb book design, thank you. Martha Bullen, for your wisdom in all things publishing, my gratitude.

To the men who have supported me along the way, my thanks. Tom Herington, you sparked my creativity and offered wise psychological insights through countless conversations. Gary Topper, for generously volunteering to take my author photos, yet again, and making it, yet again, such a fun experience. Bruce Thompson, my beloved husband and partner in all things, thank you for believing in me, for encouraging me, for loving me. From offering the smallest edits to the most profound observations, you have been with me every step of the way. I love you wildly and forever.

To all the Wild Soul Women who I have met on this journey and who have shared generously with me in workshops and retreats, and to those whose words enrich these pages, I want you to know how deeply you have influenced the writing of this book.

Finally, to the Earth and her many energies, thank you for visiting me, and staying with me, and speaking to me every day. You are my guides and my midwives, helping me and others to emerge wild and free.

Notes

CHAPTER 1
Desert Woman

1 Irin Carmon & Shana Knizhnik, *Notorious RBG*. New York: HarperCollins, 2015, p. 57.

2 Carolyn Merchant, *The Death of Nature*. San Francisco: HarperSanFrancisco, 1980, p. 249.

3 Brian Swimme, "An Interview with Brian Swimme" (interviewed by Susan Bridle). *What Is Enlightenment?* Spring/Summer 2001.

4 Carol P. Christ, *Diving Deep and Surfacing*. Boston: Beacon Press, 1980, p. 17.

5 Mary Oliver, "The Journey" in *Dream Work*. New York: Atlantic Monthly, 1986, p. 38.

6 Robyn Davidson, *Tracks*. New York: Vintage, 1995, pp. 20, 101. I have paraphrased Davidson's story and added my interpretations.

7 Robyn Davidson, *Tracks*. New York: Vintage, 1995. I have paraphrased and added my interpretations.

8 Terry Tempest Williams, *Red*. New York: Vintage, 2001, p. 77.

9 Anne Sexton, "Briar Rose (Sleeping Beauty)" in *Transformations*. New York: Houghton Mifflin Harcourt, 1971, p. 107.

10 Robyn Davidson, *Tracks*. New York: Vintage, 1995, p. 237. I have paraphrased and added my interpretations.

11 Elizabeth Gilbert, Facebook Post, June 6, 2020.

12 Joanna Macy, *World as Lover, World as Self*. Berkeley, Parallax Press, 1991, p. 187.

13 Joy Harjo, "A Poet's Words from the Heart of Her Heritage", interview by Penelope Moffet, *Los Angeles Times*, February 1989.

14 Rainer Maria Rilke, *Letters of Rainer Maria Rilke-Volume II, 1910-1925*. Jane Bannard Greene and M.D. Herter.

15 Wendy Wallbridge, *Spiraling Upward*. New York. Bibliomotion, Inc., 2015. I have paraphrased and added my interpretation to the story.

CHAPTER 2
Forest Woman

16 Scout Cloud Lee, *The Circle is Sacred*. Tulsa: Council Oak Books, 1995, pp. 196-97.

17 Marion Woodman, *Leaving My Father's House*. Boston, Shambhala Publications, 1992, pp. 109, 112.

18 The Wilderness Foundation Africa, "Nature's Defenders: Wangari Maathai, the Tree Woman of Africa," October 2021.

19 John O'Donohue, *Divine Beauty*. New York: HarperCollins, 2004, p. 80.

20 Charlene Spretnak (Ed.), *The Politics of Women's Spirituality*. New York: Anchor Books, 1982, p. 142.

21 Mary Oliver, "Wild Geese" in *Dream Work*. New York: Atlantic Monthly Press, 1986, p. 14.

22 Isla Macleod, https://islamacleod.com/

23 Charlene Spretnak (Ed.), *The Politics of Women's Spirituality*. New York: Anchor Books, 1982, p. 87.

24 Rebecca Solnit, *The Field Guide to Getting Lost*. New York: Penguin Books, 2006, p. 15.

25 Clarissa Pinkola Estés, *Women Who Run with the Wolves*. New York: Ballentine Books, 1992, p. 2.

26 Wendy Wallbridge, *Spiraling Upward*. New York. Bibliomotion, Inc., 2015. I have paraphrased and added my interpretation to the story.

27 Starhawk: *Dreaming the Dark*. Boston: Beacon Press, 1982, pp. 15, 26.

28 Joanna Macy, Anita Barrows, *Rilke's Book of Hours*, New York, Riverhead Books, 1996, p. 57.

CHAPTER 3
Ocean and River Woman

29 Toko-Pa Turner, *Belonging*. British Columbia: Her Own Room Press, 2017, p. 151.

30 Kahlil Gibran, *The Prophet*. New York: Penguin Random House LLC, 1923, p. 15.

31 Anita Barrows and Joanna Macy, Translators, *Rilke's Book of Hours*. Berkley, 1996, p. 119.

32 Diana Nyad, TED Talk, "Never, Ever Give Up." December 2013.

33 Adrienne Rich, "Not How to Write Poetry, But Wherefore." In *Essential Essays*. New York: W.W. Norton & Company, 2018, p. 264.

34 *Joseph Campbell and the Power of Myth*, Episode 2: The Message of Myth. Originally aired on public television, May, 1988.

35 Robin Wall Kimmerer, *Braiding Sweetgrass*. Minneapolis: Milkweed Editions, 2013, p. 251.

36 Elizabeth Gilbert, Instagram, September 2019.

37 Tererai Trent, *The Awakened Woman*. New York: Simon and Schuster, Inc., 2017, p. 95.

38 Eve Ensler, *The Body of the World*. New York: Picador, 2013. I have paraphrased and added my interpretations.

39 Kenneth Dickerman and Janne Korkko, "Somewhere in Finland, a village dies while a river continues to thrive." Washington Post, photo-article January, 2020.

40 Joy Harjo, *She Had Some Horses: Poems*. New York: W.W. Norton & Company, 2008, p. 69.

41 Hilary Hart, *The Unknown She*. Point Reyes Station, The Golden Sufi Center, 2002, p. 23.

CHAPTER 4
Mountain Woman

42 https://www.newscientist.com/article/2130266-early-earth-was-covered-in-a-global-ocean-and-had-no-mountains/

43 Muriel Rukeyser, "Käthe Kollwitz," from *The Collected Poems of Muriel Rukeyser,* University of Pittsburgh Press, 2006.

44 Audre Lorde, Second Sex Conference, New York, 1979.

45 Katherine Martin, *Women of Courage*. Novato: New World Library, 1998, p. xiii.

46 Lucy Jones, *Losing Eden.* New York: Pantheon Books, 2020, p. 8.

47 Terry Tempest Williams, "My Beautiful Undoing: Erosion of Self" from *Erosion*. New York: Sarah Crichton Books, 2019.

48 Jane Hirshfield, *Nine Gates*. New York: HarperPerennial, 1998, p. 6.

49 June Jordan, *Directed by Desire*. Washington. Copper Canyon Press. 2005, p. 278.

50 Patti Wigington, *Badass Ancestors*. Woodbury: Llewellyn Publications, 2020, pp. 4–5.

51 Audre Lorde, "The Transformation of Silence into Language & Action," MLA Conference, 1977.

52 Toni Morrison, "No Place for Self-Pity, No Room for Fear," The Nation, 150th Anniversary Issue.

53 Bayo Akomolafe, https://course.bayoakomolafe.net/

54 Audre Lorde, "The Transformation of Silence into Language & Action," MLA Conference, 1977.

55 Rashani, "The Unbroken," https://www.rashani.com/arts/poems/poems-by-rashani

56 Kayla Melo Costa, "Silvia Vasquez-Lavado climbs the Seven Summits . . . ," The Concordian, April =, 2021.

57 Adrienne Rich, *Blood, Bread, and Poetry*. New York: WW. Norton and Company, 1986, p. 5.

CHAPTER 5
Grassland Woman

58 Malidoma Patrice Somé, *Ritual*. Middlesex: Penguin Group, 1993, p. 49.

59 Robin Wall Kimmerer, *Braiding Sweetgrass*. Minneapolis: Milkweed Editions, 2013, p. 256.

60 Sophie Strand, "I Will Not Be Purified." https://www.artpapers.org/i-will-not-be-purified/

61 Jay Griffiths, *Why Rebel*. Dublin: Penguin Random House UK, 2021, p. 76.

62 KQED Forum, "Got Rejected? It Might Be Time to Celebrate," January 28, 2022.

63 Sophie Strand, "Confessions of a Compost Heap." https://borrowed-time.info/in-conversation-with-sophie-strand/

64 https://whatwillittake.com/covid-genderedinterview-with-blacklivesmatter-cofounder-alicia-garza/

65 Rumi, translated by Colman Barks and John Moyne, *The Essential Rumi*. New York: HarperCollins, 1995, p. 158.

Journal Reflections, Rituals, and Practices

Note: All entries not named otherwise are journal reflections. All entries in italics are practices and rituals.

CHAPTER 1
Desert Woman

CHAPTER 2
Forest Woman

CHAPTER 3
Ocean and River Woman

CHAPTER 4
Mountain Woman

CHAPTER 5
Grassland Woman

CHAPTER 6
Walking the Way of the Wild Soul Woman

Index

About the Illustrator

KATHLEEN BRIGIDINA is a nature-conscious eco-artist, creative coach, and mother of two daughters who complete her heart. As Community Engagement Coordinator and Artist Liaison for the non-profit TreeSisters, her greatest hope is that we become more conscious of our oneness with Nature and each other, that we cultivate more love, care, and compassion, and that we live in reciprocity with the Earth by planting trees and restoring the health and well-being of indigenous forest communities.

To learn more or to contact Kathleen, visit:
www.brigidina.com

About the Author

Photo by Bruce Thompson

MARY REYNOLDS THOMPSON, CAPF, CPCC, is an award-winning author, internationally recognized speaker, and a facilitator of poetry therapy. A pioneer in the spiritual ecology movement, her focus is on the transformative power of landscape archetypes and nature metaphors to reveal our true purpose and right relationship with the planet.

Author of *Reclaiming the Wild Soul*, a 2015 Nautilus Award-winner, Mary's writings have also appeared in numerous other publications and anthologies. Through her books, courses, and talks, she reaches creatives, change-makers, and seekers who long to awaken to their most courageous and Earth-connected selves and have the impact they desire.

Mary's own wild soul was awakened as a child, riding a pig called Ramona over the dusty trails of Southern Italy. Since then, she has trekked all over the world, and her connection to nature continues to sustain her decades-long recovery from alcoholism. For her, the wildest terrain has always been that of the wild soul.

To learn more, for guided meditations, or to contact Mary, visit:
www.maryreynoldsthompson.com and
www.soundcloud.com/maryreynoldsthompson

FINDHORN PRESS

Life-Changing Books

Learn more about us and our books at
www.findhornpress.com

For information on the Findhorn Foundation:
www.findhorn.org

Scan the QR code and save 25% at InnerTraditions.com.
Browse over 2,000 titles on spirituality, the occult, ancient
mysteries, new science, holistic health, and natural medicine.